# Irmgard's Flute
## *A Memoir*

# IRMGARD'S FLUTE
## *A Memoir*

# BERNARD W. BAIL

THE MASTERS
PUBLISHING

Beverly Hills, California

**The Masters Publishing Company, LLC**
462 North Linden Drive, Ste. 330
Beverly Hills, CA 90212 USA
THE MASTERS    Tel: (310) 275-0260
PUBLISHING     Fax: (310) 275-0079


Publishers Cataloguing-in-Publication

Bail, Bernard W.

   Irmgard's flute : a memoir / Bernard W. Bail. -- 1st ed. -- Beverly
   Hills, CA : Masters Publishing, 2007.

      p. ; cm.

      ISBN-13: 978-0-9795485-0-5
      ISBN-10: 0-9795485-0-0

      1. World War, 1939-1945--Personal narratives, American.
   2. World War, 1939-1945--Prisoners and prisons. 3. World War,
   1939-1945--Psychological aspects. 4. Prisoners of war--
   Psychology. 5. Ex-prisoners of war--Biography. I. Title.

D811 .B355 2007                    2007926537
940.54/8173--dc22                  0709


All photographs and images © 2007 Bernard W. Bail.

This book is printed on acid-free paper and manufactured in the United States of America by Sheridan Books, a member of the Green Press Initiative, www.greenpressinitiative.org.

*For my mother, Lillian,*
*and my father, Abraham*

# CONTENTS

# LIST OF PHOTOS

## LIST OF DRAWINGS

# FOREWORD

*N*othing transforms one like facing death, or facing love. After either of these experiences, no one is quite the same. It was my fortune to be swept up in a great war, World War II, and, at the same time, by a great love.

Of the first experience there can be no doubt. When fighter planes are coming at you, when flak hits your bomber, when German .88s shake your plane, killing and dismembering men you had seen whole one instant before, you know you are in a war.

Love is another matter.

In the spring of 1945 I was not looking for love. I thought my beloved was a sweet-faced girl waiting for me in New York, whose picture I carried with me throughout the war. Nor was I ready for love when it came, unbeknownst to me, in the worst circumstances one can imagine.

Sixty-two years ago my bomber was shot down during a mission to Ingolstadt, Germany, and I was taken prisoner along with three others. One of the nurses who tended us was a quiet, dark-haired woman named Irmgard, who played the flute and quoted poetry and left glasses of red wine at my bedside. She came only at night, when all that could be heard was the hush of sleeping soldiers and the padding of nurses down the hall, and she left letters for me under my pillow. I would unfold and read those letters where no one could see, and then secretly I would write her back. Only in these scribbled words could we speak our thoughts and our hearts.

During the long days of my captivity, Irmgard was the talisman that saved me—and she continued to save me long after that. Her prayers, for back then I did not know how to pray, would bring me back to her.

Through Irmgard, I slowly came to understand that spirit sustains and nourishes us, body and soul. Irmgard awakened the spirit within me that also graced my love for a French woman, Giselle, who was the practical, earthy side of Irmgard; a future marriage and children; and another great work: the arduous path to the Northwest Passage of the mind to find a new land in the premier healing profession—psychoanalysis.

# ACKNOWLEDGEMENTS

*I* feel honored to be able to acknowledge the heroism of Lt. Carper, the co-pilot on our June, 1944 mission. Through his quick thinking, cool-headedness, flying ability, and good judgment, Lt. Carper was able to rescue our aircraft when it was hit and badly damaged, killing our pilot, Lou Mazure, instantly.

No one, as far as I know, has ever recognized this extraordinary act of courage. He saved the plane with all his men and headed it back to England. His actions were never rewarded, an oversight that I think happened more times than one would like to think. I am paying homage to him here and I am very happy to do so.

I would like to acknowledge all the lead crews with whom I flew combat. There was about these twenty-something men a maturity that belied their age, a doing of what seemed impossible without question and without quailing.

In that period of time from pre-D-day to the end of World War II, we all wondered whether we could acquit ourselves with the raw courage of those we called the old-timers—the survivors of the important Ploesti mission which cost the 8th Air Force dearly. I think in hindsight we did, and I was proud to be part of that body of men.

Looking back, I think that all of us who flew combat came to admire the English people who withstood bombings, deprivations and destruction with what we call English reserve and optimism. We were grateful for their courtesy to all of us, their reception to all of us who were fighting this terrible and important war for the freedom of the civilized world. In his speeches Churchill rewarded them for their efforts and their confidence in him.

Though I acknowledge those men and those times, and the stalwart English people, there were also the brave Dutch, the brave French and other allied fighters. I regret that forging a character on the anvil of war is seemingly a swift way to do so, recognizing that many are destroyed or brought down by that anvil. I acknowledge all of the above in order to say that there must be found better ways for men and women to come to maturity with intactness and joy. I trust that we will find ways to that end and those ways will help mankind survive and flourish—all women and men everywhere.

I wish to acknowledge the expertise of my editor, Ms. Catherine Viel, who has worked carefully and unstintingly on this manuscript. I thank Ms. Ellen Reid for shepherding all the people and processes to bring the manuscript to a very satisfactory completion, including Ms. Patricia Bacall for her artistic efforts, and Mr. Brian Weiner, ASC, for the beautiful jacket which captures the essence of this book. I thank my secretary, Ms. Jane Jackson, for typing this manuscript and for her aplomb throughout the long process of my writing and rewriting and researching everything to satisfaction.

I wish to thank Ms. Carolyn Turgeon for her help in formulating the plan for this book. I also want acknowledge Carolyn and her mother for choosing the title *Irmgard's Flute.*

Last but not least, I want to thank my wife, Ma Lan, for her patience and good humor while I spent many hours in solitude at my desk, immersed in bringing about this book.

# 1

Ingolstadt, March 1945

*I* never slept after learning I would fly the next day. Those of us who were chosen usually turned in early. Wake-up call might be at two in the morning or even earlier, depending on the target, and on those nights I'd turn my face to the wall and close my eyes, trying to block out any ill thoughts or omens. In the best of times I would doze off, but usually I just lay there stiffly, waiting for the orderly to come in and tap me awake. "Time, Lieutenant," he would whisper, so as not to wake the others. None of us slept well when we knew we had to fly the next day. At least when we did get called up we had the great relief of fighting from the air, of not being foot soldiers on the front lines, the way my brother was. I knew that was one place I did not want to be: on the ground.

For me, the level playing field was the sky, and my weapon was the radar. Crossing the North Sea, I could see a hundred miles as the beams swept the terrain and marked out the cities. We had flown these skies frequently, so we were already familiar with the cities as they came onto the scope. As navigator, using the radar I could correct the pilot as we followed the routes mapped out before each mission. When flying lead or flying wing to the lead my attention was constantly riveted on that scope, for every other plane in the formation depended on the lead plane; the moment it dropped its bombs, all other planes would trip their bombs as well. I never got to use my sextant to take readings of the stars, though I had trained with it endlessly in navigation school.

Nighttime flying as a cadet had been thrilling, encompassing the great romance of being at one with the stars—the beauty of looking down on the clusters of light, the patterns of the cities surrounded by darkness, and the Big Dipper, which led us by the tail to the North Star. From the cockpit there were only countless numbers of stars on every side of you. Back then, I had felt an enormous pride gazing out at that sky, feeling I was part of a great adventure, one that would hurl me out of my small Jewish world in South Philadelphia where I was born and raised, and into the heavens. It was the different life I had imagined, back when we wore sweaters at night, back when my brother and I scoured around the stores on Seventh Street—the delicatessen, egg store, or hardware store—for wood or cardboard boxes. It was a richer, more colorful life of heroism and adventure, or so I had thought.

But diaries of flyers are seldom exciting, and fighting a war is often monotonous: a lot of waiting, a lot of small talk, sometimes a lot of drinking and womanizing, bridge or poker at the officer's club, or hanging out in town with a girlfriend, waiting for a buddy to call and say, "We're flying tomorrow, come on." Other than that, we had far too many hours with nothing to do but count the missions we had flown and torment ourselves with thoughts about the ones we still had to fly. The worst time was when you got into the twenties—when you had flown that many missions—for then everyone began to sweat it out, hoping for milk runs, the easy missions with light flak not too far inside Europe. For, according to our calculations, a flyer was not supposed to make it past the twenties. But no one could tell; any day we might be sent to the Ruhr or to Berlin, with its six hundred guns—.88s, those enormous guns that could find us at thirty-five thousand feet, and wound or kill us. You just tried not to think about it.

On March 19, 1945, I was awakened early, and silently put on my flight jacket, green officer's pants and high government-issue boots. It seemed a normal day. As usual, I packed a toothbrush in my pocket. I piled some wood chips in the little space heater—we took turns doing this—and left the cold Quonset hut. Then, down to the mess hall, by now crowded with fellow officers. There were something like six hundred men packed into the hall, and the atmosphere was noisy and boisterous.

We had enough time to order anything we wanted. Those flying had the best food available in the world, and I ordered my favorite, a stack of pancakes with eggs over easy in between each pancake, muffins, a glass of milk—powdered, of course—and coffee, then sat at one of the long, cafeteria-like tables with a group of men I had flown with in previous missions. A kind of nervous anticipation permeated the room, and no matter what we talked about—the mission, what we had done the night before—the talk was slightly hollow, as if each man was already withdrawing into himself, preparing for war.

After breakfast we walked to the war room, where the mood shifted to one far more sober. No one spoke now. We took our seats and waited, staring at the covered board until the colonel walked in with his staff. And then the mission was unveiled—a line drawn across the Channel in red string to the target: the point of departure, the flight path, which included the turns we would make to the I.P. (Intercept Point)—the point at which the formation would turn to the target itself, usually a distance of some twenty-five to thirty-five miles. We were also told at what intervals, and in what angles and positions and altitudes we would peel off, since we always flew in formation. Everything had to be done in synchrony. Every man listened to the colonel intently, knowing his life depended on it.

This mission was deep in Germany—Ingolstadt. The colonel briefed us on the target and its importance: German jet fighters were made in Ingolstadt, so the goal of this mission was to destroy the factories and prevent these German fighter planes from coming up against our slower fighter aircraft. The colonel described the Nazi antiaircraft guns and the fighter aircraft we would most likely encounter, and he talked about our own support fighters who would not be able to accompany us all the way there and back. Earlier in the war our support fighters were not able to follow us very deep into Europe, but by this point American ingenuity had found a way to mount auxiliary gas tanks on them, allowing them to fly deeper into the Continent—though not as far east as Ingolstadt. We loved these "little friends"; when a target was near they would stay out of range of any flak coming from the ground, and circle around, waiting to shepherd us home.

We left the war room, picked up our parachutes, and made our way to the jeeps lined up outside. My parachute was usually a chest pack that I clipped on, and this day I received it with a *good luck, Lieutenant, let's hope you don't have to use it.*

The jeep dropped me off at my plane, where the crew was gathering, and I met the two pilots; this was my first mission with them. Very young, I thought, and began to feel uneasy. I understood that they were being groomed to fly lead, so in this mission we flew in number two position, to the right of the lead plane.

As we entered the plane and prepared for takeoff, my misgivings grew. The young men crackled with the enthusiasm of the uninitiated, and their bonhomie with each other only annoyed me, but I could not show this. I did my job, and spoke when it was necessary to do so. I knew I could not let my feelings of increasing dread affect the others. My other lead crew members would have noticed immediately that something was wrong.

I remained calm as I met the chief engineer, the navigator, the bombardier, and the radio operator. I did not meet the waist gunners or the tail gunner.

In due time we strapped ourselves into our seats, the engines warmed up, and the plane trundled into position. I had never experienced this feeling of alarm with any other lead crew, even at the Ruhr with its six hundred guns. Germany protected the industrial Ruhr very well, and no one felt good about flying into that valley of death.

As we took off I readied my equipment and maps and checked out my oxygen line. I made sure that I had at least two flak suits— one on my seat and one around my shoulders to deflect anything coming in from the left side, since my seat was behind the pilots and the navigator was to my right, across the aisle.

There was nothing else I could do.

---

Mounting an airborne attack was no easy task. Gathering into formation took about two hours, and as the huge birds circled I pored over maps, memorizing landmarks, trying to keep my mind focused. We were going to enter Germany from the north and fly south. I recognized many of the names on the map from prior missions, having flown to Bielefeld, Braunschweig, Schweinfurt, Kassel, Regensburg, and so on. These names were familiar to all of us flyers, especially Magdeburg, where we had gone three days in a row. There was nothing left of the city, and today I do not even know why we leveled it; nor do I know why we went to Dresden unless it had been a last-minute alternative target. We swept that city, and it was a very, very long mission. I think we all tried to keep the people out of our minds, those who were victims of it all.

We were crossing the North Sea when the pilot gave the gunners permission to fire their guns, and we could hear the clatter coming from behind. It was something they enjoyed doing, a necessary job because they had to make sure the guns were working in case they had to use them. It was something to do. I was lucky, for I had a great deal to do, making sure the lead plane was on course in accordance with the lines drawn on the map in the war room. I concentrated on my job, and willed the mission to go smoothly.

I did not feel any more at ease as time went on. I rarely spoke to any member of the crew, except when the pilot would ask, from time to time, where we were. I would say something like, "Now we are here, three hundred miles from the target and on course."

There was nothing to do but wait. The gunners scanned the skies, and our "little friends" swept on ahead, to our flanks and above us, to ensure there would be no sudden attacks, especially from the dreaded new German jet fighters. American engineering was behind here, as we were in rocketry, at which the Germans excelled.

Though the day had started cloudy and there were still clouds over Europe, there were also great patches of clear sky. There was no way to know ahead of time if a target would be covered over—whether the bombing would have to be done by radar or whether the bombardier could use his bombsight to visually pinpoint the target.

We came down to the I.P. Because there were no clouds, bombing would be by bombsight. I watched the screen, desperately trying to drown out my anxiety over the target, anticipating the eruption of flak. I made sure my flak suits were protecting me as best they could, and I held on.

Suddenly the plane staggered, hit. There was no time to think. Fear erupted through my entire being—gut, heart, and chest. It is nothing I can even describe, the terror that consumes you as your plane begins to drop. But there was no time to suffer this feeling, or to think of anything except getting the plane back to base.

The pilot yelled at the copilot, "Feather two!" and we fell out of formation, dropping five to ten thousand feet before the plane could be controlled. The other planes were heading northwest and since there was no chance of catching up, we headed due west back to base as fast as we could in our damaged plane. We were now at twenty thousand feet and my pilots kept calling, "Little friend, come in little friend," but none came. I never knew why.

We were about two hundred miles from the lines of battle on the ground. We stayed on path, but continued to lose altitude. I told the pilot to throw everything overboard that could be thrown, anything that might make the plane lighter. He gave the order, and I think all the machine guns were dumped. They were of no use to us: any German fighter could easily destroy us now. We had been flying about one hundred and eighty miles per hour, but our speed was dropping along with our altitude.

I knew that our greatest danger would come as we crossed the battle lines ahead, where the German guns could pop us down like figures in a shooting gallery. We were a lumbering wounded bird and I prayed we would be allowed to cross that line, hoping no German gunner would fix his sights on such a helpless target. As we approached the lines, I commanded the crew to open the bomb bay door, knowing from prior experience that we had to have a way out. Without one, we could all die trapped in this closed box.

Suddenly, without warning, a terrible pain blazed and seared through my skull, and I clutched my head, then came to after having blacked out for an instant. I looked towards the cockpit, where both pilot and copilot had slid down in their seats.

They were dead. No one was in control of the plane.

I grabbed the intercom: "Whoever can hear me, bail out, bail out! The plane is going to go any second!" I could feel the death in this plane. I imagined everyone had been killed—bombardier, engineer, navigator, except for one fellow who stood frozen behind the pilots, still plugged into his oxygen tank. It was the flight engineer.

I disengaged myself from my equipment, then got up unsteadily. Blood was coming down my neck. I put my hand to my neck and saw the blood covering it, then tightened my scarf and felt my way to the bomb bay. I saw that the engineer had put his parachute on.

"Come on, come on, we have no time," I yelled, and stretched my hand to him. "I'll help you, come on." But he was frozen; he could not speak or move. "For God's sake, give me your hand!" I could feel the plane begin to lurch, and I dove out.

Many years later, after I had become an analyst, I had a patient— a physician—who dreamed he was in a big warehouse. He had reached a crossroads in his therapy. If he chose correctly he would be on the path to health, and if he chose otherwise he would remain ill, with the accompanying consequences to his children and to his own patients.

He dreamed he was in a burning warehouse. A man appeared on the roof and opened the skylight. He held out his hand and from it appeared a beam of light. "Come, give me your hand, come, I will save you," he said. My patient looked up at the arm stretching towards him and was frozen. He could not move. As I listened to my patient I recalled for the first time in years how this flight engineer could not, would not let himself be saved.

I tumbled over and over, catching glimpses of farmland as I fell. That was good—small villages, less chance of being impaled on a pole or crashing through a roof. I pulled the cord, using both arms to get the necessary strength, and then I was floating. I knew what was coming next, and I opened the collar of my shirt and tore my dog tags off. I did not want to be identified as a Jew.

Then, before I had much more time to think, I was on the ground. Slowly I slipped out of my parachute, untied my GI shoes from my parachute, and took off the electrically heated shoes I was wearing, worthless for walking. My head was throbbing with pain; I could feel the shrapnel in my skull, the blood on my neck. I sat, mechanically lacing up my GI shoes as a small cluster of people came towards me. I was grateful for this small task, for it gave me time to compose a posture for death. What else could I expect?

When they were ten to fifteen feet away, I stood up and waited. I tried to show no emotion, though my heart was racing and my mouth was dry. The people seemed to be farmers, people relatively untouched by the war.

"Let's go," one said. Now the group was becoming bigger. As I walked people hit me and pummeled me, though they could see I was wounded. My white scarf was soaked with blood. Still, they hit me, and I said nothing. I do not think I could have spoken. Some threw stones. I had to hold myself for fear of fainting, for fear of crying out. I wanted only to be able to withstand the pain, and not die a screaming, moaning death.

How can I describe the fear that stabbed through me, the terrible pain of being human, and being vulnerable? I walked along and when I was pushed to my knees one man said something that sounded like, "Enough." I had trouble getting to my feet; then somebody helped me, and I was taken into a house.

The next thing I knew I was in a room with three men and a woman. The woman spoke English and she asked me questions. Barely able to whisper, I gave her my name, my rank, and serial number. "Empty your pockets," she ordered. I put what money I had on the table, along with my chronometer, its face now smashed, my toothbrush, my escape kit, and two condoms. When they saw the condoms, all of the men laughed, and I felt a bit calmer—perhaps these were not dyed-in-the-wool Nazis after all.

The men left the room, and the woman whispered to me, "Only tell them what you did, they respect that." Then she said, "You are German, yes?" I did not correct her. Though I was descended from Russian Jews, my hair was blonde enough that I could have been German, and I thought there was no way to prove otherwise.

She was about to say something else but the men came back, speaking among themselves. "You will have to go with them," the woman said, and we all went outside. It was now dusk. Two men got in the front seat of a car, and one got in the back with me. I wondered if they would take me to the woods and shoot me; I had no idea what they would do, and I tried not to think. But though I was feeling very tired, and beginning to ache, I felt more alive than I had ever felt in my life.

They drove in silence for ten to fifteen minutes before we came to a large town, where I was taken to a prison. At least it was not to be an execution, I thought, and relief flooded through me. I was seen by the prison chief and then the doctor with him gave me a shot of what I imagined to be tetanus vaccine. After this I was led to a small prison cell with a rickety bed in it. They gave me a piece of the highly concentrated chocolate in my escape kit, but I fell asleep immediately, without touching it. Nothing could have kept me awake.

It was early morning before I opened my eyes and looked around my cell. The ceiling was probably twenty feet high, and near the top of one wall was a small window through which the dawn was beginning to filter into the room. I turned on my back and found I was in great pain. I ached desperately all over; I could not move my eyeballs without pain. My mouth was dry. I unwound my scarf and saw how much was stained with my blood, but I did not abandon it. Maybe I could use it in some way, later.

Soon the door opened, and the hallways outside echoed like those in a Lon Chaney movie. A man came in and said we were going, and then showed me to the bathroom and waited. Then he led me to a car, where two other men were waiting. The four of us drove for a half hour, passing roadways and forests, and again I had no idea where they were taking me, or what was to be done with me. I thought I would pass out from fear. Soon we came to another town, and stopped in front of an official-looking building. I was led to a room inside. As we approached the door I thought, so this is it. So this is how it all ends. But when the man opened the door, I was speechless. Three men, all that was left of my crew, looked back at me.

Two stood, and one lay on a stretcher. I did not know their names, though I soon would. I surmised they had all been blown out of the plane; they must have been in the waist when the plane was hit. I queried them with my eyes. They shook their heads; there was no one else alive.

The two men standing looked dirty and haggard, unshaven, still in shock. I supposed they looked the way I looked, and perhaps I looked even worse since my hair was clotted with blood, and my scarf and jacket stained with it. But then there was the fellow on the floor, whose name I came to know as Karl. His left leg was all trussed up with a big white bandage; someone had slit his pant leg nearly up to his waist.

I looked at them, really, for the first time. I felt myself burdened. Now I would be their commanding officer and bear responsibility for them. Strangely enough, I had no reaction, no feeling about or for them, except for Karl who was groaning and whimpering, already delirious. His cries softened my heart and made me feel helpless. I was not a surgeon, not even a doctor. I had no medicine, not even some sulfa I could sprinkle onto his wounds. There was nothing I could do. I could not even pray, for I did not know how. Nor did I think of it.

They were strangers to me. I didn't know their names. We had never spoken together, eaten together, drunk beer together, nothing—just nothing. I would come to know the two other men as Woluski, the waist gunner, and Radek, the radio operator. Karl had been the tail gunner, I would later discover.

Before much else could register in my head, the three of us were ordered to carry Karl to the train station. Woluski, the largest, took one end, and Radek and I the other. The ordeal of carrying Karl for blocks—it might have been miles—was the most excruciating walk I have ever experienced. I was exhausted and weak, and my wounds were almost unbearable. I kept biting my lip, trying to give myself the energy to stimulate the reserve to carry my side of the stretcher. Every step seemed like torture. My strength was gone and the sweat was pouring into my eyes, which I wiped with the sleeve of my flying jacket. I had but one thought: put one foot in front of the other. Do not think. Just do it. The two soldiers who accompanied us were oblivious to our struggles. They were men in their fifties, and obviously of the people's army. I knew we could not depend on them for anything.

We arrived at the station and boarded the train—an even more difficult task, but we got no help in lifting or lowering the stretcher. When we were finally able to sit down, the three of us collapsed. We did not speak or discuss events. We did not look at each other. All we could do was try to get through this, step by step, without dropping from exhaustion.

We spent several hours on this train, which dragged along, stopping every hour or so. None of us spoke, too occupied with our own thoughts and worries. We crouched in the seats as the guards watched us, and eventually the train pulled into Stuttgart, where I saw devastation everywhere. I could see homes with only the walls standing, and rubble littering the ground.

We de-boarded the train, lowering Karl onto the platform. We stood and waited, and occasionally I would bend over to speak to Karl and ask him how he felt. He was in pain, feverish, and I consoled him. There was no water available, I told him, but we were going to a German hospital. I had no idea where we were going. I could barely even see straight.

Karl closed his eyes, out of his mind with pain. A few people gathered around us, curious, then a few more, until in a little while there was a sizable crowd. I did not like crowds. I bent over Karl to reassure him. I heard a German who had obviously been to America say, "I walk a mile for a Camel," and everybody laughed. I did not search the crowd to see who had said that, for I thought eye contact would be too provocative. Our being there was already too provocative.

Then the insults started coming, all in German but unmistakable in tone, and the crowd moved closer as the two guards receded, not wanting to get in the way of trouble. We were utterly worthless to them. I could feel the tone in the voices change, and I'll never forget the feeling of fear that ran through me. The crowd gathered steadily, and my mind was shattered with fear. I could smell the crowd's hunger for violence. It was only a matter of time before the shouts would erupt into violence, and all of us would be hanging from the station posts.

We could do nothing.

Suddenly I heard a different voice, clearly from a man with authority. And when I looked up I saw before me a Luftwaffe officer, wearing the always impressive blue gray uniform with braid on the shoulders. Like that of all the other German officers, this man's bearing was erect, imposing.

He said something in a stern voice, perhaps "Herraus," *Get out, get away.* I stood up and saluted him. He returned my salute. "They're scum," he said in English. "Dogs. They won't bother you. Good luck." And he was gone. I was awed. *I was just part of a miracle,* I thought. The platform was now empty and the two old soldiers guarding us had been bolstered by the officer's presence. I was certain he'd just saved our lives.

When our train came we loaded Karl in as before—by now we were like robots, barely able to think or see—and sat down beside him for the ride. Again, the train was slow and winding with many stops on the way, and whenever we passed through the small stations there were nasty, snarling voices and ugly faces to greet us. This was an angry people, but then they were now losing the war, losing their homes, losing all the loot they had accumulated during the war. By then, I was almost too exhausted to be frightened. We tried our best to stay out of sight, hunkering to the floor beside Karl, who was now moaning continuously.

I do not recall how many hours it took, but the train stopped finally at Goeppingen, where an ambulance met us. Two orderlies carried

Karl and put him inside, and we got in with him. In a little while we came to the hospital, which, I later learned, was a converted schoolhouse. Though we did not know it then, this hospital was to be our home until almost the end of the war.

We followed the orderlies to the second floor, where they turned right and, eventually, into a room that measured some thirty feet long and fifteen feet wide. There were two large windows at the front of the room, which gave us a view of sorts—we looked onto bushes and trees and a road, the edge of a porch, and nothing else. Woluski and Radek were given two beds side by side, and the wounded Karl was put next to me, both of our beds by the wall. At the far end of the room were a small table and four chairs, two on each side. That was all the furniture the room contained.

Soon another pair of orderlies came and took Karl away, and two hours later they brought him back, his injured leg bandaged. The orderlies transferred him to the bed, and placed the covers over him. He was delirious, and when I put my hand on his forehead it was very hot, but what could be done?

We were interrupted by supper, a bit of ersatz bread—for it seemed to be made from sawdust rather than flour—and a cup of weak tea, the menu that would sustain us for the next five weeks. Two guards stayed with us all that first day and night, and would do so every day throughout our captivity. During the day they stayed in the room or took turns, sometimes going out to do other things, or to accompany us to the bathroom.

The first time I was taken down the hall, to what I had assumed was the men's bathroom, I had quite a shock. After I sat down I heard some noises, and realized another person had entered the adjoining stall. I looked down at the shoes underneath the stall; it was a woman. I was unable to do justice to what my bowels were saying then, and it took some time for me to accustom myself to that idea. The woman seemed not to mind, for she did her business and left.

I could understand that when circumstances are at their most primitive all the niceties of polite society are lost, reduced to the elemental. There is only one concern, and that is to survive. I soon learned that this entire hospital unit had been not long ago on the Russian front, and that they had been sent to this location to recuperate. They had been lucky, for to have been captured on the Russian front would have meant torture and perhaps death; the Russians were looking for revenge for what had been done to their land and to their people, and in a way it was uncanny that what the Germans had done to other peoples was now happening to them. We too were lucky for having so far survived what we had. I never forgot it.

We were all in desperate need of sleep. The guards left the room, but then a doctor came in—at least I thought that's what he was—to give us all injections. I thought tetanus again, and I didn't think to tell him we had already had that vaccine, when was it? Time had swallowed life, or life swallowed time. I could hardly recall the day before, for that was already eons go. I fell asleep after he'd given us the shots.

In the morning we got up and I went to the bathroom and shaved, for they had provided us with razors and soap. There was no hot water, so I shaved with cold and rinsed my mouth and brushed my teeth with my toothbrush, which I had retrieved along with my chronometer; the Germans had kept the money, the rest of the escape kit and the condoms. We had our breakfast together—Woluski, Radek and I—savoring the bread, sipping the tea, and trying to make the meal last as we talked.

"What do you think they're going to do, sir?" they asked, and I said, "I don't know, let's wait and see."

We had nothing much else to say. It seemed we came from different worlds back in America. Radek was a short, stocky man in his twenties, a radio operator who had worked a few factory jobs before joining the air force. Woluski, a young man of Russian descent, was in constant fear that he would be taken out and shot, for even though his dog tags identified him as a Christian, he looked exactly like a stereotypical Jew, with a typical Jew nose. I thought to myself, wouldn't that be the ultimate joke. They think that I, the Jew, am German, and the Christian, Woluski, is a Jew. Radek and Woluski did not know I was Jewish; they knew nothing of me except that I was the plane's navigator.

Those first few days all we could do was wait—wait to see what would be done with us, wait to fall into a routine, and wait to recover some energy and health. I walked back and forth and watched Karl, who did not look well. He was still feverish, and eventually a nurse came in, very businesslike, checked his pulse, and put a thermometer under his armpit to take his temperature. She wrote on her clipboard and left.

In a little while a doctor came in and addressed me in English.

"Your soldier is not well; there is a bad infection, but we have no medicine to do very much." I knew that Americans had penicillin, just recently discovered, but that there would be none here. The doctor continued, "Maybe you could sponge him down; we do not have the personnel to do that." I said of course, and, when they brought cold water, the three of us set to the task.

After, there was nothing for us to do, and nothing was asked of us. We sat, or paced the floor. The guards did not interact with us. Not so much sullen as taciturn, they hardly spoke to each other, either. Perhaps the intimacy of combat conditions narrows the range of things to talk about. The frivolous chitchat dies away, the philosophical issues die away, and you think only of your food supply and of survival. I imagine that by this time in the war the Germans were thinking only of surviving and getting back to their own families. They were considering how to surrender to the Americans, or worrying about who was going to capture them.

We could hear the big guns firing, forty, fifty miles away, on the front lines. By my calculation Goeppingen was not terribly far from Stuttgart, fifty miles at most. The train that had brought us to Goeppingen had been stop and go, so distance had been hard to estimate.

The day dragged, and two days became three, and three four. The three of us began to recover our strength. We began to feel more settled. Surely, we thought, they would have killed us by now, if that's what they were planning. None of us talked about the final moments.

Radek and Woluski were old friends, having flown a number of missions together, but they never mentioned the pilots or the others who were killed. I did say that we were lucky to have survived, that if the ME-109s had not downed us we all might have been picked off crossing the lines; our troops could only have watched our execution and thought, "Those poor bastards, they didn't have a chance." That would have been true, but on the front lines, on the beaches, in the air, chances are hard to come by and lucky is the man who grabs the limited brass ring.

---

It did not take long for tedium to set in.

Many days it was just the same thing over and over: me pacing the floor, Radek and Woluski at the table, talking just to talk. They'd have the same conversations over and over again, as Karl lay on his bed by the wall, still delirious. I tried to block it all out; I spent hours walking that room, and staring out the window, trying to forget my family, and their suffering.

At first, captivity was agonizing because I knew the pain my mother would suffer upon receiving the MIA telegram, and I thought endlessly about this. I could visualize her lying on the living room couch day and night, the endless tears, the compresses to her forehead. I imagined her lying on her right side, knees bent, with the long chain of relatives coming to visit, coming to comfort her, listening to her sorrow.

And, throughout, Woluski and Radek talked endlessly.

"Do you remember the Kiel mission?" Woluski would say to Radek. His floppy hair always fell in his face, and he'd have to push it back.

"Sure, what about it?"

"Do you remember how we got those sub-pens? Knocked the hell out of them. Then we got attacked by the fighters on the way back. I almost got one, but he was too fast…And what were you doing all this time?" Woluski would continue, laughing.

"Yeah, there was nothing for me to do," Radek would complain, "there's never anything for me to do except wait until it's over."

"You remember Anderson, the guy in the next bunk?"

"Yeah."

"Remember what he told us? You remember? He lived in Montana on a sheep ranch. His father had a small sheep ranch."

"Oh yeah. So?"

"Don't you remember what he said?"

"Fuck, he said so many things. Who the fuck remembers?"

"Yeah, yeah, that's it. Fuck. Remember he used to talk about the ranch and how all the men got horny and used to fuck the sheep and how nice it was to sleep with the sheep in the winter?" Woluski would laugh again.

Radek, the less crude of the two, would look at me without speaking, embarrassed.

"What do you think, Lieutenant?" Woluski would ask, turning to me.

"I wouldn't know," I'd say, "I'm a city boy. I don't know about Montana or sheep. But maybe when a guy's horny he'll do anything."

Woluski would laugh and turn away. He'd shake his head and say, over and over, "Goddamn. A sheep. A sheep. Damn."

This is how we spent the endless hours.

Over the course of time Woluski always initiated the conversation, and somehow got it around to Montana. Sometimes Radek got irritated, and then he would say, "If you don't shut up, I'm going to tell them you're a fucking Jew, and to look at your Jew nose."

Whenever he was threatened, Woluski stopped immediately. He was never able to gauge just when Radek had had enough.

And so it went.

These conversations brought me to thoughts of my Jewish experience. The feeling of Jewishness was always with me—when I was in college, surrounded by gentiles, or in the air force, where I was one with the young men of all nationalities—when I still felt something

I kept secret to myself, hidden from everyone else. I felt the joy and pride in being Jewish. I felt a grand elation in *being*; I felt a solace in being. It was there within me, deep inside, glowing in the reddish dark places of my inner being, of my heart.

As a child, I had never envied little boys going to the "tomatura," going every day to study Hebrew in preparation for their bar mitzvahs. There was a school two blocks away, and every afternoon I saw the boys in the neighborhood walk or run to class. Some complained of it as we played handball or baseball in the streets or the park across the street. Some said nothing. Maybe some of their parents did not care whether their children had a bar mitzvah or not.

There was never a question in my house. No one ever said that my brother and I should prepare for the ritual transition to adulthood, and since no one raised the issue, it was a non-issue for me. I was a Jew, but what kind of Jew was I? My family were Communists. Even my mother's brother had been a high-ranking commissar. There were pictures of him vacationing in the Crimea with his very beautiful wife, both of them dressed military style—he with wonderfully polished black leather boots and a long leather jacket. Both were very Tartar in appearance. He looked like a warrior, and, in fact, had been a fighter in the revolution, choosing to stay when the rest of my family left the country.

So I had this warrior on my mother's side and, on my father's side, the intellectuals. They were going to fight oppression in a different way. Of course, my uncles came upon the scene later, in a different time, a time of Stalin's ascent to power, the time of the great trials or purges, of those startling and puzzling confessions by the first Communists. My uncles talked about it endlessly, but my mother was quiet. I had understood that her brother was dead, had died in the Communist war against the white Russians, against the czar, against the landowners. My family were freedom seekers, willing to put their lives and careers on the line. As a boy, I had been told that my mother's brother had died in Russia around the time of my birth; only years later did I learn that he had been imprisoned by Stalin for years for no reason and, shortly before Stalin died, had been executed.

By that time I had already lived through the anguish my Uncle Alex suffered in America when he renounced, along with the Communist leader Jay Lovestone, his membership in the American Communist party. Soon after, in the late 1940s, he was put on trial by Congress to determine whether he would be sent back to Russia— where, of course, he would be shot. He had never become an American citizen. After a long and anguished trial, he was pardoned, and went on to work for the unions as a mediator and speaker. He and his wife spent time organizing labor in Detroit.

I think I was the only one in this family of Communists to return to the faith of our ancestors. I was only ten years old when I got up one morning, my parents still sleeping, and went to Sunday school by myself. I do not know who told me where it was. None of my friends went there. "Who sent you?" the teachers asked. I shrugged. They did not persist, and assigned me to a class with a young teacher, a man whose name I have forgotten.

For three hours I was plunged into stories of ancient Israel and God's chosen people. I felt I too was chosen, in the same way I felt chosen and special because my grandmother had the nicest house on the block, or because my uncle was a doctor. To be a doctor was to be a god among men. I saw the reverence with which my uncle was held. He was a wise man, a holy man, and I later learned he had become a Communist to help the people, and that he treated many a worker without a fee.

What kind of Jew was I to have received my call to go to Sunday school? It was as mysterious to me as the Eleusinian Mysteries are to me today. I received the call during the night. I obeyed and went to hear about my people: people like Joseph, that magician of dreams and savior of nations; David, the great poet who fought for his people and was a solace to Saul; the Maccabees, whose exploits all Jews commemorate for their allegiance to their God; Solomon of unparalleled wisdom, and the great prophets Jeremiah and Isaiah, whose language was so beautiful and so fierce that my blood raced and my heart beat thunderously to keep up.

My people became real to me during the daily Bible reading in school. Every morning I heard about my heroes, and I never forgot them. I believed my uncles also were heroes as they struggled to liberate the oppressed and slay the oppressor. I, a Jew, was not the kind who sat in school and debated the meaning of words; the Jew I always felt myself to be was the warrior.

Later I saw a picture of my grandfather Joseph, the artist, who'd been beaten by the Cossacks and, at the time of the picture, was about to be hung; he had been saved by some gentile townspeople who spoke up for him and persuaded the Cossacks to spare him. There he was, lying on a narrow bed, thin, thin, a bandage around his head, his eyes sunken and, beside him, my first cousin Sam, who was more or less my own age. He was the only son of my mother's younger sister, Eva.

The picture of Sam and my grandfather lying on a bed has always stayed with me, but only later did I understand the quietness of my grandfather and the sadness in my grandmother's eyes. Though she was always aristocratic in bearing and measured in her speech, whether Russian or Yiddish, the sad, sad eyes never changed.

There was a gentle quality about these grandparents of mine. A respect between them: the elegant grandmother and the implacable grandfather who rolled his own *paparossen*. He did it with grace and assuredness, and, though I did not like cigarette smoke, I always stayed to watch the first puffs before running away. He used to call me a little rascal; I liked that in Russian, *bondit*.

---

One midmorning I looked out the window and saw, far off in the distance, some of our own P-47s, recognizing their throaty engines and sturdy shapes. They were clearly not interested in bombing the town, and seemed much more intent on bombing and strafing the tanks and supply trucks on the road, for I was able to see them diving and attacking and pulling out. I crossed my fingers and said to myself, "River, stay away from my door." I did not relish the notion of dying in a bombing attack by our own P-47s, but of course they did not know of our existence in this tiny building with the huge red cross painted on the roof. I had no way of knowing where our pilots would respect that cross, and where they would not.

Karl gradually seemed to get better. His fever went down, though he was still very thin and weak. Even so, his rations were no larger than ours. Once a day a German nurse would come and inspect the bandaged leg and quickly bathe him. We were never asked whether we wanted to bathe, and we had no clothes except the underwear, socks, shirts and pants we wore when we were captured. I suppose that being on the Russian front days on end had created a new standard of cleanliness for the doctors and nurses of this unit. We did not complain.

Then, one midmorning early in our captivity, the alarm sounded. *Air raid.* I heard noises from everywhere in the building. Two orderlies came in and carried Karl out and down the stairs to the cellar; the guards motioned for us to follow.

The cellar was crowded but there was one light on and all the people—soldiers, patients, doctors, nurses—stood listening to the aircraft, bracing themselves for a strike. This was a strange experience for me. The soldiers looked the same as our soldiers. The women could easily have passed as American nurses, some attractive, most of them average-looking, the kind of women you meet in everyday life, as were the men—everyday-life men. This is what struck me: these were not monsters, but regular people, people I could have seen at the fish store on Seventh Street or on the trolley that passed through the cobblestone streets of South Philadelphia.

These Germans did not seem too frightened, however, for they had been through much worse. Woluski and Radek stood not far from me to my right. One dim lightbulb hung over us, and we all waited quietly in the semidarkness. Though I had been in air raids in London when the V-1s were being launched, I had never sought shelter. I was usually in bed, sometimes with a woman, and I was damned if I'd get up for a bomb. Besides, I might have guessed wrong and been hit on the way to a shelter. As for the V-2s, nobody could defend themselves from those. Everyone took their chances, hoping that whenever and wherever the bomb fell, they would not be there to receive the hit.

Because it had always been my habit to whistle to myself, I began to whistle tunes that I liked, very softly so as not to annoy anyone. "Deep

Purple," "Stardust," "Harvest Moon," "Tea for Two," and "Hands Across the Table." Nobody seemed to mind. I stopped for a while before whistling again. This time, to my surprise, a young German nurse with a saucy face and a forward manner spoke to me. Later I would learn her name, Resi, and I liked her naturalness and her spontaneity.

She said, "You are very young, Lieutenant, you must be smart to be an officer so young. I think you are as smart as a fox, aren't you?" She smiled at me. "And your music is so pretty, could you do some more?" All this she said in German; I had begun to pick up some of their words for simple, everyday living, and could understand the gist of what she said.

I did not tell Resi that there were hundreds my age over in England who were officers, and that I did not know how smart they were. As for my being a fox, it was clear that no matter how great a fox I was, I'd never be allowed to enter her chicken coop.

So I smiled and said, "Danke schön, bitte schön."

"Ah," she said, "is your family German? You look German, you have such a handsome German face."

Again I said "Danke." I did not know where this was going, and though I did not know the etiquette of being a prisoner of war, I certainly did not think it included idle conversation with our captors. I did not want to arouse anyone's anger, so I began whistling again, and looked around at all the faces that were strange to me. Some looked back at me, and obviously everyone knew we were the American prisoners. Some were looking at us intently, some with curiosity and some with hostility.

Very quiet was one nurse a few feet away. I had noticed her as I was whistling, but she did not look at me, except occasionally with a sidelong glance. She appeared very interested in the music. She did not seem to be beautiful at first glance, with her black straight hair, gold-rimmed round glasses, brown eyes, rose-tinged olive skin, and her blue dress and white apron, the uniform all the nurses wore. I smiled at her, but she only looked to the ground.

Upon seeing the nurse, a reminiscence emerged of Giselle, a lovely Parisian woman I had met and briefly loved when I was in Paris some two months before being shot down. Giselle came to mind only fleetingly during my imprisonment. I thought I would never have the good fortune to see her again, as returning to Paris now seemed impossible. My life was only the present.

As I write of my life as a prisoner of war, I think my experience may come as a surprise to many who have seen the Nazi atrocities, who do not doubt that they were committed. Indeed, my experience does not speak of monsters, who, for the most part, did not seem to exist in that small Goeppingen hospital. The men and women there were men and women you could find in our own armed forces. Though there certainly were Nazis of the brutal kind described in other books, it was my fortune to be in the company of people like us, people who behaved like soldiers the way we did, conforming more or less to the rules of being soldiers as laid out by the Geneva Convention.

Once back in our room I thought about what had just happened with the two nurses. It seemed to me that this display by Resi had told me something about the group, maybe even the nation. It bespoke a worship of rank: the officer class was the upper class, and though I was a foreign officer in this small enclave where there were no American prisoners other than the four of us, I was still of the officer class. I had not forgotten the experience at the Stuttgart train station, when a single Luftwaffe officer had dispersed a threatening crowd of fifty or sixty people. They had vanished instantaneously. But I thought this must also be due to the infiltration of the SS officers everywhere; people dreaded these grim jackals, and no one would dare challenge their authority.

Secondly, I thought that Resi's behavior was a sign of a country beginning to bend to the victor and insofar as I was American, the bending was to me. By this point in the war everyone knew the Allies had won. So, in the end I did not take this as a purely sexual gesture on Resi's part, but as a sign of submission: *You can have me if you want, I know you will be kind to me. I will not suffer with you over me.* It was the expression of the defeated wolf who bares his throat to the victor.

So I thought. What else did I have to do with my time, besides thinking how we could escape, and I weighed our chances of escape carefully. So far the odds were in favor of us staying put—our troops were not far, and soon, in a week, three weeks, five weeks, they would be here. So why risk being shot? I did not tell my companions what I was thinking. Because we were not close, I never knew what they thought of this experience. They never complained and, seeing Karl, all of us thanked God in whatever way we could that we were not in that bed.

Memories of my third flying mission often came back to me. Now, seeing Karl in his helplessness brought them back again.

On June 5, 1944, months before the Ingolstadt mission and my captivity, I was lead navigator on a bombing mission into Germany over heavily defended coastal positions in the vicinity of Wimeraux, France. Our plane had been hit badly and hard by a lot of flak from the .88s on the ground. In one stroke my pilot and good friend, Louis Mazure, had been killed—alive one instant, dead the next. He never knew what hit him. At the same moment, flak hit the mission's command pilot, Lieutenant Colonel Leon Vance, almost entirely severing his foot and lower leg. He went into immediate and severe shock.

The plane fell five to ten thousand feet, rocked by explosions, and we were carrying a five-hundred-pound bomb unreleased. Three of the plane's engines were destroyed by flak over the target. The plane fell ten to fifteen thousand feet before the copilot could gain control of the aircraft with only one remaining engine. Once he gained control, he set the plane on a course that led across a slice of England and ultimately to the English Channel, feathering the number one engine to minimize the drag from the propeller.

Then the fuel line was severed. Gasoline and fumes began to fill the cockpit and the flight deck. The engineer, Earl Hoppie, was knocked to one side. When he recovered, he immediately tried to stem the flow of gasoline from the severed line by shutting off the valves, but was sprayed with gasoline that blinded him, leading to the shutoff of the one remaining engine, since any spark might have blown the plane to tiny bits with all of us still in it.

We kept the bomb bay door open, trying not to allow gasoline fumes to gather. The radio operator, Quentin Skufca, was sitting on the step below the flight deck. The burst of flak had demolished the radio set but had not hit him. He made his way across the catwalk along the bomb bay to the waist of the plane, and then there was another burst of flak that put big holes in the underbelly of the plane, just missing the waist gunners.

Now the plane was silent, losing altitude. At this point, I uttered the last command on the plane: "Leave the plane, everybody, bail out, now!" The copilot put the plane on autopilot and brushed by me, parachuting out. The plane began to glide and miraculously continued to glide. There was no sound now, just an eerie silence that seemed to fill the plane. I was now the only crew member to remain behind— and the only person besides Lieutenant Colonel Vance and the dead pilot on the flight deck.

Once the plane leveled off, I took off my headset, disengaged from my seat and turned Lieutenant Colonel Vance around, for he was still facing the front of the plane. I had been sitting between him and Mazure, just behind Mazure, but I had not been touched—another miracle. I moved Lieutenant Colonel Vance into my seat to examine his leg. This was a difficult task because Vance was immobilized from shock—shaking, clammy, and unable to talk. Once I was able to push him into my seat, I examined his right leg, which had blood gushing everywhere from the broken main artery. I unzipped my flying suit, stripping my belt from my pants and kneeling on the floor to fasten the belt as tightly as I could around his thigh to staunch the flow of blood. This was also a difficult task, taking some four to five minutes to complete. While I was working on Vance, there was another part of me aware of a great enveloping silence, a calmness, and a peacefulness. Strangely, I was not afraid. In fact I felt at peace.

I spoke urgently to Lieutenant Colonel Vance. "We have to get out, now. You have to jump!" He didn't respond. I had to keep two things in mind: helping him, and sensing when the plane would make its death move. I then attempted to pick him up so that I could drag him to the bomb bay.

"We have to get out, do you hear me?" Vance was in such a state of shock that he couldn't move. Next I attempted to put his hands on his parachute cord to assist him in bailing out, but to no avail. His hands just dropped. An additional problem was the disparity in size between us. I was five feet six inches tall, weighing one hundred seventeen pounds, and Vance was over six feet tall and weighed about one hundred eighty-five pounds, which did not include the "dead weight" from extreme shock. I was simply unable to carry, drag, or move him in any way.

As the plane continued to descend, I attempted every other possible maneuver to engage him toward survival—cajoling him, shaking him, yelling at him—anything to revive him, all to no avail. The shock was too great. He remained completely immobile, unable to speak or move.

It had been a very long while since I gave the order to bail out, and the plane was losing altitude all the time. We were only seven or eight thousand feet above ground by now. The plane seemed to be floating, gliding, and there was a stillness in the plane with both of us. I saw that I could do nothing, absolutely nothing to help this man anymore.

We had less than a minute before the plane would crash land into the English Channel. I slipped quickly to the open bomb bay and tumbled out, leaving the silence within the plane and Lieutenant Colonel Vance's immobilized image behind me. I could see the water of the Channel and beyond it the precious green of England. I tumbled and tumbled, making sure that I cleared the plane, then pulled the ripcord of my chute, which quickly opened and brought me to land. I lay there on the ground, my mind ablaze as I drew the silk toward me. It was in this way that the Royal Marines came to me, helped me up, and took me to their base. I was later told that Lieutenant Colonel Vance had miraculously survived the crash landing and was picked up in the English Channel by a British air/sea rescue ship.

After that third mission I had been overwhelmed by the grayness of the future, the hopelessness of flying the entire tour of combat. How many men survived it? I felt I was doomed, that I had absolutely no chance to survive. And as I thought and examined my feelings, I realized, with a start of surprise, that something in me welcomed this way out of the future.

I was aghast that I had such feelings in me. I had thought all of us clung to life, fought for it down to our fingernails, but maybe it wasn't true. *Maybe it wasn't true.* Another feeling came in, however— the memory of other Giselles came to me, the marvel that suddenly fills you with the great desire to live and to love, and to take your chances with death. And I had decided to keep flying.

In Ingolstadt, the days passed slowly and quickly at the same time. Karl seemed stationary in his stride toward health. We had been in captivity a little over a week when early one morning I found myself in great pain. My joints ached, I had red raised blotches all over me, I itched, my eyes were swollen and painful, and I felt feverish. I could not get up. I was frightened and my thoughts turned to death. What did I have that I felt sure was going to kill me? Was it something that I'd gotten from Karl? Was gangrene contagious? I could not recall, but I thought I had been careful not to touch his wounded leg, and except for my head and neck wounds, my skin was undamaged.

When I had come to the hospital, a Dr. von Polster had examined my wounds and told me there was nothing to do. That I just had to let them all heal over, since they were too deep inside in the tissue and the bone. Later, in the hospital at Nancy, the doctors would come to the same conclusion. I've never done anything about these fragments of metal except to surprise doctors whenever my X-rays are taken, and these spots show up on film. They're still there today, the spots and the pieces, the shell fragments in my neck and head. I have headaches occasionally and pain on that side of the neck. A small price to pay, and one I'm very happy to pay still.

27

I could not get up out of bed. The guard came over to look, and returned to his friend, who left the room. Later, I do not know how much later, I slept, then awakened, slept some more, mumbled, cried and slept. In the midst of my delirium I thought I heard in the distance lyrical melodies like those my mother had once played for me on her mandolin. The music gave me comfort, and I thought I had been waiting for it…

I was shaken awake by Dr. von Polster, who stuck a thermometer in my armpit and placed two fingers over my pulse. He asked me if I had received an injection at the time of my capture. I said yes, and he said, "You have…," but I forget what he said I had. Not until much later, when I was studying medicine, did I realize I had suffered a severe attack of serum sickness, an autoimmune reaction to an overdose of tetanus vaccine.

He left the room and came back with a large syringe filled with a colorless liquid. He bared one of my arms, fastened a tourniquet around it, dabbed the vein with an alcohol-soaked cotton pledget, then plunged the needle in. Blood rushed into the syringe as he drew back the plunger. I looked at him. His face was calm.

Was he going to kill me? There was nothing I could do. My senses were dulled by fever, but I could see how easy death was, how nature makes it easy for us to pass from this life to whatever. I thought of the odds we used to talk about in our Quonset hut in Shipdham, the base of the 44th Bomb Group. According to our calculations, by the time you had flown about twenty-five missions, you would, in all likelihood, have been killed. The losses were that great. Such odds made stoics out of us all, yet they also made us very superstitious, and the more missions we flew, the more we found ourselves marking off various activities as forbidden.

I don't think anyone spoke of it—we did not want to appear superstitious or foolish or nervous—and yet none of us would order a pair of bespoke shoes at the best shoemaker in London, lest we be killed before we could pick them up. A pair for ten pounds. It was a great buy. Later, in peacetime, I passed that store, famous for its footwear, and not even then would I buy a pair. One could have gotten a civilian suit on Savile Row as well, from the most elegant tailors in the world, but none of us dared tempt fate enough to buy one.

I thought of my grandfather Jacob, a furrier; he had sat for forty years, smoking while he worked on the furs draped across his lap. Sitting in a kitchen chair, one leg folded under him, he would sew, fashioning mink and ermine into coats. For hours on end he would smoke, the cigarettes curling from his lips until they were so tiny that I do not know how he could take them out and replace them without burning his fingers. Forty years of chain-smoking had left him wasted and pale, though his skin was naturally dark, and he always wore an Abraham Lincoln beard. I was sure he had never heard of Lincoln. Jacob was a quiet Russian man who always let me win at checkers and casino. Weekends he prayed in his house, walking back and forth, chanting, with paraphernalia draped around his back, arms, and forehead. He seemed very tired, as if life had taken as much from him as I now felt it had taken from me.

I lay there and watched the doctor push the admixed solution into me a little at a time. Wait, I thought, how could I die this way, cut off from everything in the world—never to know marriage, never to have known peace within me, never to have known my children, my home. Never to have known my career, or the woman I would marry, or the thrill of practicing medicine, my earliest and most secret ambition. Never to have known the satisfaction of all my secret longings, the possibility of being carefree, and never to have known the answers to the questions that had plagued me all my life. It was all finished, I thought, and I was too sick to struggle.

I had wanted to become a doctor early on, no doubt due to my Uncle Harry, who because of his prestige, his knowledge, and his medical degree was able to enter the inner sanctum of all of our lives. When he visited my cousin Fanny, who was his first cousin, I went to her house with him, as he often took me along on his family patient visits. Back then, the immediate family all lived within five minutes' walking distance.

As soon as I walked in, I knew it was something serious, though I was only eight or nine. Fanny was a woman in her mid-thirties who had not been born here but who had become quickly Americanized. Back then I did not know the term, but she was a flapper. Though not beautiful, she wore perfume and the kind of wild clothing I saw only in the movies, and, to me, she was an otherworldly creature. I think she never noticed me, but then there was no reason for her to. I liked her spirit, and the air of excitement that surrounded her. She was in the garment industry. It seems the whole family was in that business. I could not imagine her life outside of the house she lived in with her parents and an older married sister. Her other sisters and brother were already married and had families of their own.

I sat down in the parlor and listened. I could hear voices murmuring, and then, every so often, I could make out the word "kidney." Something was wrong with the kidney. I did not understand, but I could tell it was serious. My uncle was upstairs a long time. When he came down, he spoke to Fanny's mother, saying she had to be in bed, that her blood pressure was very high. She needed quiet and rest.

Fanny's illness did not prevent me from imagining what my uncle did to Fanny up there. Did he touch her? Where did he touch her? These questions embarrassed me and filled me with guilt.

There was a somberness in the house, and though my grandmother kept a clean house, this house, her sister's, smelled bad. Only my uncle's being there could persuade me to come. For I knew that afterwards he would drive me to his mother's house or take me to his home—he always liked company. Our conversations were never about his patients, but of the Communist party and the evils of the capitalist system. I just listened. I didn't know enough about either to express an opinion, then.

When I was older it became clear that becoming a doctor was out of the question. I felt as though I'd never be able to have all the things I wanted. My family was too poor. My father often had no work. We often had no food and no heat for our house. Back then, the war seemed a welcome escape from what seemed to await me: a life grim and full of sadness. I did not know then that the war would open the future to me in more ways than one, that the GI Bill and my wounds would make becoming a doctor possible, after all those years of worry.

Poverty was a surprise to me. I only began to know it when my mother did not give me a penny to ride the hurdy-gurdy—all the little kids had a penny—or if I wanted a penny's worth of ice cream from the Italian man who came around with his cart. If she didn't have a penny to give me for an ice ball (straight ice, root beer was my favorite) I yelled and kicked and threw myself on the floor. I was very young—only three or four. My mother would cry and say, "Here, cut a piece of my flesh, take it and sell it. If only I could to give you a penny." All this in Yiddish. I could not be consoled and would cry in the big leather rocking chair and fall asleep.

This was poverty. No spare clothes to change into from day to day; our only shirts were washed and dried and ironed after bedtime. This was poverty. Supper was one egg between my brother Paul and myself. Then into bed, reading, sleeping, and the morrow.

This was poverty. There was no father who brought home a weekly salary; debts mounted at the grocer, the butcher, the egg and cheese store; there were fights over where to get the money, how to borrow more, how to get more credit.

All this was poverty, and I feared it because my mother was afraid and cried and fell asleep on the couch with her headaches, her perennial headaches to which I ministered by bringing endless supplies of drenched folded handkerchiefs which she put on her forehead and eyes.

I saw her grow old before me, and I could do nothing for her pain, her headaches—even the mandolin was of no interest to her. Nothing helped.

Finally the doctor withdrew the syringe, left an alcohol pledget in the fold of my arm, bent my arm to put pressure on the hole in the skin, and left. I lay there alone, preparing to die, but I could not concentrate, and sleep overtook me. Later, much later, I woke, and somewhat to my surprise was not dead but feeling better.

Later, when I myself was an intern and then a doctor, I would administer calcium gluconate just as Dr. von Polster had. Always I would feel a twitch of sadness as I remembered that long-ago scene. There was a strange irony to the fact that now I was in a hospital relieving a stranger, a patient, of his pain. I knew what to do, something tangible and helpful, and I was proud to be a doctor. It never mattered to me that I got paid only twenty-five dollars a month as an intern. The money did not matter. I used to feel the way I think Arrowsmith felt as Sinclair Lewis envisioned him in the boat floating down the river: at peace with all the wondrous beauty and at peace with his choices in life.

I had come to sense what it was that I wanted from life. I was about twenty when everything really started, when the cataclysm of December 7, 1941, changed everything for us in America. Before Pearl Harbor I had had hard choices to make, like how I could create a life for myself without any financial support from my parents, who, as immigrants in South Philadelphia, were already poor but made even more so by the Depression. My father would not have minded if I became his apprentice and, eventually, a master cabinetmaker like him. I knew that when he was only ten years old he had been sent away from his tiny Russian village, apprenticed to a family of master cabinetmakers in a different village. He had stayed with that family and worked without pay for seven years, and after that worked another several years in Russia before coming to America while still in his twenties.

My mother had no intention of my being a woodworker. I think she envisioned me becoming a master builder of another kind, and maybe all of her secret wishes had become mine. Especially the secret wish of love, for when she was sent to America to marry my father, she was sixteen and in love with a dark-haired village boy named William. She mourned that loss all her life.

My mother had a face more open to loss and suffering than anyone I've ever known. Her face, when she was in a certain mood, spoke of grief and cold dark winter evenings. In the cold, in the dark, she would pick up her mandolin and sing in a clear small voice of her little Russian village. She sang the old folk songs her grandparents had sung, songs so plaintive I would forget the cold outside and the cold inside. Instead I was in a place very far away, grieving the loss of a country, or a beloved, or a mother, from whom comes all things. Or perhaps grieving a greater being who we sometimes sense in the eerie silent moments between the pulse of the heart and the pulse in the wrist.

There in the darkness my mother plucked the strings of the mandolin, and we forgot. We forgot everything. I would feel tears in my eyes and I was ashamed lest she see them, so I wiped them away with my sleeve.

Yet even on the day I began my residency, or the day I got my wings, I never forgot how the past had held years of shame for my mother, the years when we had no money to buy food. Once, with great sorrow and reluctance, my mother had gone downtown to a government office and registered the family for relief. Later, a woman had come to our house to verify that we were indeed poor. My mother had pulled down the shades and hurried the woman into the house.

The woman looked around, but there was not much to examine: a small living room, a smaller dining room that held a round mahogany table, two chairs, a mahogany bureau pushed up against the wall, and my favorite leather rocking chair, where I would cry myself to sleep because my mother would not give me a penny.

Later I would go to the local A&P, pick up two large cans of pork and beans, and pay for them with the government coupons. My mother was filled with shame, and always sent me in her place. How cultures change—in another thirty years it might even be fashionable to use government stamps to buy pork and beans. Our tears, our humiliation were wasted, but they left a deep impression on all of us.

In spite of it all, we wore our poverty with cleanliness. Every day our clothes were clean, and every day my mother washed the four stone steps that led to the entry of the house. That stone, marbled with gray streaks, glistened white; sometimes in the summer she washed it twice a day. No neighbor would dare say my mother was not a good housekeeper. She knew where every item she owned lay, in which drawer and in which corner, and what was above it, and what was below.

We were poor but we were also proud. My Uncle Harry's was the only car that came to the neighborhood, and my mother's father had painted the two murals on the walls of our entry. I had watched him paint the flowers in their vases, watched this wonder materialize into a picture, a painting of endless beauty. I watched as he dabbed the paint on and wiped the brush off on a piece of cloth to make way for another color. My grandfather Joseph was an artist, and no other family could boast that. And I had a grandmother around the corner who owned the nicest house on that block, which was no mean honor.

So, though I was often hungry, I forgot the pangs. I played ball harder, pressed my marble shots more strongly, and swung my hockey stick more vigorously, exulting in my strength and quickness of mind—what did poverty have to do with that, I would think.

# 2

Irmgard

*O*ne night, as I was recovering from my illness, when the time was near midnight and everyone slept, I felt a hand touch my wrist. I opened my eyes and tried to rise, but the nurse gently pushed me back. "It's all right," she said, "nothing to worry about," and she continued to take my pulse.

It was the quiet nurse with the dark hair and gold-rimmed glasses who I had seen at the air raid, and I realized then that she was the night nurse. She smiled and said, "Wait, I'll be right back," and indeed she returned a few minutes later with a glass of red wine which she set on the floor by my bed. She whispered, "I'm on night duty; I see all the sick and wounded soldiers. You too are a soldier. I bring the wine to help strengthen you. You have gotten thinner since you came, so the red wine will be good for you. If I can, I will come back tomorrow night."

She turned quickly to leave, but I managed to ask her name before she did so. "Irmgard," she said, and I lay back, for a moment thinking I must have dreamt her. I was afraid to lean over the side of the bed to see if the glass was there. I waited a long while, my thoughts in a jumble. Maybe a sip would calm me. I drank the wine slowly, sip by sip, and since I had not eaten any real food for days, I quickly became flushed and a little dizzy. I put the glass down gently, and fell asleep.

When morning came I stayed in bed—a luxury I was granted because of my illness. I quickly checked to see if the wine glass was still by my bed. I did not want Irmgard to get into trouble, thinking she might have done this favor on her own. The glass was gone—she must have taken it away later in the night. I turned on my right side facing the wall so I didn't have to see Karl, my two other companions, or the lone guard sitting by the door.

I recalled how sick I had been the first year of junior high school, when I had come down with scarlet fever. My mother would sponge me down every day with alcohol and ice cubes. I dimly remembered the days and weeks I lay in bed hovering in that little space between life and death.

The room was always shaded, but my eyes still hurt. The house was quiet. I did not know what had happened to my two brothers—my older brother, Paul, or Sydney, who was born seven years after me—or to my father. There were only the two of us, my mother and I, in that world of twilight. Sometimes I would awaken to find her by the bed watching me. I was too far from consciousness to see her face clearly, but I could sense her standing next to me. Nowadays I know what a dread disease I had, and that there was no treatment for it then. Since there were no antibiotics, the regimen was simply rest and prayer.

I never saw my mother on her knees, but I knew she prayed and I knew she feared I might die. After I had passed several weeks in this twilight, something happened. I opened my eyes one morning and knew I would get better.

I called for my mother. I had not realized how weak my voice had gotten, but though I could only whisper she heard me; I know her heart would have heard me, no matter what. She came quickly and sat down beside me, stroking my hair.

I could not go anywhere in this wide world without her next to me. It was not as the poet said, "The world is too much with us." My mother was too much with me, except when I lost myself in games I played, in books I read, in various adventures I undertook. But sooner or later she came back and reeled me in like the fisherman who lets the fish go deep and far.

Many, many years later I learned after much research that Freud was not so right in his catchy phrase, "Anatomy is destiny." I do not mean to disparage Freud, but what I know from countless years of work is that "Mothers are destiny," and, of course, like all phrases, it is not the complete story. But it is a good deal of the story.

I had the same feeling of comfort when this nurse spoke to me, when she touched me, when she brought wine to me. She was an angel of mercy; her skin was soft and her crisp, starched nurse's uniform swished as she entered the room. She returned the following night, and during my sickness she came every night, not only to take Karl's vital signs but mine as well. During the night neither guard stayed in the room, but kept vigil outside. I was often asleep when Irmgard came, so she must have come some time after midnight or one o'clock. I imagined her there all those nights before my illness, slipping through the dark hallways, softly moving through our room. I could only feel regret that I had not been awake to see her then, to see the flash of her white apron in the dark as she tended to Schmidt and the others.

At night the hospital was ghostly. I lay awake, listening for her footsteps in the hall, waiting for her to enter the room. Usually she'd appear before me, place her hand on my wrist, and gently wake me. She was careful not to wake the others.

One night, when she put the thermometer under my armpit, I dared to put my right hand over hers as she took my pulse. She said nothing, though I could hear her breathing deeply. After she took my pulse she whispered, "You must not do this. It is too dangerous for you and for me. Please do not be foolish, promise me."

I nodded, but by then I knew that she cared for me, and my heart thrilled. During the first days of my fever it was hard to even understand what I was feeling, the rushes of affection sweeping over me. But even in my illness I knew that she cared for me. Human beings are simply made: we need only one person to care for us. We prosper in that alone.

The following days were full of thoughts of her, between my bouts of fever and sleep. Still Radek and Woluski spoke endlessly of flying and sheep and Woluski's Jew nose, but I no longer heard them. Still our sawdust meals arrived on schedule, and the bombs dropped in the distance. But I became absorbed in this insoluble romantic notion, which entranced and confused me. I longed for the hush of the night, the flick of Irmgard's hand in the dark, holding a thermometer over me, or carrying a glass of red wine to my bedside.

The next night I broke my promise to her; I again put my hand over hers and she put her other hand on top of mine, ostensibly to move it, but only after lingering a second. I squeezed her hand, smaller than mine, with capable, tapering fingers. She sighed, got up from her kneeling position beside the bed, and walked quickly from the room.

In a few more days all signs of my illness were gone, but still, whenever Sister Irmgard—for back then all European nurses were called "sister"—was on duty, I found a glass of red wine on the floor by my bed. She would always touch me to make sure I woke to drink it. My recovery ended all other touching, but always my eyes searched her out, and hers returned my inquiries, adding the sweet sad note that women know how to do. I would watch her move through the room, and thrill when her eyes met mine.

One night, about two weeks into our captivity, I awoke as Irmgard was leaning to put the wine down by the side of my bed. When she came at night, she always carried a dim flashlight. Though they were in shadow, I could see her eyes, and always her eyes softened when she looked at me. She realized I was awake and whispered to me, "I will put a letter under your pillow, be careful to read it in the bathroom, so that no one will see it. After, and only after, you must put it back under the pillow, and I will get it back. It is too dangerous for you to have it, and too dangerous for me too. Do you promise?"

I did, and then I lay there for hours after, unable to sleep. I wanted to shout for joy, but I lay there calmly, my mind racing, imagining her on her rounds, her skirt swishing as she moved through the hallways and in and out of the rooms of wounded soldiers. Who was she? I wanted to know everything about her. I thought back to the first time I had seen her standing quietly in the air raid shelter, and I played that scene over and over in my mind until finally I fell asleep again.

From that point on, I would slip my hand under my pillow each morning, expecting this wondrous letter. And finally, a few nights later, she woke me and whispered, "I have left something under your pillow for you to read. Would you read it in private? Do not let anyone see." In a moment she was gone. I slipped my hand under the pillow and felt a piece of paper. I shoved it near the center of the pillow to make sure it would not show. I lay awake a while, my heart trembling, my thoughts tumbling. What could she have written? Where could I read it in private? I was very careful to turn my back to the room before slipping the letter into my underwear, though the others were asleep, but then all I could do was wait until morning. I do not think I slept at all that night—I only listened to my heart pounding, and felt, again and again, the paper against my skin.

As soon as day broke I dressed and asked to go to the bathroom, where I read the letter, heart beating fast. I stayed there as long as I could, devouring the letter, reading it again and again. Not only because what she had written, "You smiled at me, and I had a deep joy," had sent my heart racing, but also to memorize her words so that I could answer them without having to unfold the letter in the room. I dared not stir any curiosity from the guards, or Woluski or Radek. Just as I had hidden my terror before, now I hid an elation greater than any I had known before.

*"You must promise to destroy this letter,"* she wrote, *"it would not be difficult for you. You must really promise it, or do you believe you do not need to do anything you have promised an enemy?"* She wrote: *"I believe that love is something holy but that one must not speak about it, one must only feel it."*

Best of all, she had copied a poem for me, one that echoes in my heart still, all these years later:

*All thoughts which you don't say I know them from you all the pains of which you don't speak, they weep in me long words which painfully listen to say your shy mouth are like the wishes which you sincerely have dreamed strangely known by me. You are living within me with such a great love. Do you wish to see yourself?*

*You must go to the far away to yourself through my soul.*

When she woke me up to take my wine I whispered, "I know your danger and mine. I will give you your letters to hold for me."

"Thank you, thank you," Irmgard said, and pressed my hand.

I said, "Whatever I think of your country is what I know from history, what I know from the newspapers. What I think of you is different. You are not your country."

"I must go, I must." I felt her reluctance but realized she could not stay too long. As Irmgard stood up I said, "You are the bravest woman I know to do this. I am bewildered; I am in a strange circumstance. It is unbelievable."

She touched my left arm lightly and was gone. I sank back. I would have to find the chance to ask why she was doing all this, talking and writing to an enemy soldier, and why it was so important that she correct me about the German soul.

I knew about German deeds, that the perpetrators had no mercy or soul, which I could not explain, nor could any Allied soldier who listened to the radio or read *The Stars and Stripes.*

I got up on my elbow and finished the wine, lay back and fell asleep.

I committed the entire letter to memory and longed to talk about it. Every swirl of an s or curve of an r was precious to me. I loved her strange phrases, her imperfect English. And I was full of words and feelings, just as she was—yet there was no opportunity to share them. Though she was free, she also was a victim of a restrained freedom.

I set about getting a piece of paper. The next time von Polster visited our room I asked him. He turned around and said something in German to the guard, so quickly I could not understand. A few hours later, the guard handed me a pencil and a sheet of paper—the square-covered paper so popular in Europe back then.

That evening I was impatient to write an answer to Irmgard's letter. I could hardly bear sitting through dinner, the same one we had and would have every evening. I could not even look at Woluski or Radek, and had to focus all my energy on containing the excitement coursing through me.

Finally, when the plates were cleared away, I sat at one end of the table and stared at the blank sheet in front of me. To my great relief, neither Radek nor Woluski seemed interested in what I was doing and returned to their usual banter. I wondered why no one had questioned me. What did the Germans think? Von Polster must have asked the colonel in charge of the hospital about the paper and pencil—nothing concerning us would have been decided without the commanding officer's approval, but what this colonel thought was a mystery. Perhaps he thought nothing; perhaps he had merely granted me this small privilege on a whim. Maybe he did not think anything more about it than yes, let him have the paper, and then went back to contemplating his own troublesome situation—for he had to have known that defeat and surrender were his future.

After all, what harm could come from a scrap of paper? One sheet of paper, covered with squares, and a pencil—yet they seemed the world to me.

I stared at the blank sheet. I was filled with thoughts and feelings, but I felt nervous all of a sudden to commit them to paper. This was the most important writing of my life. I needed to write with the economy of Hemingway, but with the flow and sonority of Thomas Wolfe. I thought how I was stirred by Thomas Wolfe with his great Bunyonesque prose, which I found so compelling that I used to yearn to write my essays in his gargantuan, torrential manner. But I was also stirred by Hemingway, and I thought his writing was so neat, so spare, so right that it stirred my longing to practice economy; to cross out, to diminish every sentence to its very essence. The small taste that effloresces into great meaning.

How should I write to her? I feared I could not, would not say what I needed to say; there was not enough time or space. As I sat at that table, pencil in hand, there was no longer a war raging outside the hospital windows; there was nothing except *how I should say it.* Then all anxiety left me. I knew I had to say simply, in my way, what was true for me, and what was in my heart. That would have to be enough.

I unfolded my hands and picked up the pencil. I wrote very small and very neatly.

My blood was feverish as I expressed, as well and precisely as I could, the answers her questions provoked in me. And I did just that, all within the allotted scrap. It was the best I could do. Though I wanted to write more, there was only this one page.

No one paid attention to me and soon, within an hour, I was done. My instructions from Irmgard, whispered in the middle of the night, were to leave the letter under my pillow. This was springtime, and the lengthening days made the hours before midnight seem interminable. I could not wait for night to fall, to fall asleep, and for Irmgard's hand to slip under the pillow and withdraw my letter. I pictured her swiftly sliding it into her pocket beneath her nurse's apron, then rising and turning to leave—herself as impatient to read what I had written as I had been to read her letter to me.

It worked like this throughout the rest of my captivity: I would leave my letters under the pillow for her to retrieve. She told me her schedule, and if for some reason she failed to come, it would be a simple matter for me to take the letter back. We spoke and wrote simply and according to the extent of our feelings, to the extent of our education, to the extent of our minds being able to relate those feelings in a situation that was timeless—a situation that was tumultuous and precarious, one we tried to encompass.

This was Irmgard's first letter to me.

*Why am I speaking to you? As first you know, as I wish to show you something of our real soul. For you told something about us which made me sure that we all don't know one from the other and it filled me with sadness.*

*I have learned to love this, the truth, therefore I will be sorry when truth lies hidden beyond a deep skin of misunderstanding, of bitterness, of badness, and though you will go back to America, I never will forget that once I showed a little of our true soul to a man who had such strange ideas of our soul. That must hurt a little an earnest person to a man whose people is an enemy. And I would have little joy in thinking that perhaps later, a man on the other side of the ocean, tells to his comrades, that I know that it is an idealizing thought, and I cannot change myself, "you don't know them right, I have seen it otherwise." Though I never wished that he should tell about me and second, it is natural that I am interested a little in a person with whom I began talking about problems. With whom I changed opinions and somewhat of who touched me after I tore away the sarcastic and bitter and proud outside.*

*But, this reason must not be spoke of, for if it were the only reason, I never were allowed to talk with you, who are our enemy and now I have a wish, please give back to me my letters, for it would not be good for you and for me if they would be found. And surely they will look at your things. I will do them all together and give you later, I promise. There no one will be lost, you do not see what I am doing. It is the worse thing when one loves his country to be looked at nearly like a treasure. You must not think I have fear, it is not truth and therefore, without sarcasm or making fun, fulfill my wish. If you cannot do it, I must finish my writing. My love of country is worth many sacrifices.*

---

One day, soon after the first letter, I heard someone playing the flute. The sound came from outside the window. I knew there was a portico on the first floor that was as wide as the building, and, in the center, stairs that led to the ground. From my window I could not see the stairs, or whoever was playing this instrument. I strained to hear the music, so lilting and sad, a gift in the middle of the dreary, dull day.

While I was looking out the window, I heard the guard enter the room behind me. I turned around to hear what he was saying, which, as best as I could make out, was to come with him. I had no idea what was happening, or where he was taking me. I followed him downstairs to the portico and there, to my astonishment, was Sister Irmgard with a flute against her lips, sitting on the second step.

Unaware of my presence, Irmgard continued to play. I was dumbfounded—to see her this close and in the light. The sun shone on her hair and skin. She was dazzling. Her mahogany brown hair was rich and full, and the flush of her cheeks played delicately over her pale olive skin. Her breasts rose and fell with each breath. I watched the breath pass through her lips into the gleaming silver instrument. Her long graceful fingers were splayed across the keys. The melody she played was slow, stately and sad. I felt such a sense of longing that I could barely breathe.

Years later, when I had the chance to watch Chinese movies set in their ancient past, there was often a character, man or woman, who would sit outside beside a pool in the woods alongside a small water-fall, or outside an inn on a parapet, playing the flute. From it would come these wonderful mournful tones, occasionally with a riff of happiness, though more often with sustained pictures of the sadness and mystery of life.

I would watch these films and remember Irmgard, her head tilted and her fingers splayed across the silver instrument, and the haunting, sweet sounds of her flute. Back then I thought of Wordsworth and the "still, sad music of humanity." To hear these melodies would always evoke a rush of feeling in me that was difficult to unravel, except that I could feel all the longing I had ever had, and I would feel full.

It was, of course, the language of the soul that unites all mankind, for the beautifully arranged notes stimulate us all whether the music is western or eastern or African. The appeal is to the sensibility of the unconscious in arousing reverie and feelings associated with earlier experiences in our lives, tender ones, loving ones, impulses to dance, sing, march, and feelings of whatever kind which have a vibration to stimulate a human being.

So I stood there, listening. There was an unreal quality to the whole scene. Could I speak to her? The guard stood on the other side of her, several feet away, but he did not seem interested in her or her playing. What would he do if I spoke to her? Would I give something away? My heart pounded, and I stood there, afraid that this was my one chance, not knowing what I would risk by attempting to speak with her. So much of the affair was like this; moments of sheer beauty bursting out of this monotonous, hungry imprisonment. It made me feel crazed. I felt I could get no handle on my situation, no sense of what was real and what was not. My world had no limits that made sense. Surely, I thought, the worst the guard could do was command me to shut up; the colonel was already allowing me sunlight and air. It was a kindness I had not expected.

Irmgard paused in her playing.

"Thank you," I said.

She looked up, startled, and I was struck, in the daylight, by the toffee color of her eyes. Then she smiled—a slow smile of complicity. The guard was indifferent. "You are much better," she said. "This is your first walk around in the outside world."

"Yes. They must have known that I was wondering about who was playing such lovely music." I did not tell her I had recognized the melody from my feverish nights.

"I've been coming here when I'm free to practice," she said. She looked at me with a gaze that was soft and grave, intimate and private. Whatever hardness there had been in her voice the night we last spoke had melted. I knew that she had been playing for me, and I felt that our roles were somehow reversed—that she had been my Orpheus, leading me up from Hades with her flute.

"You know," she said as I gazed at her, enraptured, "before the war, I was being trained for the symphony."

Suddenly, I placed her in the world of the haute bourgeois, with its traditions of literature, philosophy, and music—especially music.

"What were you playing?" I asked.

"'Trockne Blumen.' 'Dry Flowers.' I learned it as a girl; my mother accompanied me on the piano."

"It's so strange to hear such beautiful music in this place."

She smiled as she recited, "'Dann, blumlein alle, Heraus, heraus! Der Mai ist kommen, Der Winter ist aus.'"

"What does it mean?" I asked.

"Then, all you little flowers, Come out, come out, May has come, Winter is over," she translated, slowly getting to her feet. "It's Muller's poem."

"I don't know it."

"'Trockne Blumen' is one of our greatest pieces of music. The only one Schubert wrote for the flute."

The guard interrupted. "Come," he said to me. "Schnell!" I could feel Irmgard's body tense with distaste at his tone. He took me back to my room where Radek and Woluski waited expectantly.

"What happened?" Radek asked, bristling with frustration and suspicion.

"No big deal," I said, not daring to meet his eyes and show him mine. "They just wanted to give me some air for a few minutes."

"Christ almighty!" Radek slammed his fist down on the table. "Why you? Why do you get to go?"

"Corporal," I said. "Watch yourself."

"Cooped up in this fucking room. Trapped like rats."

"We got out in the raid," said Woluski.

I thought Radek might leap across the table and throttle him. "Kike bastard," he hissed.

I walked over and stood by the window. I could still hear her voice, see her there in the sun. What would she say if she knew I was Jewish? What would she think and feel? Would her response to me change?

"This is a bunch of hooey," said Radek. "This is really shit." He had calmed down a bit. Woluski grumbled, too. I felt for them, but there was nothing I could do. In the German mind, only those of the officer class meant anything. I was insurance for von Polster and the colonel. I could vouch for their humanity once they would, inevitably, surrender.

When Irmgard came that night, I was waiting. I had been thinking for hours about what to say to her. I felt a burning need to tell her that I was Jewish, but when I saw her I couldn't speak. I wanted to throw myself at her feet.

She, too, was quiet. She barely looked at me. When she put the thermometer under Karl's arm, I saw that her hand trembled. I'd forgotten how young she was—she was still a girl. A feeling of power ran through me. I knew she cared.

I helped her wash Karl down; we worked on him in silence, turning him over gently, ministering to him with our hands. I felt the nearness of her body, its irrefutable magnetism. I wondered if it was all in my head. But no, there was the tremor in her hand. Young as I was, I intuitively knew that once a certain kind of connection is established between a man and a woman there is a synchronicity at work, a congruence of impulse and feeling.

"It's good to see you well, Herr Lieutenant. I came to you when you were sick, but you didn't see me."

"I heard you playing," I said.

She flushed with pleasure.

"I have been thinking about your poem," I said. She looked at me expectantly. "About flowers and the end of winter. This war is like that, isn't it? A long winter."

"Yes," she nodded. "But you remember 'will,' don't you, Herr Lieutenant?"

I smiled.

"Everything has its will," she continued. "The flowers are the earth's will. They always grow, even after cold and snow. The flowers are the fruit of the earth's hunger, not the hunger itself. You can pick flowers from the earth, they will dry and die, but there are merely tools…Please get some rest now." I reached for her hand, but she was gone.

The next morning the miraculous happened. Irmgard appeared just before noon. "We're going for a walk, Herr Lieutenant," she said. "The colonel thinks a little more sunshine will do you good."

Radek and Woluski gaped at her in disbelief. I donned my flight jacket, which I had cleaned as best as I could. Soon we were walking down a gravel path, in the sunshine among flowers and trees, a guard trailing us at a discreet distance.

"This is amazing," I finally said. "Being able to walk with you in this way." I looked to see her reaction.

"It looks like things are turning out for you," she said, blushing. "The colonel wants you to be healthy and safe. I am so relieved. And the fresh air will do you good."

"Yes," I said. "I will be eternally grateful to him….for this."

I looked back at the building we'd just left—an elegant edifice of smooth gray stone, five stories tall, with wood-framed windows, and what looked like a hundred rooms.

"It doesn't look like a hospital," I said. "At least not like any hospital back home."

"It wasn't a hospital first," she replied. "It was a girl's high school, a very good one. Many studies were given here, and the girls had sports for their bodies. There are fields off to the left. Sports are important in Germany, but not too much for me." She laughed. "Where is your home, Herr Lieutenant?"

"Philadelphia," I said. "Do you know it?"

"Oh, yes. We studied American history in school. I know about your William Penn and Benjamin Franklin."

"There's a statue of Penn overlooking the city. I loved staring up at it." She laughed. "Where are your quarters?"

"Over there," said Irmgard, pointing to a small cluster of buildings. "That's where the nurses live."

"And the doctors?"

She pointed to another group of buildings.

"What about you?" I asked. "Where did you live, before this? Where are you from?"

"Hamburg," she said quietly, and paused. "There isn't much of a Hamburg left anymore, though. It's been bombed and firebombed and leveled. But I suppose you know that." She smiled uncomfortably, and I looked away. I had never flown over Hamburg, never helped to level the city; that had been left to the British Air Force. But I had been part of plenty of other missions, plenty of missions where I had been in the lead plane, and looked at my radarscope, called "bombs away," pressed the button, and the bombs had detached from the bay and fallen.

We stood in silence. It was an odd moment. "Thousands of people have been killed," she continued. "Thousands are homeless. Germany is now the land of the homeless."

"And your parents?" I asked.

"Homeless," she said. "They have lost everything, except their lives, I hope. Even one of their children, my brother, Max. He died in Russia, a soldier. I don't know where my parents are now. But I know that if they are alive they will contact me."

"I'm sorry," I said.

She nodded, and wiped her eyes. I could see she was close to crying, and I quickly changed the subject. "Tell me about your music."

Her face brightened. "Someday I hope to be able to play with a symphony. That was what I wanted before the war. If not all the concert halls have been destroyed."

"Have you always played the flute?" I asked, trying to keep our talk as far away from the war as I could.

"No, no. My father wanted me to learn the violin, so I learned music on another instrument. Mozart, Shumann, Schubert. Schubert's father was a schoolmaster like mine, you know. Teaching is a noble profession."

"Your father is a teacher?" Suddenly her sophistication and refinement made sense.

"But the violin is so sad," she continued, as if she had not heard me. "The flute is lighter. There is a kind of…movement to flute music that the violin does not have. There is space in the notes. There is air."

Just then, the guard called something out to her and she nodded. "We must go back," she said. "I'm sorry but there is so much to do. I learned music with my family. Papa played the violin; Max, the cello; Mama, the piano."

Before the war, she must have had a good, sophisticated, educated life, filled with music and laughter, so different from my own. I imagined the living room of her parents' Hamburg house; rich, dark rugs on the floor, shelves lined with books, elegant furniture, an upright piano around which her family gathered to play. I compared the room to memories of my own family's living room—dark and shapeless, poor, worn, and threadbare, with oilcloth covering the kitchen floor.

"What do you plan to do after the war?" I asked.

She shrugged. "I will stay here with my wounded soldiers. Our unit—I suppose the colonel—decided that a long time ago. Now it depends on who captures us and what they want. Then, Herr Lieutenant, it is we that shall be the prisoners." She smiled wryly. "And you, what did you do before the war?"

"I got my teaching degree, then enlisted in the air force. I wanted to fly."

"So you got your wish."

"Not quite," I said. "But I'm alive, so I can go on. I have to make it home in one piece."

"So you are a teacher," she said. "What do you teach?"

"I majored in English and French, but I never got a chance to teach. I wanted to go to the Sorbonne and continue my French studies."

"And now you will go?"

I looked at her. "Now everything is too uncertain."

"Ah, yes, I see." She stopped and stood looking at the hospital. "My father owns a school like this, in Hamburg, and I attended. I know a little French."

"It is so strange," I said suddenly, "how easy it is to speak to you. We are a continent apart, a people apart, and yet you are so familiar to me."

She looked at me thoughtfully. "You don't look like an American. I know that is what you are, but you look more like a German or French student. There is about you the feeling of Europe."

I was secretly pleased to be identified with the sophisticated Europeans rather than the philistine Americans. But in my heart, I felt I had her fooled; I knew all too well where I came from.

We were approaching the portico again, and I knew our time was almost up. I felt desperate, unwilling to leave her. Should I whisper to her now that I was a Jew? The guard lurked behind us. I couldn't bear the thought that I might alienate her. Would we ever have this chance again? I wanted to know everything about her, to lose myself in her. I had never felt this way before; I had had fun with girls, at the movies, at bars, in bed. But I had never had this overwhelming desire to know someone so fully. I felt loss, desire, and hope all at once.

As we climbed the steps, I turned to her suddenly, and whispered, "Please come tonight. I want to talk to you more, learn all about you."

She looked quickly back at the guard. "I can't," she whispered.

The guard was approaching now, to take me back to the room, away from her. I felt—for the first time—as though, perhaps, the colonel and his kindnesses were not to be trusted, that perhaps he had intended this kind of torture—more precise than any physical pain. Was he watching this from somewhere in the expanse of the hospital building, taking his own kind of pleasure in knowing that I could only suffer for the crumbs that she'd been permitted to drop for me? In a last desperate attempt, I whispered, "Walk with me again tomorrow."

"Only the colonel can permit these walks," she said, shaking her head. "I cannot promise."

"Tell him how good it is for me to get outside in the fresh air!" I urged, quietly. I was afraid the guard could see my insistence; his pace quickened. "I must know more about you. Tell me what you really feel. Explain to me what's happening here. Tell me about your family and your music. Let me know your heart. *Please.*"

The guard stepped in front of me. Irmgard began to turn away. For a moment, our eyes met, and, for the benefit of the guard, she shook her head. But the guard did not know how to read the fire in her eyes that afternoon. Her public refusal belied the private message she conveyed. I tried not to smile, but I felt like laughing out loud. With or without the colonel, I, Bernard Bail, from a Jewish ghetto in South Philadelphia, had fallen madly in love with my German nurse.

On the way back to my room, I thought about how precious it had been to listen to Irmgard's flute, and to be able to talk with her, no matter how constrained the circumstances. Our meetings and glances, our scribbled letters—all were brief and wonderful, and always we both felt, for I knew she felt the same, that we had more to say. We feared we would never have the time to hear each other out, to feel the great peace between us that we knew was possible. We suffered hurt desire, but I knew we were lucky to feel such in the chaos of the war.

I gathered she suffered more deeply than I, as she was more available to her feelings, and, also, because the older of her two brothers had died on the Russian front. I wondered how many of these soldiers, doctors, and nurses carried a similar grief in their hearts as the war wound down.

As far as I knew, my brother was still in North Africa, or maybe he was one of the soldiers who landed in Italy to fight the beleaguered Germans on the top of the mountain. I had heard that the First Division was in Italy. I knew nothing for sure, however. In war nothing is certain. Not even the German population could feel secure with the bombers coming day and night, taking back whatever joy they might have felt earlier, when everything was going their way.

The universe has a way of balancing things. One has to live a long time to see this phenomenon, but it does exist. I have seen communism rush to fall, a regime in power tens and tens of years. No one fifteen years ago could have imagined it; many dictatorships in Eastern Europe have fallen, and despots, who seemed invincible, have been killed. When history moves to rectify and balance, men are matchsticks that can break so easily we have to wonder, why did we ever think we were impregnable? It's as if men are given the chance and the choice to behave correctly, to think correctly, until eventually history comes in and gives us the chance to start over and do it right. So far, I do not believe we have learned to do it right.

That night, Sister Irmgard came to my bed and whispered, "Thank God you are safe." She had tears in her eyes. "A few hours ago, the colonel met with his staff to decide what to do with all of you—they can keep you here or they can send you by train inland. The order all over Germany is to create as much chaos as possible for the Allies. Who knows what would happen to you on a train?" She squeezed my arm and was gone.

Fear and shock seized me. I wanted so badly to talk to Irmgard, to ask her what she knew, if she had heard any more details. I also knew that I did not stand a chance of being able to have that kind of conversation with her. I was utterly helpless.

Throughout the night and the following day I was pure nervous energy, unable to think of anything but what she had told me. I said nothing to the others. What I found appalling was that my life, whether I lived or died, was being decided by men who knew nothing about me. Their motivation for sparing me could only have been how valuable a pawn I was. In my favor was the fact that I was an officer. By their standard, I was worth something. I could think of only one thing they needed me for: to stand as witness for them when the Americans came. We all knew it was only a matter of time.

I would have to rest and wait. In my shock, and my helplessness and futility, the thought came to me—was this any different from flying combat, being assigned to certain missions and not to others, having where I was, when and how and why, be completely out of my control? Indeed, these were not options any soldier has or has ever had, but one thing was sure: I vowed never again to be in a situation where I did not have some control or some choice in my life's course.

Looking back, it seems so pretentious a vow, and, in light of my life's events or indeed anyone else's, I realize that one's choices are really fewer than they seemed to me years ago. Then, the entire world had been before me, and I could believe the lines of Henley's poem, "I am captain of my fate." The years have taught me to not be so grandiose, and there is a lot of grandiosity in that poem, which had stirred me in college.

Two days had gone by. Only the wine glass told me she was thinking of me. There was the slightest of touches now on my left cheek. I opened my eyes, but she was gone. After my lunch of ersatz pumpernickel, she came in and stood at the threshold, saying, "We are going for a walk, thanks to the colonel."

Once we were strolling on the path, I said, "How can I be so happy when I am a prisoner. It's crazy."

"I want to think it is because of me," she said, blushing.

I said, "Of course, it is all because of you. It is all about your being, your letters, your thoughts and your feelings."

"Oh, I think many German girls are like me who have been to the University, had a good family, loved literature, music and talked about them."

I thought that world was strange, for in my house we talked politics. In my Uncle Harry's house we talked about the communist party, about the 1938 trials in Moscow, the future of communism. We never talked of literature except Marx or Lenin. Uncle Harry was the physician in the family and inspired me to become a doctor.

I said, "I think of everything you told me about your family, the pain of losing your brother, you loved him so much. I wonder about my brother in Africa. Now maybe in Italy. I try not to worry, not to think about it." We were silent and then I said, "I try to imagine we are on a date and wonder when I can hold your hand." She withdrew from me a bit, always aware that a guard was walking behind us and that everything would be reported to the colonel.

A hell of a way to have a date, I thought, and continued,

"I had dates like this with a girlfriend walking in the country while I was in teacher's college. It was on the edge of town. It was the most beautiful place I ever lived in. Trees, fields, flowers, no crowds. Everyone so very nice. Nearly all of the students were from German communities in a radius of twenty-five miles. They were known as Pennsylvania Dutch."

"Maybe it is what draws me to you. What were the girls like?"

"Very cute—sweaters, socks, saddle shoes—you know, brown and white—patterned wool skirts, very sweet—all looking for husbands to settle down with, have children with, teach school, retire in the communities into which they were born and raised. That would have been a successful life for many. But I wasn't looking to marry, only to get an education and go on. My thirst was great. I wanted to do something challenging…Am I boring you?"

She was listening intently, her head cocked toward me, as if she was listening to more than words and facts. I said, "Do you think God arranged that I meet you in this way?"

"Ah, your arrogance has to come up. I think you are becoming afraid."

"I wasn't aware of that," I said.

"No, your arrogance is large and you were starting to lose it and then you asked a question, but you can't imagine that as a truth or that you are afraid of that as a truth."

"No, no, you misunderstand me," I said. I realized she did not know English as well as I'd thought. "You may be right about the arrogance, but I was asking if you believed in destiny, a destiny that brought us together."

She blushed in confusion and said she was sorry. I replied, "No need. I think you are too smart for me, but I enjoy that you are. I really like women, smart women, the way other men adore a shapely woman…and by the way, I have never seen you in a civilian dress and I guess I am never likely to, but you look great in that uniform."

She sighed. "Men are such children. Everything with the body. German men I think are not like American men, fascinated by their movie stars—so silly." We were now back at the hospital. She added, "I will tell the colonel you are doing better. You seem a bit stronger. Maybe the red wine is helping."

---

The hours passed interminably. By this point Karl's temperature had begun to spike, and it was an ominous time for all of us. Karl had seemed to get better for a few days and we were naively full of hope for him. The shock came with his spiking a temperature which told us truly this was a dangerous development. Still, we were not aware of the potential consequences, which the German doctors knew only too well.

About eight or so in the evening a soldier came and said, "Come with me." I did not ask where, but followed. Woluski and Radek looked up, confused, but there was nothing I could say. They had no idea how close we were to death at that moment. I tried to appear calm, though my pulse was racing and I felt I would pass out from fear. What would be done with us?

The soldier led me through various hallways, upstairs and down-stairs. I could never have found my way back to the room if he had disappeared. There was nothing in the hallway that seemed to make sense—the day people were off, the night people were beginning their shifts. Patients were quieted down. Soon lights would be out, and then only people like Irmgard would be walking around the var-ious wards taking temperatures, pulses, and doing what they do, even bringing me glasses of wine. But I knew that such activity did not come until later at night, when most were asleep.

The soldier stopped before a door and knocked, then motioned for me to enter. There behind his desk was the colonel who headed the entire hospital unit. He was alone in the room, his desk covered with papers and, I think, some charts, as well as the wine bottle standing to his right.

I was scared, my heart beating fast. I had no idea what was coming. I remembered what Irmgard had said about sending us away by train—had he changed his mind? What did he want of me? These were some of the thoughts racing through my mind.

I controlled my face. I knew Germans respected courage, pres-ence. I stood straight and saluted him. He motioned with his hand, acknowledging my respect for his authority, then motioned for me to relax. As he spoke I realized he did not know English or French, only German, maybe some Russian. He knew some words in English and tried them out. It was a hopeless mixture, one I could barely under-stand. What I did realize was that he was trying to convey friendliness to me, this man who I could only describe as stalwart, a man with substance in his body, high cheekbones, and a tanned square face with lines that ran from his nose to his mouth. A handsome man's man, five feet nine or ten, with strong, agile fingers. I had heard from Dr. von Polster that the colonel was a surgeon.

Finally the colonel said to me, "Waren Sie schon mal in Paris? Très bien, beautiful...Sie bleiben hier im Lazarett; sie sind mein Zeuge." I said, "Ja, Oberst Arzt, ich verstehe." I understood he was saying that Paris was beautiful and then in German he said that he would remove the guards if I would promise not to try to escape. I had to say "no" to this because to have said anything else would have diminished me in his eyes. I remembered what the farm woman said, "They appreciate toughness and pride." I also said no on the psychological grounds that I had to be regarded as a prisoner still, and that he had to keep watching me; otherwise it would feel too much like fraternization, like we were buddies making a deal.

I think it was because I said "no" that he let me see Irmgard even more. The colonel knew, not only from his conversation with me but from conversations he must have had with Dr. von Polster, that I was not stupid nor was I a fool. There was no place to go in any case.

I surmised that he had said something about Paris; he had been there, yes, Paris. Wunderbar, beautiful, he said, and when I nodded, it was as if our both having been in Paris had created some sympathetic bond between us. We were now united by a common experience, and the feeling I got was one of meeting a fellow American in an out-of-the-way place, in a foreign country.

We went on in our conversation, or really his monologue, for there was nothing for me to do except nod, very seriously. He poured liquid from the bottle into two water glasses. It was not wine, for I heard him say schnapps, which I knew from my experience was probably way over one hundred proof. I began to sweat. I knew I could not do the tip-the-glass-down-the-hatch macho business, that if I began to sip the stuff, in no time I would be sweating even more, flushed and totally drunk.

The colonel took a deep swallow from his glass and emptied more than half. I picked up my glass, sipped from it, and held onto it. He filled his up again, loosening. I wondered how long this would go on. Every so often I would say, "Ich verstehe, I understand," for I sensed that he wanted me to be a witness for him when the Allies came.

It was clear that the colonel had been very decent. I knew that other American flyers had been shot or hung, while we were kept alive and Karl was tended and cared for. He sat there for a while, drinking, laughing quietly, saying Paris was wonderful, do you like Paris, "Vous aimez Paris," to which I nodded, I understand, "Ja, mon colonel," "Je comprends," alright, alright. I took a bigger sip, feeling that our meeting had to be almost over. I was holding onto myself as tightly as I could; it was a race against time, especially as my body was even more denuded of fat than before. I began to feel the heat of the schnapps in my belly. I began to worry that I would fall over drunk on the spot and that, to my shame, I would have to be carried out by two orderlies and dumped onto my bed.

When I felt the heat rush to my chest and throughout my body, he stood up and shook my hand. I saluted him as smartly as I could and again he made a gesture resembling a salute. He was definitely not a Hitler man. No "sig Heil's" here. The orderly took me back to my room rather quickly. I felt the time returning was much shorter than the going and I wondered about that, for it seemed to be true in so many situations in life—going is long, coming back is short. It must have to do with time and Einstein.

My thoughts were blurring and I could feel my body giving way. I clenched my fist, I bit my tongue, I rubbed my face, then finally in the room I just fell into bed, dressed fully except for my shoes which I kicked off before I was gone, and too drunk even to look for a letter from Irmgard.

# 3

Days in Captivity

During those five weeks of imprisonment, I was often shaken by the intensity of my feelings for Irmgard. I did not see her only as Sister Irmgard, my German nurse, for I knew that was only her superficial persona. Another side, a deeper layer, came out in her whispered words and her letters.

At times I'd write things to provoke her. She would retort that I was an arrogant American, that if I had arrived under other circumstances, as a conqueror, she would never have approached me or spoken with me or given anything of herself to me.

*When they will come, they will have a manner and this is natural, which forbids for me to talk with them and so I never knew anything about them. Therefore, when I shall be too much hurt by their, in this moment, natural manner, I will think of their friendly enemy who I knew a little bit. Yes, you don't believe it but you never have had the heart and feeling of a woman. This would make all any easier, though he too is very arrogant.*

Irmgard was right when she called me arrogant. What was strange was that I did not feel I was that kind of person. I knew I could be proud, and that if pride could be inherited, I had inherited it from my grandmothers.

For me my two grandmothers had been emblems of pride. My mother's mother, Elizabeth, had sympathetic eyes and very high cheekbones, and seemed like she might have been of American Indian or Tartar or Mongolian ancestry. Her bearing was erect, and a quiet wisdom emanated from her. Women from the neighborhood would stop by with platters of cookies or knishes or pastries, and would sit for hours with my grandmother, asking for advice.

My other grandmother, my father's mother, Mary, had the pride of silence. Though she was uneducated and illiterate, she was always a consummate wife and mother, and ruled her house with the assurance of an English butler. She could do anything in the kitchen, and my fondest memory was of her sitting in the late afternoon on the bench in front of her home, in her favorite cotton dress, hands folded on her lap and clean hair combed back smooth. She would sit silently, often for an hour or more, not even talking to me as I ran in and out of the house with my marbles or trolley cars. Sometimes I would watch her face, and the timeless, still quality about her that was so lovely. I feared that I might tumble into that stillness and go falling, falling into a place where there was no bottom.

My father's mother was also the richest woman in the family. My grandfather Jacob was a furrier who had worked hard and had been very well paid even during the darkest hours of the Depression. He died in 1938, and his widow, Mary, had the most elegant house, all made with love by my father, her eldest son, who was a master craftsman and could do anything with wood. He had that gift.

Somehow I always felt I'd come from royalty. Irmgard and others have always interpreted it as arrogance, and some people read it as coldness. Irmgard even cautioned me in her next letter:

*You must not always say my opinion is wrong, you must say, it is strange to you. For there is no straight answer in the world about our questions. Why should only your answer be a right one? And you may find in the world then people would think, did you only like them because they think no matter what they think? I know that you try to find the truth in life, the deep sense of life but, it is no great fate when you say, I believe in myself. Look, it is true that one at first must know their own heart. That one must confide in oneself, but this is only the foundation on which one must build, on which the heart must grow.*

But I knew that my heart was hot and passionate, my mind quick and imaginative, and that my fantasies traveled with such speed and over such distances that my heart would beat even faster.

It was crazy to think and feel such things in the middle of the war, but to say that our falling in love was impossible would be to deny the infinite possibilities nature puts before us. This woman, younger than I, was already far wiser than I. She had already divined the emotion that drew us together and she dared to write it down to me in a letter. The written word was better than spoken words—like signing your name on a legal document, there it was, irrevocable. Women do that more quickly than men, for they know that terrain and make their home in it. We men have a hard time with it—in it, and out of it.

At the time, this speed did not seem strange to me. Everything in war is accelerated. We have to live more quickly, eat more quickly, go places more quickly, and make friends and lovers more quickly. We knew we could be dead by tomorrow, that we could be dead in twelve hours. Andrew Marvel, the English poet, said it well:

> Had we but world enough, and time…
> We would sit down, and think which way
> To walk, and pass our long love's day.
> But at my back I always hear
> Time's wingèd chariot hurrying near;
> And yonder all before us lie
> Deserts of vast eternity.
> . . . . . . . . . . . . . . . . . . . .
> Now let us sport us while we may…

Poets always say it better than those plodding the path of ordinary human life.

I thought back to Giselle—only three days together in Paris and we had been in love, both of us. I thought of Sofi, my girlfriend in college, how after one kiss we had been in love and inseparable for over a year. Was I in love? I was with Sofi, deeply and terribly so. This was nature's way, all from one kiss.

All this was different with Sister Irmgard, it truly was. Soberly different, startlingly different. There was no holding, no kissing. Our love unfolded in stolen moments, scraps of paper, and whispered words and glances late at night while wounded soldiers slept. It took place in the breathy notes of a flute, played as fighter planes inched closer and closer to our sanctum in the German countryside. "I believe that when we find ourselves really, is when we have given up ourselves," she wrote.

Irmgard opened up a different vein in me, and what I felt for her seemed more spiritual than anything else. But I recognized even that was not quite accurate, for she had reignited something in me, in my being, that went back to childhood when I had felt a proclivity for a nonphysical, mystical world. These stirrings had prompted in me a great moral debate, one that had left me nonplussed, about the morality of loving. I had envied my older brother Paul and his life with his friends: partying, playing cards, going every week to the burlesque theater on Arch Street in Philadelphia, going to the whorehouse, drinking, dancing.

The burlesque house was a hallowed institution for my brother and his friends, a weekly ritual that I, the younger brother, was never asked to attend. I did not think of asking to go with them to the theater with the large gilded sign out front. Neither was I asked to accompany them to the whorehouse. I knew about their visits by their joking on the weekends as they played cards in the neighborhood park, where others strolled, pushed baby carriages, sat on benches, or set up card tables and folding chairs to play chess and checkers all afternoon. My brother and his friends would sit on the grass playing pinochle or poker or blackjack. I was allowed to be on the edge of these games, and heard all the banter about burlesque girls and chorus lines and comedians. This world of burlesque was something I never got to see, a brighter, wilder world that deserted our city while I was still young—too young to ever see it in person. But now, there was a richness to Irmgard that

I had never imagined possible during those afternoons when I heard about the dancers and the girls at the brothel, or during my passionate days with Sofi or with Giselle.

---

When I was eleven or twelve I used to stand before the mirror in our kitchen, determined to find out what lay behind my face. I thought if I kept looking into my eyes, sooner or later I could read what lay deep in my head and retrieve the secrets that made me, me.

I lost track of time as I stared, but got no further than watching the pupils widen and constrict, and the color of my eyes change from blue to blue green and back. I figured after twenty minutes it was not going to work. I no longer recall what prompted me to do this. Though I was usually a genuinely carefree and thoughtful child, the problem niggled at me.

I was also curious about people, about couples. I could not understand why this man was with that woman. I never understood why my cousin Etkis was with his wife. They fought all the time. I did not understand why my Uncle Harry lived with his wife who seemed so cold and denying. I hated to be alone with her when I visited my uncle, which was often because I loved to thumb through his Tolstoy and Gogol and Chekhov, and his medical books, with their pictures of skeletons, muscles, nerves, blood—a world hidden from me like a great, magnificent secret. Sometimes it was hard to relate those pictures to me—that I was all of these pictures, that every person is all of these pictures and more.

I observed the relationship between my Uncle Alex and his wife, Eve. They frolicked, held hands, even kissed in front of me and his mother (my grandmother) when they visited from New York. Their relationship seemed right. It was natural, and I was lucky to have this one example of what two people in love looked like. I never forgot it. Their presence gave me the model I was looking for, as I had never trusted the movies and the models of love they presented. They were fun to look at but too far away from my reality to come into my life. But unconsciously I was looking for a model and when I was in the presence of Alex and Eve, I knew I had found it.

───────

After I received the first letters from Irmgard, I made sure to do what I'd always done, and not to betray my feelings for the quiet, dark-haired nurse who tended us at night. So I continued to pace, to stare out the window, and to sit at the table with Woluski and Radek, who talked endlessly in low voices. I had long stopped trying to understand what they talked about. The guards were, as always, a little saggy in their uniforms, wearing pistols in their holsters. I wondered if they could really shoot the guns they carried. They did not mind the talking or the pacing, or my looking out the window, and would break their own boredom by taking turns on the inside watch.

After the appearance of Irmgard's letter, everything had changed for me. This was a new voice, an exciting voice. This was a woman who could think, and who had feeling and courage. I did not know if, under the same circumstances, I could have done what she did. I know enough to say that we can never know what our actions might be if we are faced with choices with potentially alarming consequences. Only in that place do we have to say yes or no, and wartime choices are not those of peacetime.

My mind no longer seemed vacant as I paced. I looked out the window but had stopped listening for the American aircraft or the big guns in the distance. I no longer thought of home, or the girl whose picture I carried. I was lost in thought and reverie, transported back to the air raid cellar where I had first seen Irmgard, or to the nights when she first whispered in my ear, or when I first caught her eyes in the glimmer of the light she carried with her.

Suddenly I forgot what came after "you filled my heart with joy" and I had to read the letter again. I asked to go to the bathroom and there, with my pants over my knees, I read the letter once more. She was worried about the letters—no I did not want to destroy them, yes I would be careful, yes in an air raid I might put them under the pillow, but I would rather carry them with me.

She had my letters, too; what was she thinking? Did she read them again and again, the way I did, as if something new would appear each time? Back in the room my pacing and staring continued and ah, what can one do with time? There's nothing but time to get through. I recalled movies that showed a clock with its big hand moving slowly, ever so slowly. Time, no one can hold it and shake it, no one can nudge it forward. One just has to endure those gaps between the minutes, and they can be as wide as the Grand Canyon.

One letter and my life had changed. Though my status had not been altered—I was still a prisoner of war—everything was different now. A German woman had reached out and taken my hand. What was she thinking or doing, while I paced my room and stared out the window? Was she sleeping now? Or playing the flute somewhere? Was she writing me another letter? I could not imagine her life, for I had never seen the living area of the hospital. We were neatly sequestered and I never saw any of the nurses "off duty"; I could not even imagine Irmgard wearing anything other than her blue nurse's dress and white apron.

Lunch came and then it was the same agony of waiting, the slow passage of time. Woluski and Radek were solving the problem in their way. Karl lay unmoving, as before, as if this momentous event had never happened. I asked to go to the bathroom again and again to re-read the letter.

Ah, she was sensitive, she had pride, she did not want to hurt my feelings by telling me things that might do so. She was intuitive but then she was in a place—this German hospital—that was, for her, normal. I was the upset one, the wounded one. How old was she, eighteen? I knew she was no more than nineteen. I was knocked out of time to suffer time all because she had dared to write, "You smiled at me, and I had a deep joy." I could not suffer the time until I saw her again, and there was nothing I could do to make this happen, nothing. I'd sit or pace or stare out the window, imagining her hand on mine. Later in the days that followed Woluski and Radek would talk to me and I would lose them.

I could not tolerate their conversation, or Woluski's constant anxiety that they would mistake him for a Jew and kill him. That set me to thinking—what if Irmgard knew I was Jewish? I decided it would not matter to her: it would simply not matter. I hoped for another air raid, anything to break the monotony, but none came. I did not know what other happening I could wish for, except the Allies coming. But I knew that would end the beauty of what we had, and so there I was, suspended between two worlds. Neither world would ever bring any lasting satisfaction.

I remember the last line of the poem she quoted in her next letter, from a famous Milton sonnet: "they also serve him who stand and wait." She wrote that for me.

Now and then I returned to memories of the narrow confines of my world back in South Philadelphia. In the Jewish neighborhood where I was born and raised, the limits of my world had been very clearly, definitively marked. To go even a few streets beyond the familiar landmarks traced out by my mother on her shopping trips would occasion a kind of panic.

I could play and run through every corner of my known world— Seventh Street on the West, Ritner on the South, Fifth to the East, Snyder to the North, and, perhaps, to Eighth Street in the West, where my grade school was located, though between Seventh and Eighth the territory already became a bit foreign, more Italian than Jewish.

I had lived year after year in this neighborhood with the brick houses of varying shades of weathered red. The houses small, the streets small, the men and women familiar—there was safety in the smallness, even in the wet heat of summer, when the smell of pitch oozed from the streets as they softened under the sun, or the smell of the factories making whisky engulfed all of South Philadelphia with a scent that was both sweet and suffocating. I never knew whether I liked this smell or not.

The trolley cars passed by us, and all the gentile-looking conductors seemed big with big hands as they fingered the change machines strapped on their bellies. I admired how they knew how much change to give back so quickly—click, click, click and there it was, transferred to your hand and always right. This was an urban world with a small mentality contained within. If you dared go forth from this world, suddenly another village mentality surrounded you, though one unfamiliar, like Italian or Polish or English. The faces were different in these other enclaves, as well as their clothes, their speech.

Some summers I had spent in the country, in Vineland, New Jersey. I felt at home there, for there too all the families were Jewish except for a sprinkling of Polish people, only a sprinkle. I loved my summers there helping my cousin Etkis in his labors. He used a real horse, a real plow, and made real furrows in soil that was dark and moist. I reveled in the sweet corn in the last days of August, in the peppers, the tomatoes and the wonderful vines of grapes, red or purple or just a few white ones. The smell of the grape juice was heady and so was the wine, which my aunt made secretly for the consumption of people I was not supposed to know. For me the extreme pleasure of my boyhood was to walk around in shorts, barefoot, picking up pebbles with my toes or sinking my feet in dark wet soil.

Our world in South Philadelphia contained all we needed, with stores of every kind serving every need, from sewing a button onto a shirt to supplying fishing equipment, shoes, girdles for women, or every kind of meat or spice or bread or pastry you could ever want. On Seventh Street the curbs were lined with pushcarts: here was the woman who sold hot potato, meat, or cheese knishes that made your mouth water; beside her stood the snowball man with his cart, syrup bottles, and the little ice scrapers he'd use to fill your cup with ice chips; beside him Tony the Italian ice cream man sold chocolate or vanilla cones for only one penny each, and stood with an umbrella over his cart to shield him from the sun.

I remember the live fish store and the store next to it with its cheeses and eggs, brought fresh from the farm twice a week. You could smell the chicken coop in them, or the chicken that had sat on it, almost. The butcher store with its live chickens and the schochet who would kill the chicken as soon as it you bought it. This store had its own smell, of sawdust and blood and chicken entrails, and when the butcher opened the refrigerator door you could see massive pieces of beef hanging up.

There was something awesome about it, and about the bakery with its sweet smells and countless variations of cookies and cakes and icings. There was the hardware store with its array of scissors and knives, parts for machinery I couldn't name. The husband used to peddle in the neighborhood, selling or sharpening knives and scissors while his wife, Chika, minded the store. The notion store with its seemingly inexhaustible supply of wool and ribbons and buttons and tchotchkes of all kinds. My mother would buy wool to knit me sweaters. I loved to hold the wool looped between my hands as my mother wound the wool into a big ball which she would later manipulate with her needles. And before you knew it, something was growing right before your eyes.

Each store displayed its wares on outside stands as well, so that the sidewalks were full of stands and pushcarts. Every day the women poured from their houses and onto Seventh Street—to shop, buy, browse, and talk with the other women, whose faces were familiar, or with relatives who lived on neighboring streets. With these women came scores of preschool children, holding their mothers' hands or dresses or sometimes, if adventurous, scouting ahead.

Sometimes I held on to my mother's skirt, and sometimes I wandered away. There was no real problem with traffic, for cars were seldom seen and the trolley cars passed these stores very slowly. The stands were put out all through the spring, summer, and fall; in the winter they appeared only on Saturdays, and no matter how cold it was the women and their bundled-up children once again crowded the street.

My friends and I played cops and robbers or cowboys and Indians on Seventh Street, or on Wolf Street, which ran perpendicular to Sixth and Seventh. Our fighting could range over several blocks. The stands were good hiding places to pop out with a good *bang bang*, or a *bang, bang, bang*! with appropriate gestures, hands shaped like a gun and arm jerking forward while yelling, "You're dead!"

We did as we liked, sometimes pretending to be killed and sometimes going on shooting even if we were "dead."

Although our parents talked about times being hard, we children really did not know what that meant. We knew our life, we did not know a better life, or a worse life, whatever that could be. We played with sincerity, with ferocity and with endless energy. For us, there was no Great Depression, there was only this, our childhood.

This was my world before the war. I've gone back there a number of times since but cannot find that quaint and beloved time or place, for nothing is the same there now. The red brick house, once as familiar to me as the Sphinx must have been to the Egyptians, is now gone.

I regret now that I did not ask my grandparents to tell me about their village, about life in the village, their families, their genealogy, my genealogy. Now all is gone, all is forgotten, except they're not forgotten, nor the deep pleasure, the profound security, which knowingly or not they extended to me.

I regret that it never occurred to me to ask my father or my uncles how it was growing up in Russia. How it was to come to America: how did they do it? Where did they have to go, cross what rivers, what mountains, what barriers, to board a ship to land on Ellis Island? And I never asked my uncles how they went to school here, or what was it like growing up in South Philadelphia at that time. Now all is lost. I imagine we have plowed under countless civilizations that have existed, cultures that have flourished, people who lived and worked and died, and were forgotten.

One afternoon, one like all the others, Radek and Woluski were making their usual murmur as I sat listening to them, looking at one and then the other. I became distracted, thinking of nothing but the boredom, when suddenly the rich notes of the flute trailed into the room. Woluski and Radek seemed not to hear it. This always astonished me—their utter indifference to these sounds that filled me with joy.

I did not call the music to their attention. They never knew who it was playing the flute, and I never told them. I'm not sure they even noticed Irmgard, or were awake to watch her as she moved through the room at night. I am sure that if they ever did notice her, she would have seemed no different from the other nurses.

I got up quietly and went to the window, though I was not able to see her from it. Already wisps of spring were in the air. The trees were leafing, the bushes were green, flowers were beginning to open, and I could smell the spring air, so clean and sweet and nourishing. The beauty of this April belied our circumstances, and the flute with its notes took me to the rushing water of streams and rills, the smart, smacking sounds of the water divided by stone and rocks, and then to meadows and tall, lonely pine trees. All this in a foreign land, and myself a prisoner.

I felt insane for a moment, for I could not reconcile these contradictory feelings, and as I was trying to make sense of it there was a quick burst of notes. I could see her fingers move in my mind's eye—agile, rhythmic, with minds of their own—and then suddenly there was silence.

But I had already stored away my treasure. And I kept standing at the window, repeating the music, repeating the feelings, wanting it to last the way a child puts a cookie in his mouth and waits for it to moisten and to melt, and to slowly dissolve. I leaned my head against the windowpane, closed my eyes, and let myself drift from the joy to the sorrow, through the infinite variations and combinations of the flute. And through them, I knew she was speaking to me of her heart.

---

I had received two letters from Sister Irmgard and was electrified by her words and the danger she had set into motion with these letters. "The soldiers cry with pain," she wrote, "and I must hear their cries without helping." Around that same time Karl took a sudden turn for the worse. He was again delirious and we resumed our regimen of cooling him down. One day I smelled something awful, so stinking that I gagged. When I realized it was coming from Karl, I told the guard to please call the doctor. I knew this was serious, that gangrene had set in. There is no other smell like it.

When Dr. von Polster came and looked under the bandage at the wound, he remained silent and hurried from the room. Later that day the guard moved Karl's bed away from mine and next to the windows, which looked out on the trees and bushes and the edge of the porch where Irmgard often played her flute. They moved the rectangular table to the center of the room—a change that allowed us to breathe air uncontaminated by the awful smell of rotting, blackened flesh. Karl lay delirious; God had blessed him with this forgetfulness. How could he have withstood the sight and smell of his own decaying body?

That evening I was again taken to the colonel's office, but this time there was no schnapps, no levity. I noticed how the colonel's black hair was going gray, especially at the temples, and how neatly the color of his hair blended in with the gray blue color of his officer's coat. Dr. von Polster was there and translated for the colonel.

"Your soldier has gangrene. We are sorry to see this but we knew there was that possibility. We tried to remedy it when we took him to surgery before. Now, the leg has to come off; if it does not he will die in a few days. If we take it off there is no guarantee that he will live, but it gives him a chance. Do you understand?" I nodded, saying, "Ich verstehe." Dr. von Polster went on, "The colonel wants you to attend the surgery so that you will testify that no brutality was done to your soldier. That all due surgical procedures were done as they would be done to any one of our own soldiers, do you understand?" Again I nodded, "Ich verstehe."

Now I could better understand why the colonel did not want me to leave the hospital, and why he had shown such kindness to us. I was going to be a star witness for him, just in case.

"Would you be able to stand by and watch?" von Polster asked, and I said I would do whatever was necessary. The colonel said, "Good, good." I saluted, and von Polster took me back. We did not speak much; he left me alone with my thoughts, my apprehension about watching such a procedure.

"Have you seen many of these cases?" I asked.

"On the Russian front we had a fair number."

"How did they do?"

"Some lived, the lucky ones, minus an arm or leg. They recovered, and were sent back to Germany to recuperate. Many did not recover." He was silent after that. He had his own history to reflect upon and I continued to do the same with mine.

The next morning I was awakened earlier than usual. I dressed. There was some tea on the table for me but no bread. I suppose they did not want me vomiting up sawdust in the operating room. Karl was already gone. I followed the guard down several stairwells until finally we came to a door that opened into an operating room. I saw nurses and doctors and it was much like what the movies show.

I watched them set Karl up, the anesthetist behind him. I could see the doctors who were going to perform the surgery washing their hands and arms over and over in the sink and finally drying off with a towel, each his own towel, tucked into his gown by the nurse. I was given a surgical mask and gown to wear. I did not understand the procedure, and no one explained it to me. The doctors worked quickly. They would take the leg off at the hip; experience had taught them to be safe. Better to lose a little more leg and be alive than to cut too close to the infected area and be dead.

I stood watching as the leg came off, black and full of pus, and I wondered how these doctors could tolerate the terrible, terrible smell. Once you've smelled it you will never forget it, nor the nausea nor the rising gorge in your throat. The surgeons wrapped up the leg and passed it on to a nurse, who took it carefully and left the operating room.

Then began the procedure of dealing with what was left. I could not really see how much they sewed, or how they applied bandages and pressure to close the body where the leg had been separated from it. And then it was over.

Von Polster appeared, and the colonel, who had been there throughout watching, spoke to von Polster, who then spoke to me. "We have a German soldier who caught a bullet in his throat, and it has to be removed. The colonel asked if you want to see the operation." I said that I would. So I stayed and in twenty minutes or so was at another table with two young doctors, new surgeons, using what I thought were probes to jab into this man's throat. I could see they were trying to locate the bullet, to get a fix on it the way I would get a fix on two stars to establish my position in the heavens. The injured soldier was anesthetized, so the two probes caused ghastly choking and coughing, so horrible sounding I thought he would die on the table.

After a considerable amount of jabbing both had their probes on the bullet. They had isolated it. A third surgeon now went in with a scalpel and delivered the bullet, but not without the most terrible retching and writhing from the unconscious patient. The colonel had stayed and watched but after a little while left the room, saying, von Polster told me, that he could not stand to watch these new surgeons work. It was traumatic, both to the patient and to him.

Karl was brought back to the room later that day, smelling of antiseptic. The nurse came in several times a day and throughout the night to take and chart his temperature. I thought all was well. He had had gangrene of the leg; I figured take off his leg, and he'd be cured. Karl did not sail into serene waters, however, but remained feverish, sleeping or muttering. At the request of the nurse, I began again to apply compresses to his forehead.

Woluski and Radek took turns with me applying compresses, a monotonous and sometimes difficult job because Karl would twist and turn in his delirium. We were lucky that no air raids sounded for it would have been tortuous to try to get him into the basement.

It was odd, the relationship among Woluski, Radek and me. I had not known them before this mission, and there seemed to be nothing that could draw us closer together, despite the fact that we spent so many days and nights in one room. They were a twosome who had an affinity for each other, based on a past I was not privy to. I felt no desire to inquire into their lives, and this surprised me, for I was usually a very curious person. Together we ate in that room, walked in that room, slept and sat at the table in that room. We all talked softly, for there was something about being a prisoner that gave rise to a feeling that we had lost our right to speak in ordinary voices. Always our voices were lowered, though the guards did not pay attention to us or to our speech.

The one occasion when I had been able to speak to Irmgard on the porch had been exhilarating, for we had really talked, exchanging ideas and feelings in normal speaking voices. Everything had come alive, my mind had lit up, and I could feel my heart beat strongly and color come into my thin cheeks. Nights when Karl lay ill again, Sister Irmgard would come and tend to him. Woluski and Radek slept soundly, and only I would know when she had come to check on Karl, taking his pulse and temperature, and trying to cool him down. As she wrote in one of her letters, "the sick would call for her all night," and she was busy tending to them. I always knew she'd been there because of the wine by my bed.

*I do not speak about these questions to all people, I know I'm different from them, with all my soul, I am somewhat obliged to speak to you about these things, but I often think if it has a use (if it's useful to do it) for you too are quite different from me. You may not understand my wishes, my striving, you may be sarcastic at them. Perhaps you may any way later tell with other Americans from the German woman. You may show them my letters, you all will laugh at them or discuss about them. I would freeze in thinking of it when you did not have anything written by me it would be better, when you could not speak about me to other people, at least not in this distinct manner.*

Time was heavy. We had nothing to read, and I had only scraps of paper to write my thoughts down for Irmgard. No one was curious about these jottings; the guards did not ask, Woluski and Radek did not ask. Mealtimes we sat and ate slowly, sipping our lukewarm weak tea, commenting on nothing. After the meal I would walk the length of the room or stay at the window looking at the trees and the sky, straining to hear again the sound of the flute. My mind would play tricks on me; I'd think I heard a note and my heart would soar, until, one second later, I realized it was the wind or something else.

Sometimes the three of us talked of how nice it would be to have a bath. I do not know what Radek and Woluski did, but I shaved every morning, and I assumed they did in their turn at the small bathroom sink with the small mirror over it. After shaving I would strip to the waist and wet myself in what my brother would call a "whore's bath." It was better than nothing, and luckily no lice ever appeared. We all wore the same clothes, underwear and socks we had worn that ominous day when we first entered the plane.

I spent long hours at the window looking for Irmgard, and sometimes I could see our P-47s flying, diving, bombing and rising once again. All the time I would hear the really big guns, now thirty to fifty miles away. Aside from Irmgard, that was my only comfort. I knew my freedom was close—another few days at the most—and yet this same freedom could only bring me anguish. And so there I was, caught.

Mainly, I recall pacing the floor. Woluski and Radek seemed more placid and once I reassured them, after my talk with the colonel, Woluski especially relaxed. We looked forward to our meals—not because there was any nutrition to be had, for sawdust does not satisfy, it only blows your gut up—but the arrival of the one slice of pumpernickel bread and cup of weak warm tea marked the passage of time. It was also something different to do, and though we did not have much conversation between the three of us, we did share this common activity.

Sometimes Woluski or Radek would say, "Don't you remember those sausages and pancakes and eggs we had for breakfast? Or those steaks?" For those who wanted meat before missions, steak had been available. The best of everything had been put before us as we walked along the counter cafeteria style. It seemed there were endless trays of eggs cooked in every fashion, along with bacon, sausage, pancakes big or small, butter galore, syrup, pitchers of milk on every table and coffee and bread, mountains of bread.

Our stomachs, though blown up after our sawdust meal, did not feel full, and we were always hungry. Yet there was a cleverness to the sawdust meal, for it left us with a discomfort in our bellies that made all food seem distasteful. Eventually we stopped thinking and talking of food, and I never knew whether or not our captors knew of the consequences of our meals. Nor did I know what they ate in their mess halls. I suppose the colonel and the officers had genuine food, for that's the way it works in the military, whatever side you're on.

I thought of how I had comforted myself at home as a young child when things seemed boring and gray on cold winter nights and the passage of time seemed endless: I whistled songs I enjoyed and I listened to the radio, which came into our lives one day, a surprise from Mr. Braverman.

One Sunday Mr. Braverman had arrived carrying large packages, from which he assembled a rectangular box with complicated wiring and tubes inside, and a speaker that sat on top—our first radio, made by Silvertone. My father had done some work at Mr. Braverman's house and this was Mr. Braverman's way of repaying that favor.

The only place I had been able to hear music before this was at my grandmother's house. There, against the wall, between the two windows that looked out over Sixth Street and onto the park, stood a beautiful black piece of furniture as tall as the windowsill. There was a round form covered by green velvet to place the record on. The substantial arm was folded on the side; you would place the arm on the record as soon as you wound up the Victrola. Again and again I would play my favorite record, "My Bonnie Lies over the Ocean."

This was visible wealth. None of my friends' houses had a Victrola; I doubted that anyone on the block had one. My grandmother may have been illiterate, but she was avant-garde. She had the money—her husband and sons saw to that. Later, I puzzled as to what she did with all the dollars they dropped in her lap. She had very few possessions when she died, not even jewelry, for she never wore any piece of jewelry other than her gold wedding band.

Once we had a radio, our world changed. My father could get the news more easily than he had reading the newspaper. He was hooked on "The Lone Ranger" and never missed an episode. I was hooked on "The Shadow," but I'd already come across him in magazines at the candy store. I would read through an entire magazine whenever I waited to make "phonies." In those days, the 1920s, people did not have private phones. There were three or four public phones in nearly all candy stores. When they rang, the owner would ask one of the young boys to fetch Mrs. Cohen or Mrs. Schwartz a block or so away. For this effort, the boy would be rewarded with a nickel. This was the custom. To not give a tip would be courting not being summoned the next time Mrs. Cohen or Mrs. Schwartz had a phone call waiting at the candy store.

But there was another great attraction to the candy store. Among the many magazines the rack held were the lurid covers of "Spicy Detective" and other titles with provocative pictures of beautiful women whose dresses barely covered their breasts. All the fellows looked at these magazine covers, and dreamed.

The radio opened a new world. On Saturday nights there was the hit parade, and we would all sit and hear the countdown of one beautiful song after another sung by the famous singers of the day. We listened to Amos and Andy, Fibber McGee and Molly, the evening detective stories, and Jan Pearce singing "The Blue Bird of Happiness." There were so many riches to hear, so many evocations, that my imagination always took hold and flew.

But as it flew I also knew that one foot was tied to the ground in this house, in this street, in this poverty, which wrenched my heart. The weather in the winter—cheerless, gray and cold—only aggravated the pain. I would be bored with reading, and there was no one with whom to talk. It was too cold to be outside. No one, not even a dog, would be out. On those evenings the radio was my lifesaver. I listened to the music and escaped into reverie.

---

One night in prison we went to bed around ten p.m. as usual. I took off my pants, shirt, shoes and socks. The lights were out. The guards stood outside. I fell asleep, but suddenly was awakened by a noise outside the door. I heard loud voices coming from the hall, and then the door opened. Two younger men—not the usual guards, who were older and slower in their movements—entered. I did not see our usual guards as real soldiers, but more like middle-aged aides turned guards with guns. It was clear they were not accustomed to them.

The light came on. I sat up, threw my covers off, and began putting on my pants and shirt, and hurriedly pulling on my socks and shoes. I felt that old feeling in my gut and down my spine—that unmistakable shiver of fear. I wanted to be ready.

I could see that these younger men were real soldiers. They handled their guns as if they had lived with them, used them, and cleaned them. They motioned me back to bed—"schlasen." I stayed sitting up, and by now Woluski and Radek were also awake, still under the covers. I lay down reluctantly, pulled my feet out of my shoes, and covered myself with the blanket. Tonight I was going to sleep with my clothes on if I could. The room was dark now. The men stood facing the door.

My pulse was racing. Something was happening that I could not understand, or could only guess—that the die-hard Nazis, those not too wounded, were planning some kind of assault on this part of the hospital—against us.

I waited. Suddenly there was a tumult in the hall. I heard raised voices, and shouts and counter-shouts, but I could see nothing. The two men in the room raised their guns. The noise outside continued until I heard what sounded like a command. I imagined I heard the colonel's voice, that he had come to quell the ruckus. In a few minutes all was quiet.

Von Polster entered the room, looking agitated. He was properly dressed, though it was well past midnight. I got up and stood before him in my stocking feet. The others remained in bed, fear on their faces, trying to listen to our conversation. Von Polster was brief. A few SS men had gotten drunk and then a little out of hand. Word had quickly spread to the colonel, who headed off their threats only after ensuring our safety.

"The colonel wants you to remember that," he said. He paused before adding, in an embarrassed tone, "This is not how many of us are." He stood a moment, not knowing what to say. I imagined he wanted to talk his heart out, but it was not seemly before an American POW.

I said, "I appreciate the colonel's efforts, and yours. I will not forget."

Von Polster left, and after a while the two young soldiers went outside. I do not know what happened after that, since the door was locked. We were forbidden to exit, in any case.

I did not get undressed, but lay back in bed. I spent the night restlessly, twisting from side to side, sleeping fitfully. As if from far away I became aware of a hand on my shoulder, and I awoke with a cry.

It was Irmgard. She put her face to my ear. "Sshhhh, shhh," she whispered, and pointed to the glass of red wine on the floor. When she left, I drank the glass at full tilt. "My angel," I thought, again and again. I slept until morning, and the day began like every other day, as if nothing had happened, with the same round of dull events. Nothing to do except sit, wait, stand, stare, walk, think, reflect, reminisce, conjecture, and listen to our P-47s and our big guns, now a little closer. There was nothing for me to do. Still, I preferred this monotony to the problems of the night before. That was finished, and was never mentioned again.

Four or five days after Karl's operation, the old stinking smell of putrefied flesh returned, and I knew he was going to die. One night, after I'd sponged him down and gone to sleep, I was awakened by a touch. It was Irmgard, kneeling beside me in the dark. She said, "Your friend has died. I will get Dr. von Polster."

In a little while von Polster entered the room, followed by two soldiers with a gurney, to confirm that Karl was gone. The room was silent and heavy with death. Radek and Woluski had awakened and were watching from their beds, half sitting up but quiet. What was there to say? We did not speak as the two soldiers lifted Karl onto the gurney and carried him out of the room. The stench of gangrene was staggering.

Once they had all left, I went to the window and stood for a while, benumbed. The other two drifted back to sleep. I had never even known Karl as a healthy, conscious man, and now he was gone.

We were not shocked, and yet his absence seemed profound, and the following morning none of us could find the words to express that. I knew Woluski and Radek had become close to Karl on their many missions together—it is always that way in war—but there was nothing to say about it, for any of us. He was simply gone.

———

We were now in the fifteenth day of our captivity. Von Polster appeared. He said, "I am sorry about your comrade, but you saw his leg and his whole body was infected. We have no cure for gangrene." I nodded. I didn't know what to say or even ask. "The colonel sends his regrets that we could not save him."

I asked, "What about antibiotics? There is penicillin."

Von Polster nodded. "But only you have it, we don't."

"What if you had taken his leg off before all this happened?"

"We just don't take off legs like that, not even on our own wounded soldiers. We hope the wound is clean, stays clean, and we watch." After a moment he continued, "We will bury him in the local cemetery. The colonel asks if you want to go to see for yourself."

I recognized again the wisdom of the colonel, from the beginning to now, deciding not to send us away to oblivion, to show us his humanitarian and ethical physician's duty. I appreciated it all.

Von Polster said, "You must promise not to try to escape. There will be a guard with you." I nodded. I was conducted to another part of the hospital where I saw four men lift an ordinary pine wood casket, and begin to exit. Von Polster told me to follow them outside.

———

What most impressed me as I followed the four men carrying the casket was the cleanliness, the smell of cleanliness. A fountain spout emerged from a dragon's head carved into a wall, and the water poured fresh and clean as we walked by. The houses were old-fashioned, painted saffron or deep brown, and they stood among shops with ornate iron signs hanging over their doors. I saw a tavern with windows full of beer mugs—shapes of every kind, colors of every kind.

A man in a wagon rode by, his horse trotting down the street in sharp clean clips.

The few people we came across looked at me with some surprise, although I'm sure the townspeople knew that there had been four Americans in the hospital, and that now there were only three. We walked fifteen minutes and came to a cemetery that I thought could not have been too far from the center of town. I could not tell for sure.

At the gravesite there was already a mound of freshly turned earth. Overseen by the keeper of the cemetery, the four soldiers lowered the box into the grave and then turned to me with a gesture. Did I want to say something?

This caught me off guard. I was not expecting to recite a eulogy, and I didn't know what to say. I hadn't a thought, for I had been totally occupied with the walk through the town, and smelling the sweet air, feeling the freedom and slow living of everyday life, imagining Irmgard walking through these same streets. Life was too strong for me to think of death then. But I nodded and bowed my head at the foot of the grave, and thought about Karl.

I had not known this young man before our mission began. I did not even know where he came from. He was one of those young Americans who had come to Germany to die; that was clearly his destiny. In those days I had hardly a notion of the great God, though I had already been struck by the thought that the sweet hand of the divine hung over my head and had helped me to get this far. What happened on my third mission reified a belief, though I never spoke of this to anyone. The fact that I had been wounded and not killed on this mission was truly a miracle, as was the sudden appearance of the Luftwaffe officer at the Stuttgart train station; as was Irmgard. Already, deep in my heart was the sure knowledge that whatever problems I might encounter later in life, this force of the universe would be there. However bruised I might become, this greatness would shield me and lessen my wounds.

Finally, I began. "Oh Lord, I did not know this young American, but I see that it is not important, for you know everything about him. You also know the reason for taking him. Lord, I know only one psalm, which I will say," and I recited:

> The Lord is my shepherd; I shall not want.
> He maketh me to lie down in green pastures: he leadeth me beside the still waters.
> He restoreth my soul: he leadeth me in the paths of righteousness for his name's sake.
> Yea, though I walk through the valley of the shadow of death, I will fear no evil: for thou art with me; thy rod and thy staff, they comfort me.
> Thou preparest a table before me in the presence of mine enemies: thou anointest my head with oil; my cup runneth over.
> Surely goodness and mercy shall follow me all the days of my life, and I will dwell in the house of the Lord for ever…

When I finished I bent over to pick up some dirt, flung it onto the casket, and said, "Dust thou were, now dust you are, amen." I stepped back and watched them fill in the grave. We turned and retraced our steps, or so I thought, until at one point we stopped and one of the soldiers said "inside" in German.

I was surprised and curious, but realized soon enough that we were at the town bathhouse. The soldier motioned for me to bathe, so I took my clothes off. This was my first full bath in almost a month. There was a wonderfully hot shower, and I soaked and soaked and washed and let the water fall over me, enjoying it beyond imagining. I stayed until the soldier appeared and told me it was time to finish. So I got out and dried myself with the towel they had provided and combed my now-long hair with a comb they had provided, then got dressed. Unfortunately I dressed in my old underwear and clothes, but, nonetheless, I felt renewed.

On the way back, I thought about the colonel's gesture in allowing me to attend Karl's burial. My thinking was that he had decided to use me as a witness of his benevolent treatment of me and my comrades. I felt it was why he wanted me to see the operation to remove young Karl's gangrenous leg and shared with me, through Dr. Von Polster, his frustration at not being able to do anything more to help us or his own patients. They had heard of penicillin but obviously had none, nor any medication to fight infection. Everything was a matter of luck. It was also clear to me that giving me the wine was with his approval, but Irmgard's writing me of her heart and mind and soul—that was all hers.

When we returned from the cemetery, I was met by von Polster in front of the hospital. He said, "Your President Roosevelt has just died. We are very sad; we know he was a kind and great man and would have dealt with us fairly in the time to come. Everyone is sad. We feel his loss almost as much as the American people do. We do not know anything about the new President Truman…It's Easter Sunday, do you want to go to church? We have service in the hospital." And we walked down some hallways, and into another building and into a large room filled with soldiers and nurses. The priest was at the altar.

The service had already begun. I thought it was incredible that I could find myself in this situation, for I could have been in any military base Catholic church anywhere in the world and this is what I would have seen and heard. I stood with von Polster and the rest of the congregation, listening to the priest, though I had no comprehension of what he was saying. I was sitting on the aisle, above the middle of the church. I noticed people turning to glance at me but they would look quickly away. I saw no unfriendly eyes; if there were any, they were not cast in my direction. Because of my time at West Chester, the small Pennsylvania town where I went to college, I was familiar with many of the Christian hymns.

After the service von Polster walked me back to my captivity. The room seemed different when I returned. Although the four of us had not been close, and though Karl had been sick from the moment he was wounded, the room was changed without him there. Though never part of our daily routine, he had always been there in his feverish state, twisting or muttering. His presence, his moans and sighs, had altered the feeling in the room. It seemed that with his death the three of us turned inward, Karl's death sobering us and making us aware again of the swift and terrible deaths of the majority of the crew. We did not talk of it, and I never told them how the engineer had died, standing with his parachute on and the look of terror on his face, unable to move. I doubt he had even heard the words I shouted to him before I flung myself out of the bomb bay doors.

That night Irmgard came. I had made myself stay awake so I would not miss her. Quietly she entered the room, walked across the floor, and put the wine glass down. And when she put it down, her hand gently touching my shoulder, I said, "Danke, danke schön." She held my hand for the briefest instant and said, "I am sorry about your friend, your young friend. I am sorry about all the young men who have died in this terrible war." Though it was dark I could see that her eyes glistened. I could feel the pressure of her feelings come toward me, in sympathy. It made tears come to my eyes. She turned and left. I gazed after her for several minutes, then drank the wine quickly, and fell asleep.

The next day von Polster sent for me, and again we spoke of Roosevelt's death. I agreed with him that this was a terrible loss for all of us, especially for the Germans. We Americans revered Roosevelt, for we felt he had done so much for the country, and all of us had listened eagerly to his radio-broadcast "fireside chats."

Von Polster and I spoke as our thoughts impelled us. I could not say anything about Truman, for I did not know the measure of the man. I explained that vice presidents do not play a stellar role in the governing of the country. I imagined the Americans would be as curious as the rest of the world to see what this man was made of. As it transpired, he was the man who would drop the atomic bomb, and he was also the man who would say, "The buck stops here."

Truman would turn out to be a man of great stature, but we did not know that then. Von Polster did not, in turn, talk much of the politics of the Nazi State; he reddened when the topic came up. I could tell he was ashamed, the way Irmgard was—for she had told me this directly. It was clear to me that von Polster was first and last a doctor and a humanist.

I understood too that the colonel had prompted him to sound out what I knew. I said, "I don't know anything about Truman, but there are no more Roosevelts and I am sorry too for America."

It seemed these deaths were a prelude to changes, to endings, like Karl's life and death. Fatal disease was an ending—like Irmgard's song about the end of winter, spring and flowers beginning—for endings also intimate new beginnings.

The sound of the guns was closer. That night Irmgard left a letter, which said in part, "*Would you ever tell to a conqueror or to a man who feels like a conqueror, 'Here am I, here is my heart, deeply look into it'? Now, when you wish to show anyone something of yourself, you must always stand upon the same bottom. Why am I speaking to you? At first you know as I wished to show you something of our real soul for you told something about us which made me sure that we all don't know one from the other. It filled me with sadness.*"

When Irmgard and I walked again, I spoke of her letter.

"You wanted me to see you deeply. Am I not to see the German people as well? Am I to forget the German flyers are shooting American airmen who were unlucky enough to lose their planes and had to parachute out? Should I forget the soldiers being killed by Germans on the ground?"

"I have no answer for war," she replied. "I have no answer for Max being killed. I have no answer for any of this."

"You say you love the truth. What is the truth?"

"I do not know the truth of my country now. I know my truth in me and I think I know the truth in you and I will be sorry when truth between us lies hidden beyond a deep skin of misunderstanding, of bitterness, of badness. I don't want that to happen between us." She looked at me imploringly. I was silent. I retreated, thinking, why am

I badgering this girl anyway? It is as bad for her as me, losing a brother, losing her home, losing her parents somewhere in Germany. Maybe I will be lucky. I may get out, but she will be in a mess. How big a mess I could not even contemplate.

It seemed I loved her all the more.

———

As I went over the events of the past two days in my mind—that little stretch of the town that I saw, the burial, ceremony, the psalm I recited—I found myself thinking back to my grade school's morning assembly, where we saluted the flag and listened to the teachers read from the Bible. I used to love the psalms, with the lines I never forgot:

"If I ever forget thee, o Jerusalem, may my right hand lose its cunning.…"

"When I was a child, I spoke as a child…"

"By the waters of Babylon, we sat down and wept…"

"For the earth shall be full of the knowledge of the Lord as the waters cover the sea…"

My imagination had soared at the images the words evoked. Later, when I myself taught school and was asked to read from the Bible, I picked the same psalms and parts of the Bible that I had heard as a child. This was really my introduction to my heritage, for my Jewishness was secular. All the history I knew I got from Sunday school.

I recalled how one Sunday morning I got up early before the family awakened, got dressed, brought in the milk and, as if in a dream, went to the Sunday school on Snyder Avenue about a mile from our house. I had never thought about the school even though I knew in the edge of my mind where it was and what it was. I heard no voice. If there were one, it was certainly inaudible. I just walked there and what I heard from my teachers was the glorious history of the Jews, the poets and singers, the prophets and the warriors, and the kings. Their great discovery of only one God, a jealous God, a vengeful God but a forgiving one—who forgave David—and a giver of wisdom to Solomon and Joseph, he of the multicolored coat. In this story I heard of envy, betrayal, forgiveness, and of a gift of prophecy that astounded me. It was a great forgiveness as Joseph forgave his brothers. It seemed to me a thread of feeling for the greatness of the Jews, of their fickleness, their weakness, their hardness, their persistence, their intelligence and their will to survive ran throughout their history. It was this quality of pride that ever quickened my blood.

I was ten years old and I had found my people.

I thought back to my magnificent shower and the surprise of Roosevelt's death. I relived the church service bit by bit, and it freshened and re-freshened in my mind.

One day after Roosevelt and Karl died, von Polster sent an orderly for me. He and I stood on the lawn in front of a small folding table and on it were two glasses of wine. He gave one to me and said, "I think soon it will be over. Your guns are louder and your planes are fearless. There are no German fighters left, and what a pity."

"What is the pity?"

"That we are fighting on opposite sides. The Russians are the real enemy. You will see, though they seem to be your allies now."

I uttered an inanity. "War makes strange bedfellows."

Von Polster replied, "You Americans are more like us than you are like the Russians."

I dared to say what came to mind. "And what about the Nazis? The whole world knows their story—their rise to power, 'krystallnacht.'"

As I spoke his complexion flushed. He was silent for a moment and then said, "They are different from any Germans, believe me. The colonel is an old Army surgeon. They [he meant the Nazis] have a different ethic than ours. I know war makes it difficult to differentiate but we are doctors, not at all politicians." As an afterthought he said, "Germany used to be a beautiful country. One day you may want to come back."

He stood, self-absorbed. We had almost finished talking. I lifted the wine glass to get the last trickle. When I put the glass down I said,

"My thanks for the wine and the talk. I appreciate your talking with me and I appreciate everything the colonel has done for me and my crew. I will never forget that."

***

As the days went by, the P-47 sorties became more numerous and the boom of big guns much louder. Our troops were closing in. I was gripped by feelings of turmoil, even states of mindlessness as I thought of the time when we in this room would be overtaken by American forces. I did not want to leave Irmgard, yet of course I knew our affair was doomed. I knew this as I sat down or paced back and forth or stood at the window looking into space, though ostensibly onto the trees and bushes and the grass—I did not see them at all. I was in consternation. I knew that I was helpless to do anything. No suggestion, no plan would work. I would be liberated. We three would be freed and immediately sent back to our units after proper identification and debriefing.

What Irmgard felt in this time I did not really know, though it was clear to her as to all those in this hospital that the days of things as they were, were numbered.

The end came sooner than I expected.

# 4

Liberation

*E*very day I had watched the P-47s fly over to bomb and strafe the road. From the windows of our room I had not been able to see exactly where they were. They might have been fifteen or twenty-five miles away, so their target was impossible to see. It had been clear from everyone's demeanor that the end for them was near—in another day, another week at most. My captors' faces were glum and they became more and more deferential towards me. That was the clearest sign of how close our troops—American, or French or English—were. After all, I might be the commanding officer who could order them all to be shot. They inferred this, and I let them have that opinion. This state of things did not, however, improve our food ration—still weak tea and a piece of ersatz pumpernickel, both with the usual bloating aftereffect.

Every day during my captivity I looked forward to seeing my Sister Irmgard, and every day that I did not see her was a day wasted. I was aware of a tug in my heart, a heaviness in my chest, and I wondered if I was in love. Or was it just a connection with another person who could speak English, and who had feelings and thoughts that revealed her education? But the persuasion of her heart, as well as her love for music and her sensitivity, which she let me see in her letters—all of this had struck me to the core.

I yearned to be with her, to look into her eyes, and once more to watch her fingers as she played the flute, when her face was lost to the world and to those around her. She was most beautiful then, and when I told her this, she blushed, and said she was glad she could make me happy.

───────

She had written me a letter containing the lines, "I know two French songs which I will tell you. Are they pretty?" I knew she meant "aren't they pretty."

*You call me your life, you call me your soul*
*I want a word from you that lasts more than one day*
*Life is ephemeral. Just a breath blows out its flame.*
*But its soul is immortal, just as is love.*

I knew at once what she was saying. Today I know even better what she was saying. I was lucky. The day after von Polster and I talked, an orderly came and asked me to follow him. I found myself on the portico and Irmgard was sitting on the steps, flute in hand. She played for a time. I looked out away from her and at times at her. The music stirred me and when she stopped for a moment I said, "That French song you wrote me is so achingly true. This moment is ephemeral. The past moments are gone forever, only to be lived in memory. Do you know that when you play, you entrance me; you are lost to this world. Then you are simply beautiful."

She blushed, laughed and said she was glad she could make me happy. I said, "You do and you have. Maybe the soul is immortal, maybe love is immortal. Right at this moment, I do not even see the guards over there. With you and me alone, I can believe that a soul has a reality like love." Then she wrote out the second song in which I read her dread of impending loss—hers of me and mine of her. This wrenched my heart.

*When one loses through sad occurrence*
*One's hope and gaiety*
*The remedy against melancholia*
*Is music and beauty*

*Which obliges more and is more able*
*to put on a good face than an armband*
*And nothing is better than to hear*
*a soft and tender tune loved long ago*

This wrenched my heart, as it must have hers for she knew more of the current events than I did.

---

She apologized once, in a whisper, for being unable to play for me every day. The nursing staff was so shorthanded that many of the women worked two shifts. "I know how you feel," she had whispered. I said, "When I do not see you on the parapet just a few feet away from me, I have an empty feeling in my heart and I think, is life worth anything without these feelings that sweep through me, a hot fire, but I still would not let myself know and feel the fire of the truth of love."

---

The morning began like all the mornings, our breakfast over in ten minutes. I went to the window facing the portico, which I could barely see. All was quiet. I resigned myself to another day hopeful I would see Irmgard again later yet not wanting to get my desire up too much. That would only make me feel worse. Thinking about the situation concerning her and me, I could find no consolation. I would have to be mindless with no thoughts of a present or a past or a future.

I thought of a butterfly. Do they know of now and later, today and tomorrow? Or a butterfly just is and one day sometime that it does not know, it is not. Is this the way of nature? It is not the nature of man who has a mind and memory and desire. I turned to Irmgard and to her letters from memory, bits and pieces from this one and that one, the love of the French woman for the German officer, her insistence on my giving back her letters, which I had done—all of them. Why was she writing about it again and again, the German soul and her chastity, her waiting for her true love—that would be me—the little French song, her family losing everything and somewhere my family who did not know where I was or if I was alive or dead.

All these ramblings flitted across my mind. It was not easy this morning. I felt a little unsettled. I could not find a reverie in which I could lose myself. Max, her brother, her beloved brother—did I remind her of him? I had already asked. She said, I recalled, "Yes, but you don't look like Max nor are you as tall as Max. You have blue eyes." She looked at me carefully. "It is nothing physical. There is something about you, a comfort, like that of being with Max. It is a feeling deep. I can't explain anymore."

I was lost in this—going over and over it—then attending to myself—what was this feeling she speaks of? But I felt blocked like when she spoke of the soul. She seemed to know more about that than I.

Suddenly someone came in, breaking my reverie. I whirled around. It was a soldier I had never seen. "Get ready," he said, "you are to go with the colonel." He motioned to my jacket. He spoke German but I understood enough to know what he meant.

Radek and Woluski came to their feet and then stood rooted and speechless beside their beds. The soldier waved them away. "Nein." It was only me that was to go.

He spoke matter-of-factly, as if he were not ripping my heart from my chest. My pulse began to race. I panicked—there was no way for me to get to Irmgard, no way for her to know. I looked around the room, eyed my two companions wildly, longing for a post to hold onto, a doorknob from which I would have to be torn. Where were we going and for what purpose? Would I see her again? Yet at the same time I imagined my freedom might be at hand, and I felt divided, torn, suspended between two great impulses—one for life, and the other for her.

I was on the verge of breakdown. My life was with her, tied to her. She had given me a new life. How could I be torn away so cavalierly? No one noticed my panic. The orderly waited for me as I turned around, trying to catch the sleeve of my flying jacket. I began to say,

"Tell Irm—" but the words were strangled in my throat. I didn't want them to know anything; I did not want to give anything away. Woluski and Radek were frightened, too; I knew they depended on me as the buffer between them and the German captors, that they felt safe as long as I was with them. So I reassured them as I took my jacket and put it on. "Don't worry," I said, "I'll be back soon."

I never saw Radek or Woluski again.

I was taken outside and when I saw a white Volkswagen with a big red cross painted across the roof, I began to sweat. Where was she? Where was I going? My eyes searched the hospital for any sign of her. After the endless minutes and hours, how could I be snatched away so suddenly? Everything seemed unreal. The colonel appeared, and in a mixture of phrases, some pidgin French, German, Russian and a word of English, told me we were going to another hospital some fifteen miles away. I had had no way of knowing that he had two hospitals under his command. It was gracious of him to tell me—after all I was his prisoner, and there was no obligation to say anything.

I nodded, but all I could think of was Irmgard, finding a way to glimpse her once more. I willed her to appear. The colonel got into the passenger seat after I squeezed into the small back seat behind him, and I took one last look at the hospital as we sped away. My heart was in anguish; I had no reason to believe I would see her again, and yet part of me thrilled to leave behind that small hospital room, where I'd spent so many days and nights. I was in turmoil. Somehow over the preceding weeks I had avoided imagining the end of Irmgard and me, the wine and the letters, but of course the situation could not last. Even so, I was not prepared for this kind of ending.

The roads were surprisingly clear, though we saw small groups of German soldiers walking along the roadsides carrying their weapons, their faces grim and as dirty as their uniforms. Mortar fire and machine guns crackled in the distance. It was a warm, sunny day, and the sky seemed to be empty, with no plane in sight. Every time we passed a German contingent I slouched down in my seat and tried to make myself invisible, never sure whether the car would be stopped or whether I would be dragged out and shot. It did not happen.

I was relieved when we pulled up to a building much like the one in which I was held in Goeppingen. I do not remember the name of the town in which this hospital was located. I was conducted to a room, where the orderly told me the colonel would return in a few hours. We would return to Goeppingen shortly after. He closed but didn't lock the door, for, of course, there was nowhere for me to go. I stretched out on the bed. There was not much to see or do in this room, with one table and one chair, and a window addressing an empty courtyard.

There was nothing to do but wait, so I waited one hour, two. The orderly reappeared and said the meeting was taking a little longer than expected, and again shut the door. Another hour passed and then another. It was now midafternoon, and I'd heard all kinds of noises, voices and movement outside my room. Footsteps, but no one entered. All I could do was think, the same thoughts scrambling through my head. How could I get back home where they knew me, and where my chronometer hung on the wall beside my bed? The chronometer's face was shattered, so I had not touched it for fear of injuring the hands. How could I get back to my chronometer? And Radek and Woluski, how could I get back to them? I thought of them, though I had hardly spoken to them. They relied on me, these two, and I had to get back for them. And then, above all, there was Irmgard. Finally I had to shut off these thoughts. I could not stand the thought of never seeing her again, of not having even said goodbye to her.

I steeled myself, spoke to myself, and might have even prayed. All I recall now is the feeling of anxiety, unlike almost anything I have known in civilian life. In the midst of this uproar of thought and feeling the door opened once again. The orderly said the colonel wanted me to join him and the other officers in the garden. I thought they must have had a great many documents to destroy before the Allies came and relieved them. These days, the shredding machines would have been going.

I followed the soldier into daylight and onto a beautiful cropped lawn where some ten to fifteen officers were standing about with drinks in their hands. Most were smoking. I was offered a glass of wine, and I cautioned myself to sip; otherwise I'd make a fool of myself by passing out drunk. That could have happened quickly, so I let only my lips get wet. The colonel introduced me to the other officers and many of them spoke English with a British accent. I placed their age from thirty to forty-five—all dressed in the natty German gray blue uniform. All were attractive. No one was blond. They greeted me in a friendly way—a fellow officer. I didn't detect any hostility.

I imagined the colonel had briefed them. One said, "You came on a holiday. We are celebrating Das Führer's birthday. Later we will listen to Herr Goebbels's talk." I nodded. What could I say to that. One of them said, "We meet only to say good-bye." I asked what that meant. He replied with a suspicion of a smile, "We will not be staying the night." The others smiled, one or two snickered.

Again I didn't know what to say. Were they doctors or administrators? When I thought about it, it didn't really matter. One said, "All this must be very unusual for you."

I said, "I could not imagine this in any book I might read, maybe in my dreams."

They laughed. None of them seemed particularly nervous. It was as if they shared a secret and they found a comfort in that shared secrecy. They raised their glasses to each other and toasted. I couldn't understand what they were really saying. The few that could speak English even raised their glass and wished me luck. I returned the gesture. Noblesse oblige—on to the big room.

I could not distinguish whether they were all doctors, soldiers of rank, or officers in the various controlling organizations of the German army. But there was no question that the colonel was the boss. Tough, with strong shoulders, thinning hair, a strong, lined face, he was an obvious leader. They treated me as a fellow officer—though unlike me, they wore a regal arrogance as if they'd worn it all their lives. It seemed natural, almost, rather than arrogant: it was the way they were.

Gradually I came to understand that a number of these men were planning on not being captured by the Allies. They were going to elude the Allies and go somewhere outside Germany, though I didn't know where. I picked up the fact that this group already possessed forged passports and papers and would disappear wherever they wished. But no one seemed rude; certainly no one was rude to me. We could have been at a cricket match in England, everyone was so civil.

The hum of conversation was broken only by fits of laughter, and the officers asked me many questions about America and the war, though I could see they were not really interested. It became clear that they all hoped—for those who were not fleeing—to be captured by the Americans, who would treat them best. Some asked if I knew where the American armies were, but of course I did not have that information.

I was then told that we would spend the night and return in the morning. I was asked to join the large hospital staff in a room filled with officers, doctors, nurses, and soldiers. As I entered I could feel a great hysteria beginning to sweep the room. Herr Goebbels was to speak to the German nation on the occasion of the Führer's birthday, April 19, 1945.

This must have been the recreation room, for it was big enough to accommodate some fifty or sixty people. People were scattered about everywhere. Everyone had a drink in hand and the conversation was loud and came in waves. The room was never quiet—laughter was a nervous edge that passed through the room, and I began to feel uneasy.

Some of these personnel sidled near me to take a better look. Since I was with my officer captors, no one came close enough to talk to me directly, though it seemed some of them wanted to. Because of der Führer's birthday, "heil Hitlers" were heard intermittently as people came into the room or as the officers were addressed for various reasons.

The room filled with smoke, but no one seemed to mind it except me. The alcohol, the smoke, and the excitement reminded me of my Uncle Alex's Communist party meetings when I was younger. The meetings were held in town, and my uncle had been a prime speaker along with his boss, Jay Lovestone. Those meetings had been full of men and sprinkled with women, some surprisingly young, but all apparently devoted to the party and to the party line. They were going to change the world, they thought, and I remember the sober urgency of these meetings, the idealism that energized the room. I was quite young but interested in these matters, especially because my uncle was considered very important in the party. I knew he and his wife had spent several years in Detroit organizing workers, foregoing their own plans to have a family.

When they all began to realize that they had been misled, that Stalin was little better than his counterpart in Germany, my uncle's heart broke and so his wife Eve's heart broke as well. They were the only couple I knew in all my life who truly, honestly, devotedly loved each other, were never bored with each other, who talked to each other endlessly and enjoyed playing with each other like two children—tickling each other, wrestling, giggling.

But here the feeling was much different from the idealism of my uncle's meetings: more manic, and desperate, the end of a powerful, corrupt regime. Standing in the smoke-filled room I had to tolerate the burning in my eyes and throat. I could not walk into the hallway or outside as I had done at my uncle's meetings.

Little by little I noticed that out of the clustered officers who were at the lawn party, only a few were left, maybe two or three. They stood with me, sighing, saying, "You know, Lieutenant, the sides are wrong. The real enemy is Russia, and America would be wise to join Germany. It is plain that the Russians are the common enemy to all of Europe." Sure, I thought, isn't that what they say now, at this point, when all is lost.

But I held my tongue. Such feeling among the Germans was not new, however, for I had heard this statement before at the prison hospital in Goeppingen. Even Dr. von Polster had made such a remark, though of course he knew the Russians in a way that I did not. I hadn't argued with him either, only listened. Prisoners listen; they hold no aces.

The words were prophetic, however, in the sense that the Russian holocaust was probably as great as the German. Stalin had shown his hand early in the game with his staging of the trials of Bukharin and the others. The famous "Darkness at Noon Trials."

Many who had accepted the party line were as heartbroken by this betrayal as my uncle was. It was clear that Stalin was never to be trusted, and Stalin was Russia, being no mean propagandist himself. During the war their slogan was, "Fight for Mother Russia, not for Communist Russia." "Mother" always does it.

It was now close to eight o'clock. A radio sat high on a shelf, and a large picture of Hitler was hung across the wall above it. Flags and swastikas were draped all about the room. Many soldiers held mugs of beer and some held glasses. The officers with me were drinking schnapps, and their glasses were half filled with the colorless liquid. The pitch of hysteria was high and the room was loud with voices. Then, suddenly, the room quieted and Goebbels began to speak by radio from Berlin.

Everyone was rapt and even I was mesmerized by his voice. Not for nothing, I realized, was he the master of propaganda. He knew how to put on a good show, and, even better, he knew how to talk a good show. The Germans listened, quiet and rapt. An officer translated for me. They, the people, were to be encouraged, for they had done splendidly by the Führer, and they were to continue to fight for the Fatherland. They were not to despair in this grave moment when all seemed hopeless, for the Allies were about to receive the surprise of their lives. Germany was about to unveil a secret weapon that would dazzle and destroy the enemy, one that would make the enemy capitulate and beg to surrender.

Goebbels's voice rose and fell and the group became elated. A wild hysteria swept through the room. In one moment they had been snatched from imminent death, and turned from vanquished to victor. I could feel myself caught up by the tone in the voices, by the contagion of mad feelings that spread around the room. I was more terrified here than when I had sat on the ground about to be captured, watching the straggled line of villagers approaching. I was certainly more numb then than I was now.

During this speech I saw a few German officers leave the room. I guessed they were on their way to their rendezvous with their forged identity cards and civilian clothes. To be in German uniform right now was not safe or wise. Only later did I hear of South America as being an inviting place for exiting Nazi soldiers. Later I found out also, along with the rest of the world, that not long after this speech Goebbels poisoned his wife and children and shot himself, committing suicide rather than face the disgrace of defeat.

Another German officer said to me, "Hitler has secret weapons that will destroy the Allies." I thought, what kind of insanity was this; the Allies were here, and the German cities were rubble. The German army was stopped on the western front and retreating on the eastern front. What were they thinking? Of course I said nothing. I had no idea what these people were capable of, with such madness all about.

The room had gone wild. I looked at the faces of the officers near me, and now only two were left. There was no elation in their eyes. The officers were not laughing, nor, as I noted from their faces, were they near any state of happiness. Somberness, and even grimness were outlined on their faces. I could only guess what they had in mind. Tomorrow might be their last day of freedom, and if not tomorrow, the day after. The speech was, after all, only a gesture, a grand gesture in words by the master propagandist, Goebbels. Just as six months ago the Battle of the Bulge had been the grand and final gesture by the German military. Our air power and troops had stopped them short—the way Joe Lewis would stop an opponent, ending the fight with one right hook.

The noise in the room was deafening. I shivered and moved backward toward the door. One officer, apparently assigned to be with me, moved in consonance with me, and soon, feeling my discomfort, took me back to the room.

A small glass of schnapps awaited me on the table; the colonel had ordered it for me, obviously as a goodnight gesture. I imagined he worked with the staff late in the night to make sure that nothing visible and incriminating was left for the Allies to find. I did not undress, just took my shoes off and lay awake a long time. Only the fact that the colonel needed me, I thought as I lay falling asleep, saved me that night.

Suddenly I awakened. The orderly had come in with my usual ration of bread and weak tea and said something like, be ready in half an hour. That was not a hard command. Breakfast only took five minutes and I opened the door to find the orderly in the hallway; I motioned to him that I needed the bathroom. Afterwards I was ready.

The day had come up sunny and already it was warm. It was eight in the morning according to my wristwatch, and I waited. I began to feel anxious. I did not want to think of the ride back, passing through the battle lines, yet I could not control my thoughts and feelings. I could think of nothing else, not even Irmgard. I did not know how to interpret the tightness in my chest. I recalled the bad feeling I had had as I walked up to the plane on that mission to Ingolstadt. But there was nothing I could have done then; I would have had to get on the plane no matter what, even if I had known for certain that the mission would leave more than half the men dead, and myself a German prisoner of war. I did not have that kind of feeling now, but there was a tension in my gut and my pulse was fast. I took a breath, a deep breath to relax.

Finally the knock came and I left the room, went out to the car, and got into the back seat with the colonel in front of me. As usual he seemed unperturbed; but then, he ran a station hospital on the front lines and was what we called battle-hardened. I wasn't even air-battle-hardened. I had never flown a mission with equanimity nor with the feeling that all was in fate's hand. I had thought that all was in my own hands. How little I understood of the universe and its laws, and how much anguish I would feel as a consequence. I used to think my adrenals would give out because of the stress, and what would I do with the rest of my life with those hormones missing?

Soon we were on the way out of the small town where we had spent the night, and onto what I would consider a country road, lined by grass with sometimes a hill to the side. The road was narrow, with room for only two cars to pass. A few minutes later I heard the familiar mortar fire. The car kept going, but more slowly now, as if it were feeling its way through a dark room. The road turned and up above, not a hundred yards away, I saw some heavily armed German soldiers crossing the road. The colonel spoke to the driver, who turned the car around and took us back to a point where there was a divergence of roads. We took a different road, but before long found ourselves in the middle of gunfire.

We were in the middle of the front between the American and German armies. Even the colonel did not know exactly where the lines were for certainly in war they shift unevenly and suddenly. At this point, the sides had not joined in battle but elsewhere, not far, we could hear the machine guns, the mortars, the rifles. Each had a different sound, a different crackle, and we didn't want to get caught in the crossfire. We wanted to find the American army disengaged, not actually fighting.

Soon I could see the German soldiers alongside us. The colonel spoke to one and after that the driver turned again, and we went back to the fork and took still another road. This time I could feel the urgency in my entire being. There was the crackle of machine gun fire, mortar fire, and rifle fire in the distance. I could hear grenades exploding. The little white car had become a cornered rat running this way and that way, with no way out. My fear was so great I thought I would lose control and begin to scream. My body was so tight I thought it would break.

A rat in a trap—which troops were closing in, the Americans, the French? If the colonel knew, he did not tell me. Though I was sweating and almost deafened from the pounding of my heart, he remained cool. He spoke to the driver and we retreated from the active gunfire and the German troops swarming around us.

The little car chugged along and we could hear the gunfire, but only at a distance now, and we soon pulled into a town.

We stopped at a house and got out. Inside the driver showed me to a small room with substantial furniture, bookshelves filled with books, a beautiful desk. The furniture smelled of fine wood. Though the immediate danger was over, who knew what would happen one hour, two hours later? No one came to explain anything to me. I was used to this. I just waited.

---

I waited in that little room, skimming through some of the books, which were all in German. I could not have focused on them anyway. I shut the books and re-shelved them, sat in a chair and waited some more. Finally, the door opened and I was taken to the colonel, who was standing by the car. He looked tired. Both he and the orderly spoke to me. From their words I pieced out that an American tank had come to the center of town twice, and that each time it had stopped, stayed a while, then turned around and left. He said there were more tanks at the edge of the town.

The street was quiet and empty. The colonel said, "We will go and surrender to the Americans."

So this was it, I thought. It was over for me—the war was done. I felt numb. We got into the car, he in front and I behind him, as before. Our car moved slowly down the street, then very slowly made a right turn. The colonel motioned the driver to stop. I could see an American tank some two hundred yards away and several soldiers around it. Another soldier stood behind the machine gun on top of the tank. Seeing us, they assumed an about-to-fight stance, each holding his weapon at the ready. I didn't know it then, but there was someone in the tank and the man on top had his hand on the machine gun.

The colonel motioned the driver to go forward slowly. We advanced a hundred yards, and again we stopped. We were now about a hundred yards from the tank. The colonel said to get out of the car.

I felt suddenly as if I were in a movie in slow motion—the driver, the colonel and myself. I knew the blue and cloudless sky, the sounds of spring and its smells. It was warm but I did not feel the heat. There was silence as we walked forward. I was light-headed as I held my arms slightly out from my sides; the colonel had his arms raised in classic surrender position. I was not a German and I was wearing an

American officers uniform. I trusted they would sense no danger from me. We walked toward the tank.

The movie came to an end suddenly. I felt a great part of my life was over as well—alive so far, made it so far, too tired to exult—but I knew I could not let go yet. There was this to go through now.

About thirty feet from the tank a soldier said, "Ok, stop. Who are you?"

I said, "This is Colonel Prilippi. I'm his prisoner. My crew and I were shot down a month ago. I have two men left in his hospital at Goeppingen. We were headed back there when we ran into you."

I had not thought before about how it would end. I knew the town would not end up in rubble, but I never imagined exactly how the finish would play out. The tanks rumbling through the town, or columns of our GIs marching through, coming to the hospital and freeing us—none of these had crossed my mind, until now. Like so many things in life, the end came as a surprise to me.

I suddenly felt tired. It was all over. But I realized it is not over until it is over, really. There was a ways to go before I would be safe.

We stood silently as the American soldiers looked us over.

Finally one said, in a thick Brooklyn accent, "So, you say you're an American. Well then, who are the Yanks?"

"We are, and if you mean the baseball team, the best in the American league."

"Who's Babe Ruth?"

"The legendary player of the Yankees. He hit sixty home runs."

I could see and hear myself talking to the GI astride his tank, as the other soldiers stood beside him, and still others stood on the ground, guns in hand, at the ready, but I was numb.

"Who's the first baseman?"

"Lou Gehrig."

"Where are the Red Socks from?"

"Boston," I said.

"What is the St. Louis team called?"

"Cardinals."

"Who's Lefty Grove?"

"The best pitcher the A's ever had."

"What other teams are in New York?"

"The Giants and the Dodgers."

"You're an American, you're an American alright," he said, smiling at last. "Wait here."

In a minute he came back with the captain who commanded the tanks; there were at least five more down the road. I repeated to the captain what I had told the soldier with the Brooklyn accent, who now said to me, "Ok Lieutenant, take his gun."

Motioning to the colonel, he added, "He's your prisoner; take him back to his hospital. Tell him to continue his duties until our men take over command of the town. I'll send you back with two men and a jeep." I told him we had seen Germans retreating. He nodded, looking at his map, and said, "Show me." I did. "Ok, Lieutenant, ok, go. Get your two men, good luck."

I shook the soldier's hand. We exchanged names, and slapped each other's arm with affection. He grinned, and said something unimportant. What was important was the feeling that passed between us—one Italian American and one Jewish American, but here, in this time and this place, just Americans, just buddies.

I turned to the colonel and held out my hand, motioning to his gun holster. He took it off his belt and handed holster and pistol to me. I didn't open the pistol, just stuck it in my waistband. I motioned the colonel into the back of the jeep and followed him into the backseat, settling down for the ride. The two soldiers rode in front, the one in the passenger seat riding shotgun with a rifle across his lap and his pistol on the floor. The driver had his rifle across his lap as he drove.

I turned to the colonel and said, "Everything will be all right, no problem. We go back to the hospital. You are still the doctor in charge." He looked at me calmly, this man twice my age, and slowly nodded with a sound in his throat. Did he say yes? I shrugged my shoulders. I felt I was paying him back for the decent treatment he had especially given me.

"One more thing, Captain," I said to the soldier in the front seat, flicking my head toward the colonel. "He treated us decently. He is a doctor. For me he is a good guy."

During the ride back, I felt no elation. I knew, inevitably, that a piece of my life, an extraordinary piece, was over, and would never exist again. My freedom did not exhilarate me. There would be no more letters, no more glasses of wine, and no more hands to touch, if only for an instant.

I looked at the colonel beside me. He sat erect, his ruddy face more haggard than before. He looked grayer. The war was over for him, yet the changes for him would not be as spectacular as they would be for me.

Of course he knew nothing of the letters between Irmgard and me, and if he had known, I think the whole matter would have seemed trivial to him. He had his command, his two hospitals, and a considerable number of personnel. Even in captivity his job would be more or less the same, except now he would report to an American officer.

But my life was in the process of crumbling, just as was my heart—coming apart without a visible sign, without a murmur.

The trip back took less than an hour. I was not aware of the landscape, the colonel, or the two soldiers in the front seat of the open jeep. The soldiers talked, not a lot. It was clear that the one riding shotgun was very careful, scanning the road and to the sides.

I sat quietly, the colonel's pistol in my waistband, thinking of what I would say to Irmgard, how I should say it, and what I should do. Was there a choice—was there any choice of action? Even as I asked myself, I knew there was none. I became even more depressed, thinking of how I might have looked to a bystander—no levity, no joy, no clapping of hands, no jumping up and down or doing a jig. On the contrary, I felt I weighed a ton, though my pants were loose and my chest felt like pure bone.

The Volkswagen with the red cross painted on the roof followed us and soon we were back at the hospital in Goeppingen. My feelings were a jumble. In one second everything had changed. I was not accustomed to the difference and deep within me I preferred the old arrangement. I wanted my Irmgard as I knew her. Freedom without the rush of love of seeing the beautiful girl, waiting to see her, listening for her arrival, or the reedy sounds of the flute, and all the tones possible with the sounds—trills of laughter, sounds of water, wind, trees, clouds, love— did not seem worth much. It was slipping out of my hands. No—it had already. And I was feeling the heaviness of my loss.

There was nothing I could do, like taking Irmgard with me. I knew the soldiers would not allow that. More, I knew Irmgard would never leave the hospital. The war was still on. I was still just a pawn in the game. Where I would be sent, the interrogations, all had a pro- tocol which would have to be followed, and over which I had no control.

Back in the hospital, I talked to von Polster. "Tell the colonel he is to continue his duties as head of the hospital until the American authorities come and decide what needs to be done. Tell the colonel I thank him for his courtesy and respect, that I'm grateful." When von Polster had translated, the colonel saluted with a hint of smile. I saluted him.

The colonel spoke to von Polster. It was our eyes that spoke as well. I know they saw the gratitude in mine. The colonel said, "Wait, I want to give the Lieutenant a remembrance. It will be a moment." He went to another room and when he reappeared he had a postcard of the hospital, and signed his name on it. I saluted him. He acknowl- edged it with a friendly wave of his hand and left.

Years later, as I was rummaging about for this book, I heard that Colonel Prilippi had become the mayor of the city some years after the war.

I went upstairs to my old room and saw my navigator's watch, with its broken crystal, hanging on the wall by my bed. The room was empty; only the chairs, the table, the beds, and the watch were still there. Sadness overcame me. I felt the way an archeologist must feel when coming upon a site, finding a broken ball, or perhaps one broken tool—knowing the object contains an entire history of people and loves and wishes long gone. Now there was only this empty room. Who would ever know the story of the people who had once lived there? It was not the same, and would not ever be.

I returned to where von Polster was waiting for me. I asked if he could send for Sister Irmgard. "You don't have to come back," I said, "but I want you to know how grateful I am to you. In a way, this has changed my life. You have changed my life. Who knows, maybe we'll meet again, some time, some day." We shook hands and he left.

The two soldiers stood by me and leaned against the wall, watching this. Now one said, "Lieutenant, the captain ordered us to take you to Heidelberg. So we ought to be going pretty soon, we're still not one hundred percent safe."

"Ok, ok," I said. "There's one more thing I have to do."

Those moments of waiting for Irmgard were some of the most terrifying moments of my life. I tried to bring a resemblance of order to myself, straightening up, but I could not stop the quiver that caught me.

I felt a shaft of lightning burn through my head; I knew I was half crazy, and the last twenty-four hours were awash in my brain. I bit down hard with my teeth, trying to provide some kind of stability in my being. I could feel my right eye twitch; that I could not stop. My eyes blurred.

I had no idea what I was going to say to Irmgard. Should I tell her of my desperation? Should I tell her of my inward shaking? My legs were weak. I stamped my feet and tried to energize them. And what if I told her that yesterday I'd become like a terror-stricken child because I feared I would not see her again? But then I thought, how would she react? What would she say?

I heard the two soldiers moving about. I turned around; they were crouching down on their haunches, rifles nested between their hands. For the time being they were patient.

I needed time to think this out. I had no plan; that was the problem. I had not prepared one. Suddenly I felt sick, for I did not know what to do or, for that matter, what I could do.

I remembered when she told me of the decision to be made by the colonel—whether or not to send us by train to the center of Germany, an order by Hitler to disrupt the Allies in any way. What was I to have done with that information about things beyond my control? Later she came in the midmorning when she should have been sleeping to say, *I prayed all night for you.* She said, *For you.* She did not say *for all of you.* I thought, pray? What is prayer? I did not know what that was, and I had no place to put that information. It was not the same as "William conquered England in 1066," or "Bogart played the lead in *Casablanca*." Those things I could place.

But prayer? Suddenly I did not want her to come. A great fear came upon me. I knew this was a historic moment in my life, and I was not up to it. I was not old enough or learned enough to make any sensible statement. I dreaded her coming, for I knew it was the end of us. This time was over—and there was still a war going on. I was under orders to go to Nancy, France, and Irmgard was under orders to remain on duty in this hospital.

And then, before I could stop history, she appeared. She walked towards me, dignified. Her usually red cheeks were only tinged with pink, and I could see that she was as affected by this final goodbye as I was. I felt weak. I wanted to stoop, to put my head down, for I was now light-headed. We went a little way off so as not to be heard, and I spoke.

"What shall I say to you? Now that we have time to talk, we can't; the soldiers have orders to take me to Heidelberg." She tried to smile, "So now the Americans are the captors and we are the prisoners," she said, and shook her head, sighing. "How God arranges things."

"I will no longer call you Sister. That's all over. Now it's Irmgard, just Irmgard. There's so much I want to say to you, but there is not time, not now. Let me at least have your letters back so I will know this was not just a dream."

"Everything is a dream," she said. "Our little time on earth is a dream, it feels like a dream."

Then she looked at me, her eyes sought mine. She looked at me very closely and said, "You are not as arrogant as you were."

"You have taught me in your letters and in your silence and in your music and I'm grateful that I have known you. I will never forget you." I looked into her face, memorizing it. She said, "Wait," and turned. In a little while she came back and handed me a packet of letters in a thin coffee-colored envelope. "Here," she said, "is evidence that we've existed, even if only for a little while in this place in this time."

I looked at the packet. The name "Madralena" was on the coffee-colored envelope that I still have and look at as I write.

"Who is that?" I asked.

"That is my second name and I want you to remember me by that name. Irmgard was the nurse. Madralena is the woman with whom you talked and walked and who wrote to you. My family calls me by that name so it is a precious gift I give you to remember me. Irmgard was my duty. Madralena is my love for you."

I held her in my arms. I kissed her forehead, her hair. Her body was thin but feminine. I kissed her mouth gently and we put our faces cheek to cheek. She was quivering and crying. I asked, "What is the name of that fruit?" She laughed through her tears and shrugged. I said, "I know. I was talking about the kiss, the fruit of paradise. It has no name here on earth."

She hugged me and drew back to look at me, still holding onto my waist. She said, "You must go. They are waiting."

"You are living within me with such a great love. Do you wish to see yourself?" For a moment she cried deeply and she said, "My heart, my soul." I kept on holding her until both of us were quiet.

I reached into my pocket and withdrew my navigator's watch that had one hand, the little one. The watch had a silver chain. I said, "Here is something of mine. The little hand is on twelve when the world stopped for me and for us. The time will be eternal like the union of our souls. I want you to wait for me."

"I will wait, but I know you will have much to do and will do everything. I will wait. Women know better how to wait then men." Her face became sad, sadness I could not erase. It seeped into me.

As an afterthought I said, "And you have my letters."

"You must go," she said finally. The soldiers were getting impatient. We heard their nervous movement and their mutterings. "You must go."

She withdrew her hand, gently. Her eyes began to tear, as did mine. She blushed. She said, "I wish you well, Herr Lieutenant." And she turned and left, leaving me in silence. I knew this woman's pride, I knew she was turbulent with feeling she could not express to me. I suppose she could never imagine a future for us. I really didn't know what she could or could not imagine. But I did know her pride, and how she could never show weakness. Only when she told me, in one of her letters, the story about the French girl who put her German lover before her own country, had I understood that she was talking about us.

And then the soldier's voice brought me back to the present. "Come on, Lieutenant, we have to go. We want to get there before dark."

She was walking down the hall away from me. Right before she'd have to turn left into another hallway, she turned around and looked at me—I could see the tears coming down her face as they were mine. And then she was gone. In all this there was only anguish; my freedom brought me only anguish. For I felt that I had reached the zenith of my life. I could imagine no other situation which promised you death and gave you love—and then took both away. How could I live the rest of my life now? What could bring me joy or bring a smile to my lips? Nothing could equal what I had already had and lost.

With the letters in my hand, I went back to the two soldiers, who hurried me into the jeep. We sped off on our way to Heidelberg, my head reeling. I could not truly think. I was too full of feelings, of sadness, so full of the moment that I did not have the objectivity with which to think. The jeep sped on, wind rushed through my hair, and I was numb.

# 5

Nancy, France
April 1945

The drive from Goeppingen to Heidelberg was one of the longest I have ever taken. I thought, with a controlled sense of victory, that I had made it, survived it, as we rode through the countryside towards peace, but my mind was only beginning to grasp what I had lost.

I closed my eyes and let myself feel the pain in my heart. There was little time for reflection or grief, however; I had imagined there'd be no fighting in Heidelberg, but as we rode in the open jeep I noticed how my two guardians were listening intently to a sound in the distance. They did not want to talk, and I soon found out why we had been hugging the edges of the road, close to the ditches and the brush.

Suddenly the driver stopped the jeep and yelled, "Go for the ditch!" and we all dove in. I flattened myself so deep into the earth that the hard dirt scratched my face. Sweat beaded on my face and I heard the machine guns clattering from the planes. American troops controlled the skies, with our P-47s, P-51s and P-38s, but here were some rogue aircraft, German pilots determined to fight until the end. Now, with my face on the ground, my body pressed down as tightly as I could press it, I lay dug in, light-headed, my heart beating to bursting.

The minutes passed slowly, until, finally, it was safe. The driver said, "Let's go," and we boarded the jeep and resumed our journey, but soon enough the clattering returned. There was nothing we could do. Again we hit the ditch and sweated it out, letting the rogue aircraft blast and swoop above us.

Later, after we had suffered these attacks, we could see clumps of men in strange uniforms walking along the sides of the road, and even from a distance we could see they were not armed. As we drew closer we saw that their uniforms resembled striped pajamas—black and white and filthy. They were in terrible physical condition: gaunt, heads shaven, bones protruding, some in wheelbarrows or pushcarts, too weak to walk, many without teeth. The stench was terrible. But all seemed triumphant as they walked to freedom.

I was seeing the first of what the world was yet to see and obviously not the worst, images of which would later be emblazoned across the world—the concentration camp survivors. These men were going to France, home, or who knows where, and we did not linger, but drove quickly past the scattered ghosts of our conscience. Occasionally small convoys of American trucks went past us, waving. Their presence did little to allay my fears about the big guns and the little ones not too far away.

Finally we entered a small town where there was an American field hospital. Here I was transferred to an ambulance, and here I met my friend, the P-51 pilot Tyler Wyans, for the first time, along with another man, who lay quivering and moaning on a stretcher, covered heavily with blankets. My friend, whose name I did not know then, told me how the wounded soldier had been a victim of the Battle of the Bulge. He had been shot and left for dead, and afterwards had suffered from frostbite. Later this man had been retrieved by the Americans and was now going back to a general hospital for better care. After this Tyler and I did not speak. The ambulance drove on through the valleys towards Heidelberg. The wounded soldier, a member of the 106th Infantry, was one of the men who, after almost no training, had been thrown into the battle to staunch the rush of the German army. He was in bad shape, shaking, muttering, and crying the entire time. We said nothing.

Suddenly we heard mortar fire and big guns, maybe .88s; the atmosphere was so clear, so quiet, and so clean that we could hear the reverberations of these guns. Tyler looked at me and I at him—were the Germans counterattacking? We listened to the sounds and I began to sweat again—would I make it, would we make it? After everything else? Neither of us spoke, but I'm sure we both were thinking the same thing. The ambulance drove on, and the guns crackled and continued to fire for several hours. I had no time to think of my experiences, my anguish or my joy—all I could focus on was getting through that drive. Our vehicle kept to the now-empty road, crawling up the hills and rushing down them over and over, second by second. And then we were in Heidelberg.

The ambulance pulled up to a hospital where we got out to stretch our legs. Soon Tyler and I were asked to follow an officer, who debriefed us individually. He wanted to know where we had come from, which army we had been in contact with, how many guns we had seen and where we had seen them. I told him the Tenth Armored Division had freed me in a small town not far from the hospital where I'd been held. I was freed by Captain Randolph, I told him, having remembered the name of the young, rugged man in charge of the tanks. I told him all the details of that encounter, and that was all.

That evening I had my first real meal in five weeks and I ate voraciously. Fifteen minutes later I threw it all up, and didn't eat again until I got to Nancy and the station hospital.

The doctors at Nancy brought me and the other freed prisoners of war back to as good a state of health as they could. Since I had not eaten real food for more than a month, they were very careful in what they fed me, for at first I would vomit almost anything up. It took time for my digestive tract to get used to food instead of sawdust. Our minds and bodies adapt quickly to misfortune so that it seems natural, and all things healthy seem suspect; many years later, late in my analytic career, I would find this principle to be exquisitely true and the most fundamental obstacle to a patient being cured. In Nancy I lay in bed, resting, and was later taken by wheelchair or gurney for laboratory tests. I was young, and my body recovered quickly. Though I did not have to be in bed, I spent a lot of time there in the luxury of having a room to myself.

Finally I had time to think about the entire experience, which I played over and over again in my mind. The days and nights at Nancy were not easy. Memories only too fresh crowded my mind. When I had been with Irmgard I could not talk—too limited, or too full of feelings. Those last moments it seemed as if my tongue had been stopped, and my mind blank. I had not found the words to tell her all that was in my heart. Here, during the long days and nights, rushes of words would come. All I could have said to her, in words and gestures. If only she could have heard them so that she might have known my heart better.

Sometimes I thought that Irmgard could not have been real, that I had made her up. At these times I would get up and go to my blood-splattered flying jacket and feel for the packet of her letters. It was real; she had been real. It was hard to bridge the gap of time, the experiences of these minutes. For, all in all, that's all they had added up to—just minutes.

And I thought: oh Gods of old, as I have read, strike us into stone so that we might be together for ten thousand years. Or entwine us into trees so that we will have time enough to say all that we ever wanted to say, or into butterflies that we might pursue our beauty, together. This is how I thought about her, in all those days and nights. I felt crazed with a hundred thoughts and feelings and regrets.

One afternoon, as I sat on a bench outside the hospital reading a letter, I thought of that ill-fated train that was to have taken us away, and I thought of how, for a little while, this dark-haired nurse and I had met in that little station called Goeppingen, and, within moments, another train had taken me away from her. Throughout my stay in Nancy I would sit on that bench, so lost in reminiscence that I'd forget to move, to blink my eyes or swallow, until suddenly I'd begin to choke and cough and tear. They did not send you away, she had said the next day. Joy had been in her eyes.

My body began to mend at Nancy, but for me Nancy was a station of remorse, sorrow, and guilt. I never wanted to return to it, and even now the thought of it makes me shudder. Then, my heart lay heavy in me.

In Nancy I was finally safe. I could let go of my constant pre-paredness and anticipation, but I knew what was coming was not joy, only an ever heavier dose of sadness. We were taken care of in every way physically, but I and my fellow ex-POWs were more dis-abled by our emotional experiences than anything else. Nights were often interrupted by soldiers' nightmares. The yelling woke us all up with fear, and during the day, as I took my walks alone, I could hear sobs and laughter and then sobs. Sometimes I would laugh out loud and say, "I beat the odds, I beat the odds, damn, damn," but more times I was sunk in gloom, the letters in my hand, loosely held.

When I looked into the mirror now, I saw a skeleton. I might have weighed only ninety pounds or so; flying combat before all this, I had weighed in at one eighteen. But I could walk, skinny as I was, and I knew in time I would get my weight back. Though my body was Gandhi-like, the face was still mine, though very, very thin, and my blue eyes the same, though sunken a little deeper in their sockets. There were raised welts on my neck, and I could still see where the shell fragments had entered my body, though I could not see the wounds in my skull. I thought and thought as I lay and sat and walked, sometimes in the garden, where we were allowed to wander once the doctors had found us fundamentally sound, no matter how we looked. Sometimes I sat on a bench in the garden, where other men had also gathered. No one intruded with questions or conversations; the other released prisoners from all parts of Germany were alone with their thoughts, as I was with mine.

And gradually, as the days went by, my thoughts passed from reminiscence to the future. What kind of life could I have now?

What had once been my safety, my little South Philadelphia ghetto, the streets with their cobblestones, the tiny houses of brick, and the streets uncluttered by cars, still sounding with the clatter of horses, hooves and iron-clad wheels—all that had been dear to me, all I had felt a sweet nostalgia for, was changed in my heart. What had once been my ambition—to become a teacher—no longer seemed like enough, not after this. A revolution had occurred within me.

I could not go back. I did not want to go back. I would fight going back—else what had all I'd suffered and seen been for—just to go back and pick up the plow?

But after I said all this to myself, as quick as lightening I would imagine my mother, who was already in great pain and sorrow. I knew she would never lie peacefully in her bed until I was found or at least identified as dead. I knew she would lie on the sofa day and night, and cry and have headaches and put compresses on her head. But, even so, I dared think the unthinkable, of hurting my mother. I dared! And amidst this guilt and longing and anguish I had a twinge of doubt—I wondered would I be able to do it, and where would I go and what would I do?

I forgot for periods of time, except when I would have nightmares. Then it would all come back as I sat up in bed, or dangled my feet over the side, breathing fast and shallow: the guns firing, my mother's face, Irmgard's hand in the dark, a tumbling of thoughts and images that shattered my heart. The rest of the night would be finished for me, as I paced the floor or lay remembering. Many nights the letters remained in their manila envelope, but my soul never forget them, not for one instant. I too wanted to do something for "my soldiers, the wounded, who lie and moan with pain, and I have nothing to give them." And in the quietest hours of the night I dared to think that one day I too would have something to give the wounded for their pain, the pain of the heart and the mind and the soul.

My life as I had planned it would be a lifetime of dullness, I thought. Going home to the dreariness of the houses and the streets, to the dreariness of being a schoolteacher filled me with so much anxiety I began to retch when I let myself go deep into that monotonous scene.

After the hurrahs at home, after the noise would die, after the hugs and kisses of people both distant and close, I could not imagine ever feeling again the range of feelings I had experienced in one day with Irmgard.

There would be no expectation, no letters slipped under the pillow, no glasses of red wine by my bedside. No furtive reading of her letters, no quick answer that I jotted down for her to read, no more nervous expectation of her response, no more wondering how she would read my words and receive my thoughts and feelings. Where would I ever find that again back home?

And I wondered and worried whether I would be able to do the rest of my life—or would I just be putting in time, waiting to die?

One night I dreamed I was on a mission to Ingolstadt. Everything was familiar. The engines were hit. I was standing up, manipulating the aircraft's various mechanisms, trying to stabilize the plane. I knew we had lost altitude and we had lost two engines hit by flak. Now we were cruising about fifteen thousand feet, going lower, when suddenly the plane rocked with jolts and deafening noises. I could see my two pilots slumped over the controls; I could see the navigator dead with blood on the table. And then there was the lead navigator who held his head.

It was all in slow motion. The man screamed, but I did not hear it. He jumped down on the bomb bay bridge and yelled something to me. He held out his hand, convulsively working his hands, his fingers. I saw it all but I could not move. The plane lurched and began to nose over. The lead navigator was gone. The plane was silent. I still could not move. I watched myself die, now caught in the plane's gravity, no way to get out.

And then I heard myself screaming. The night nurse and orderly ran in and woke me. I was screaming and screaming. They sat me on the bed. The nurse gave me a shot to quiet me. I realized as I was going under that I had become the engineer who had frozen as the plane went over and down. Had frozen with terror and numbness, watching himself die along with those already dead or dying in the plane.

I could not escape these demons. I could not face a life without what I had felt for Irmgard. I could not return to my little brick row house, where my family waited. I did not know what to do, where to go, or how to do it. My future stretched out flat and bleak, and my mind tormented me from all directions. I knew that sooner or later we would all be sent to Paris and then on to a staging area from which we would board a ship for home. Could I get on that ship?

Then Giselle in Paris came to mind. I remembered the hotel where she worked, and the more I thought, the more the idea came to me: could I stay in Paris, could I stay in France? I do not remember having dreams in my life before I began to have nightmares during my captivity. Now, in Nancy at the station hospital, these dreams continued and then I had a dream which echoed much of what I had thought about Giselle and Paris, Giselle whom I already knew back in January.

I had no idea about Giselle except that we had spent a few days together in January. Now it was coming on to May and I had no idea really whether I would ever see her again.

But during this one night the dreams turned into a bad feeling for suddenly an image of Irmgard appeared before me, smiling. I woke up, my heart beating fast. I knew nothing of dreams, of their meanings, except I had a great feeling of guilt about what I was thinking. It seemed all so pre-Irmgard and pre-Irmgard it seemed reasonable. At least I tried to convince myself of that. My common sense said slow down.

My practicality began to kick in. How to live, where to get money, what to do just to survive and with another person to support, I could not see how to do this. At least not now. That was my mother, worried about real life like how to pay the rent, is there money for bread, the butcher. I hated this reality.

I regretted one thing, which was that now the authorities knew I was alive—wounded, but alive—and back in American hands. I regretted this, for now that I was safe I felt my former missing in action status had given me the freedom of choice to do whatever I wanted with my life.

I formulated a plan, that in Paris I would see Giselle. I went so far as to consider the notion that I could disappear, and that, if I were ever found, I could simply plead loss of memory. The wounds to my head would have shaken the contents of the skull, the brain. I went on like this almost obsessively, each time going one step further until I felt a rush in my chest and my heart beating too fast, as if I had betrayed a taboo, I'd gone too far. So it was in those days and nights at Nancy: trying to imagine a future, trying to come to terms with the past, wondering if I could face going home.

———

As my thoughts became more clear and sharp, I realized that the one thing I had to have in life was freedom. I did not think that, after the war, I could ever go back and be a high school teacher of English or French. I simply could not have stood it. It was like the WWI song, "Once they see Paris, you can't keep them down in the farm." So I lay in bed, looking for ways to do my life, the rest of it, and slowly my old dream of being a doctor returned to me. I think that if I had not been shot down and captured, that old ambition probably would never have resurfaced. I might have rekindled my dream of going to the Sorbonne—yes, I might have done that, for I found it distasteful to even think of going back to Philadelphia to resume my life with old friends, to walk the old streets. It was so negative a feeling that I felt myself shaking my head, NO, and I laughed. Alone as I was I could do that. I did not have to explain.

I regretted that there was a record of my existence, and now there was. I could not remain missing in action or if so, I would have had to somehow disappear without a trace. This time, however, I'd be listed as AWOL, another unpleasant label with consequences. Looking back, it seems clear that not all of my thoughts were rational, but what also was clear was that I had had it. No doubt I was still suffering combat fatigue—being freed did not cure that. As an analyst, years later, I read about how several of the first analysts had been doctors in service in WWI and had treated soldiers who'd suffered shell shock, war neuroses, and traumatic neuroses. Though I might have suffered from any one of those conditions, it was not until some years later, when I began my analytic training, that I began to learn about a new and infinite space—the unconscious, as vast as the universe and as complex and as fascinating.

I began to feel something new, something that told me I would never be frightened again, that nothing in life could be worse than what I had experienced in these last ten months. There was a photograph of the four of us officers who had survived that third mission. We were sitting in a jeep, two in front and two in back, and a B-24 behind us with the insignia on the tail blacked out, should the photograph fall into the wrong hands. It was a picture for the *Stars and Stripes*. There we were, our faces grim and gaunt.

But I did not think then of my twenty-fifth mission, of what I had seen on the way to Ingolstadt. The corpses lying around in the cockpit—what name should I give to that? To a large extent I believe I've been unafraid in my life, though I had to take orders from a lot of people, many stupid ones at that, until I could get to a place of real freedom. And whenever I've been in some civilian jeopardy, I have recalled what real jeopardy is, and I have hardened my resolve.

As I recovered my strength at the hospital, I read and re-read Irmgard's letters. It began to seep into my mind that everything would have to be judged by the war experience as my touchstone. I knew that vaguely, with disquiet because I was now to look at everything from a different vertex. It was easy to say this to myself but I had no idea how long it takes "with help" for a new idea to really possess one, for one to emotionally live it. It would take me years to find that out as well as many other things.

My mind returned to Giselle and the idea of being in Paris and finding her there. I even dared to think of the possibility of eventually locating Irmgard after the war was officially over. I knew the war would not last too long. In the chaos there'd be no problem for an American traveling across France to Germany, to Stuttgart, to Goeppingen. But now I would be returning to Paris. My heart raced at this, and my mind raced at the idea of finding Giselle in Paris again.

When I stopped and took measure of where I had been, I realized that my thinking began to veer away from Giselle. I was occupied with the rest of my life, with how I proposed to live it. Irmgard and Giselle were there as problems, but my life was my biggest problem.

Of course, perhaps I did want to think of Giselle—to think of possibilities. I feared Irmgard coming in and I did not want to break my word to her. Now that I was free, I thought—was it true, all that happened with just one kiss and one hug? I knew some people would jeer at it and dismiss it. I could not do that. The times we met and talked, what she had said written here in my hand, I might have placed in an opera or a play on Broadway, even a movie. In real life maybe I was weak and promised too much. I was certainly weak physically, being starved. Is that a good place from which to make up my mind about a life course? And how would I manage to put Irmgard in this picture, which was not even clear to me?

I knew I had to go back to service and probably fly B-29's in the Pacific. That was looming ahead of me. Everything I might be thinking was idle, a fantasy. It had no ground, it had no feet which in a way was how I thought of Irmgard—a spirit—and that was something very far from my family ground in the realism of the class struggle of communism.

I gave it a rest, this and Irmgard and Giselle, concluding I would wait and see what would happen. It's not only my life. It is also theirs and I know already that even if I were not fixed in her life, Giselle was certainly fixed in hers—very grounded in the reality of survival for which I admired her as much as I did Irmgard for her life in spirit. So I decided to leave it for the time being.

---

Thinking and writing about this time years later, I recognized the confusion between Irmgard and Giselle and the problem of having to live my life and the question of whether the war would last and would I have to go to the Pacific theatre. I realized I was in an entirely confused state—one which psychiatrists term "post traumatic stress syndrome," except that I did not know it at the time.

# 6

Paris, May 1945

*I* had met Giselle four months earlier, in January, when our bomb group was diverted to France because of bad weather in England. We did not have enough fuel to wait out the storms in the air, and so we were forced to land at Orly. The only alternative had been Scotland.

So, for the first time, I had been in Paris, the city I had longed to visit in college. But I had not come to enroll in the Sorbonne, as I had once dreamed, and I was not exactly thinking of medieval literature. We arrived at about three o'clock on an already gray, darkening day. Jack Wales, my best friend and copilot, and I were assigned to the Hôtel des Deux Mondes, and a military truck took us to the subway, which carried us into Paris. The people on the train looked at us curiously, saying nothing, hunched up in their sweaters or coats like workers in any big city, any place in the world. We, on the other hand, were loud, happy and eager to see Paris, even if we could only stay a short time. It was a treat none of us had expected. Some of the crew sat, and some stood looking at the maps that measured off the stations. We traveled an hour, more or less, filling the air with our laughter and excitement.

When I walked up the subway stairs to the street, I saw what I took to be an opera house, and I began to quiver internally. Place de l'Opéra was cold and dark, but not so dark that we could not make out the shapes of the buildings. I had the unmistakable feeling that I had been there before. I said nothing, not even to my good friend

Jack, to whom I was the closest. We shared a fondness for good talk and literature, and together we planned for the future, returning to one of those dreams time and again—"After the war," he would say, "let's go to China."

The crew scattered to wherever, and Jack and I found our hotel at about seven o'clock. We were giddy as we walked into the lobby, which, though plain, seemed wonderfully luxurious to us after months of barracks living. We were in Paris!

And it was there, behind the counter, that I first saw Giselle. I was at once drawn in by this slender dark-haired woman, so self-possessed, with brown clear eyes and dark well-fitted clothes. She stood like a dancer, with one foot tilted out. Her eyes widened when she saw me. The lights threw glints of red from her soft wavy hair. This was so intimately feminine a woman. My heart was already stirring, and my energy came into me with a burst, despite the fatiguing day. The war was forgotten, and the mission we had just flown was forgotten. This was the Paris of my dreams. Giselle's smile was delicious as she handed the room key to me.

Up in the room Jack and I washed our hands and faces as quickly as we could, anxious to head back out into the streets of the city. We agreed that we would ask the woman behind the front desk, as well as the woman assisting her, to dinner. The other woman, I soon learned, was Irene, younger than Giselle. Irene had a face with that flushed look, though she wore no rouge, and a concentrated body, with curves around the waist, and strong thighs and legs.

We headed down the stairs. I put my best French forward, and Jack, who could not speak French at all, charmed both Giselle and Irene with his wide-mouthed, toothy grin. We were rewarded by them agreeing to come out with us to a nearby café.

Later, as the meal progressed I felt a great pull towards Giselle and she to me. Several times as we spoke across the small table, she put her hand on mine, as if to emphasize a point, "n'est-ce pas?" or refilled my wine glass when it got low.

So much had happened since that giddy day in January, when Giselle and the city had seemed to encompass all I'd ever dreamed of. When I returned after the war, it was a different world.

I returned to Paris with Tyler Wyans on May 1, 1945, after my imprisonment and my stay in Nancy. We sat in the train car by ourselves, looking out at the dry, scrubbed country that passed beneath us. Neither of us spoke. I knew his Mustang had been hit by flak as he accompanied a flight of bombers, but if he had told me what the mission was or what the target had been, I had already forgotten.

The train shook, and we fell into cadence with the rocking wheels. I kept reassuring myself that it had all happened by touching the thin wrinkled pages I kept in my left pocket, the letters Irmgard had slipped under my pillow. Evidence, she had said, that we had existed. As the train passed from the countryside and into the outskirts of Paris, I again thought of disappearing forever from American view, becoming whatever I imagined I could be, free from the density of the war and of my own past.

Tyler did not tell me what occupied him. We had both been prisoners of war, and if I never saw him again I would feel closer to him than I would to many people I today call friends, who cannot truly know my heart.

I paid no attention to the landscape slipping past us, and I could see that Tyler too was absorbed in himself, hunkered down in his seat.

Despite myself, my mind returned to that ill-fated morning of my last mission. Once again I recalled my great misgivings, the feelings of dread that had warned me, to no avail. And before I could stop them the memories swept over me: the flak over the target, the impact of the plane being hit, the turn to the right as we lost altitude, and the task force—our "little friends"—leaving us, crossing Northern Germany to alert all the German anti-aircraft installations.

I remember the terror that took hold as our air speed dropped, our two engines feathered—of no use. Suddenly the explosion: my head, my head! I could see myself shriek, and fall unconscious for a moment, only a moment, before blood began streaming down my neck. I saw my pilots slumped down in their seats, the navigator's blood gushing, and the flight engineer frozen in place.

The scene stopped there. I could no longer breathe; I was gasping, someone was shaking me. I heard a voice. The shaking became more urgent.

"Hey! Hey!"

It was Tyler. I slumped back.

"Man, I thought you were about to go," he said, and I saw the stricken look on his face. "Man, don't do that to me now. I've just about had it. Are you ok?"

He poked at me again.

"Ok?"

I blinked my eyes. I'm ok. I'm ok.

But my heart was still racing and my chest was still heaving. And my legs had no bones. Was I ok? Would I ever be ok?

We pulled into the station, where it was frantic and panicked as trainloads of soldiers pulled in. None of it seemed real, even as I talked to the soldiers in my command. I could not think; my mind was jarred by the din within the station now clogged with soldiers, their families and belongings. I could have been in a thicketed forest, forced to hack my way out, on the verge of screaming for fear I would not be able to escape.

Once outside, I stood for a moment on the sidewalk. The whole city seemed to line the streets; the French soldiers marched by, the French anthem blared, and ex-prisoners of war pressed forward in the haze of the crowds. I had to order myself to focus, to slow down and rest a minute. It was hard to do. It was too much compressed into too small a time. I had to focus; why I was there? Whom had I come to see? Where were they and why I was there to see them? My mind raced. I feared passing out or going crazy, and at the same time.

And then it came to me: Giselle, I would find Giselle again. I know where she is. Quickly yet slowly I set my compass for this task. I knew I was at a breaking point, the way I had been when the colonel and I passed through the front lines, the machine gun and rifle fire surrounding us, the mortars firing just beyond. Then I had let all my feelings drown out. I knew how to do this; I had learned as a child, back when we had no money to heat the house, and I had to will myself to ignore the cold. It was my trick. I never told anyone how to do it, but I was no longer cold or afraid afterwards. In the car with the colonel, I knew that if death were to come at that point, I could meet it. But, then, what of my life? Goddamn, what about my fucking life? I calmed myself once more. Nothing had changed outside—then or now. The white VW had still zigged and zagged like a crazy rat, and here too, in Paris, the crowds continued to celebrate.

And it hit me: I was in Paris. It was all over. Today, May Day, was already a day of celebration. Though the war wouldn't officially end for another six days, everyone knew. It was over.

As I write these words now, over fifty years later, I have no recollection of how I found myself curbside on the Champs-Élysées watching the May Day parade, alongside of thousands of French men and women who cheered as the French soldiers marched by. Perhaps memory has been falsified, but I see De Gaulle with his military bearing and his kepi, marching in front. Somewhere down the line hundreds of skeleton-like men followed, all wearing what looked like black-striped pajamas. I had already seen men like these on the way to liberated Heidelberg. A long column of them—some walking, some with canes, some with crutches, many being wheeled along in carts or wagons or wheelbarrows—passed by, waving to the crowds, which fell into silence. This was the city's first glimpse of concentration camp survivors, and the crowd seemed struck down, as if what I would later learn to call the universal unconscious were trying to tell them of something fearful about to be unleashed upon mankind. You could almost feel the clutch in the chest.

At one point in the parade, and only for a moment, a man stopped in the middle of the street, perhaps fifteen feet from where I was standing. He looked very old; his hair was white and he had the cadaverous look that spoke of concentration camps. I remember how, looking at the crowd on the sidewalk, the man shook his head at us, and how his bright, sad eyes seemed to hold all the pathos of what had been and what was to come. I knew what I had felt and I knew that this man must have felt it one thousand times more, but in this we shared the common ground—the feeling of impending death.

The man walked on and the crowd again became noisy, and I was also more alive to where I was and to my purpose. I had to find Giselle. But then what? I hardly knew her, but I had to fly to her like a child runs to his mother.

When the man moved on, and when all the victims had passed, the crowd seemed relieved and eager to cheer and to wave again.

A woman beside me asked, "Vous êtes américain?" Not hard to tell, I guess. I was hatless, but still wore my officer's green shirt, green trousers, and flight jacket. "Yes—oui," I said, and looked at her more closely. In her thirties, attractive, slim—but wasn't everybody slim, with the food shortages?

"What are you doing here?" she continued in French. I responded in kind. "J'étais libéré, j'étais un prisonier de guerre, comme ces hommes—I've just been liberated, I was a prisoner of war, like these men I said, nodding towards the emaciated men in their striped prison camp clothes.

"You look so young," she said, putting her hand on my arm. I thought that she looked old, as if she had aged too quickly, but, then again, this was natural with the way things had been for the last four years. Suddenly I no longer saw the parade, I no longer heard the music, and I was not aware of anybody around us.

"Can I help you?" she asked, and leaned toward me.

"You are very kind. Très gentille, mademoiselle." She looked at me closely, then her eyes wandered to my flight jacket, where she saw the large stain of dried blood. She said softly, "So, you have suffered for us."

"I was lucky," I said, "I didn't lose my life; I think I really found it."

It was the first time I had said this out loud. Suddenly I felt elated. I wanted to embrace this woman, to feel her cheek against mine. It felt right to do so, but I didn't. As she held me by the arm, I held her likewise, by her arm. She gently squeezed my arm and caressed it, saying, "Vous êtes un homme très fort avec beaucoup de courage. Vous me semblez très, très français, vraiment." She smiled, then said, "I have to go," and withdrew from the crowd. I stepped back, watching her, at times losing sight of her, and when she was about a quarter of a block away, she turned around and waved.

She thought I was strong and courageous, like one of her countrymen; and at that moment, I felt it too.

———

I watched her as she faded from my sight. We could have been companions on this May Day, instead of watching a parade like this and all these other men and women who had been beaten down by war. How deep our desire goes, once ignited almost impossible to extinguish. But I drew myself back to the parade, and watched the soldiers marching. I felt calmed now, and once again felt for the letters in my pocket. The people around me waved their small flags, the band began playing the "Marseillaise," and a thrill swept through all of us as we listened—about peace and liberty, lying bleeding, about hateful tyrants, march on, march on, resolve on liberty or death. The presence of the prisoners must have been somebody's idea, a way to begin introducing the sad knowledge. Somebody always orchestrates these events, with something always in mind. But nobody was yet ready to contemplate the tragedy at this immediate time of the war, when the costs of the war had yet to be reckoned, and when the dead had not yet been counted.

———

Things had changed in the few months since January, when I had first come to Paris with Pete and Jack and the others, and when I had first met Giselle—only four months ago, when the weather had been cold, and the skies a dirty gray. All of Paris had seemed to reflect that sky, and no Parisian had wanted to venture out. There had been few people on the streets, fewer in the perfume shops we visited, buying bottles for the girls in London, in Norwich, and for the girls back home, if we ever got there. All of Paris must have been in the cafés, for I remember seeing the people huddling together in the windows and spilling out onto the café sidewalks. Anything to get away from the loneliness and the cold of your room.

Only four months after liberation and the shadow of occupation had not yet disappeared, though maybe, we thought then, it might disappear by spring. And would I be there in the spring? Back then it had not seemed possible. So much had not seemed possible then.

This was a different Paris now, Paris in May. De Gaulle had come and established clearly the victory of the Allies, of his free French army, and it was clear that he was the man of the hour. He was, as he sought to be, France. Later, the outside world would know people around him, like Andrew Malraux, but on that day Paris was more cheerful than it had been four months before. The day was sunny and warm, the women were more gaily dressed, and the men seemed cleaner in their suits and sports coats. There was a sense of joy in the air, as if people were realizing that now was the time for all things on earth to come to life, despite the forlorn spaces where corpses lay, some burned, many buried and others still alive, soon to die. We would see them for the next fifty years and we would never understand why or how it all happened.

But no one thought this now and here. It was enough to breathe deeply, to go into one's favorite café and to seek out one's favorite companions and talk, talk the way French do.

I do not remember exactly where the Place de l'Opéra was in relation to where we were now, on the Champs-Élysées. I might have asked the French woman where to find the Hôtel des Deux Mondes. She might have told me. Finally, I found myself at the Place de l'Opéra, which was the only landmark I knew. When I saw its elaborate façade—the row of columns, the winged stone statues—I knew that in a few minutes I would be at the Hôtel des Deux Mondes. As impatient as I was to get to Giselle, my thoughts sprinted ahead of me, already seeing her, embracing her, telling her what had happened to me. Suddenly I stopped in front of the hotel. What if she were no longer here? What if she had forgotten me, or was no longer interested? I felt a crush of fear imagining her turning away with a carelessness that would leave me burning with shame.

And what if she were here? What if she were overcome with joy at seeing me—then what? And if she asked me what I wanted to do, or what we should do; how was I to answer?

I had no answers. A thousand thoughts ran across my mind, crushing out order. I could not think then. I would not have been able to speak.

I stood immobile for a long time, until slowly, feeling came back, my thoughts ordered themselves, and I held myself open to a solution—any solution now that would get me to move forward.

I thought I had to move, to go in, and in the motion, ideas would come. My mind seemed to work at these times. Words would come and Giselle would help. Yes, she would speak to me and as she did, with her calmness and her logic and her questions, all the answers I needed would come.

But I knew I was off balance—one moment calm, and the next elated or terrified.

I did not notice the people passing by, who must have thought I was a bit crazy. No one said anything. No one tapped me on the shoulder, asking if I needed help. I would not have cared, in any case. Then I walked back and forth and after half an hour I walked into the hotel, my heart beating so fast and loud I thought it would come out of my skinny chest.

A young woman sat behind the desk. I said "Bonjour, je suis Lt. Bail. Is Giselle here?" She said, without a trace of surprise on her face, "Bien sûr, attendez, s'il vous plaît, monsieur." And she left. In a few minutes Giselle appeared, dressed simply in black, and looking more than ever like the famous French actress Arletty with her smooth auburn hair, brown eyes, and red lips. Giselle was about ten years older than I, and I found her as glamorous as any movie star.

Her eyes widened when she saw me. "It's you," she said, "my God, what has happened?" She hugged me and kissed me on both cheeks. "Have you gone AWOL," she asked, "how are you here?"

"No," I said, "I'm not AWOL. I was a prisoner, and now I'm going home."

"Oh my God, oh mon Dieu," and looked at me closely, seeing the blood stains on my jacket and some stains of blood on my white flying scarf. She hugged me again. I could feel her body very close to me, and I pressed up against her. Relief washed over me. I was safe. With tenderness Giselle said, "Later, later, maintenant parlons," *now let us talk, now we can talk.*

---

It was five or six o'clock, and I was hungry, so we went to a café to eat and talk. Giselle and I walked on the rue de Rivoli, with its grand stores on either side, their windows almost bare. In May 1945 there was still not enough milk for the children or enough meat for the adult, and no one could think of the kind of material goods such stores would sell. We crossed the street and walked on the other side. The night was so perfect I could forget everything but her, Giselle. It was exactly right. As we crossed on rue St. Honoré Faubourg, there appeared a line of cafés where we could see men and women drinking coffee, smoking their Gauloise cigarettes, and reading the newspaper. I could not see the headlines, but the men seemed absorbed in what they were reading; perhaps there was a special delight in being able to sit and drink and smoke, in not having to worry about the approach of a German soldier. It was the freedom seen in the long, leisurely inhalation of a cigarette, the enjoyment in pulling the smoke deep into the lungs. We walked up to the Ritz and were silent, her arm through mine. We stopped at a café, where we let the red wine warm us. My cheeks became red and she laughed at the color, enjoying my visible pleasure. All my pleasure was in her. I could not eat much and the wine immediately went to my head. Two glasses were enough for me.

It was dark and getting cold when we arrived back at her little room in the hotel. My belly was warm from the food and wine.

I took her into my arms and began kissing her. I still do not know what had compelled her to my side and to bed with me four months

132

before, why she had not chosen to be with Jack. He was boyish, engaging, and tall—taller and more handsome than I—and he had a rakish tilt to his cap, which he had broken in as carefully as we all did. Jack was one of those men who had an impish gleam in his eyes that made him desired by women, and he could have had pretty much any woman he wanted. But here I was with her again, and her hips nestled into mine as we stood against the door.

Womanliness exuded from her along with the magical scent of her perfume—the way she stood, the way she tilted her chin and smiled. Giselle pulled away from me to turn the lamp on. It was dim, and the room was cold. No hotel had heat in those days, and I doubt many homes had it either. The war had been hard on everyone.

She quickly slipped off her things, and I once again saw the loveliness of her body. "Quick," she said, "come into the bed," and she held the blanket up for me. I undressed and joined her and she looked at me, all over. Touched my protruding ribs. "The Germans," she said, "they made a scarecrow out of you. Are you strong enough?"

I felt a pinprick of fear pierce through me. How had I lived through these last six weeks? A group of SS soldiers had been patients on the other side of the hospital, and of course had known of our presence there. I still remember what Irmgard told me about them, and how her words had haunted me when I was still a prisoner. I repeated to myself: But now I am in Paris. It was over. The war could not last more than a few weeks more; everyone knew it. Still, these images, images of the German soldiers, came in, occupied me as I lay with Giselle. I had to shake them away to revel in my present.

We made love for hours, until the early morning. And when I finally slept, I dreamed of her legs, her thighs, how readily she welcomed me between them. It was all in the welcome, in the tenderness, in the slow riding of the hips, in the muscles of her pelvis contracting to give me greater pleasure. And always kissing me, and searching out my mouth and teeth and tongue. We were together and it was a miracle, that I was alive was a miracle, that I was in Paris, the city I had dreamed of in college. I was alive. I was alive.

133

When I awoke, Giselle was gone, but on the small dark brown table were a razor and some soap, and I got up and shaved. The water was cold, so I did not bathe. I knew that Giselle had gone out to do her business in the black market that flourished everywhere under the Allied dominion. She never told me what she did exactly, but there were big markets for cigarettes, sulfa, penicillin and whatever other commodities the civilian population wanted and would pay any price for. There was a lot of money about and I knew only that Giselle had cut out her share.

The girl at the front desk told me that Giselle would be back after ten. I settled into a deep armchair in the hotel lobby to wait.

Left alone, I thought again of Irmgard. Had it only been a few days since I'd seen her? I would have given anything to know where she was, what was she doing, what would be done with her. I began to feel guilt over the way I had seemed to flee from her, the way I might have betrayed everything I had said to her when I was still a prisoner. A hot feeling of shame passed through me. I was so uncomfortable that I stood up and stamped my feet, raised my arms and swung them around. I tried to think of Giselle and myself, of our lovemaking the night before, but thoughts of Irmgard intruded with a threatening finger. She would never have condemned me like that, but I imagined it nonetheless. For me it was as if I had defaulted in flying combat after all my training by saying, "I'm sorry, I'm too scared, I simply cannot do it." Having Irmgard's letters in my pockets did not help, and I was deep in despair and shame.

Giselle came back, finally, cheerful with a colorful scarf around her neck. Her perfume scented the air around her. When she saw my expression, she sat on the arm of my chair and pulled me to her breast. We sat like this for a few minutes, and I did not speak what was in my heart and mind. She looked down at me and smiled. Giselle had the kind of sweet, upturned smile that could only inspire joy in those around her, and soon I was able to laugh with her again. She hugged me as I stood up and I could smell her perfume. Come, she said, let us get a croissant and coffee. After, we'll eat something more.

I know but do not know how we walked, all the places we went; we walked along the Seine for a short while, we walked on the Boulevard St. Germain de Près. We sat at the Café Flore, we sat at Café des Deux Magots. We may have even sat there with Sartre and Camus. It was this Paris that drew me most, this wonderful enchantment of people sitting. This is what I had dreamed of in college—a life in the Paris cafes, so far from the weathered red brick row houses that lined the streets back home. And there we sat, mostly all strangers to one another, yet with an invisible strand draping and connecting us. Though we did not speak to the people at the next table, we were all together, sharing ourselves, our minds and our hearts.

But the dead were never far from us. Even now I can see my pilot friend Lou Mazure as clearly as if he were standing before me, as alive and glittering as he once was. I remember his face and his smile and his kindness to me, much younger than he and scared as hell to begin my journey. In one instant he was killed, right in his pilot's seat, and me across from him, helpless. When we told his dark-haired lover who worked at the Red Cross that he was killed, it killed her, too. For within two weeks she went home. I missed her, just as I missed everything of beauty, for without that death was near.

Is there an easy way to die in war? Already there is terror, even if death comes quickly, a .50 caliber bullet in the head, an 88-millemeter shell that explodes your plane and you with it. Even being in a Paris hotel room with the kind of auburn-haired woman you dreamed of in college, a woman who calls you "mon chéri," and who smells like hyacinth, her pale dancer's body soft and quivering under your own— not even that could erase these thoughts.

I returned to thoughts of my life. What will I do, I kept asking myself, with the rest of my life? Could I really remain in Paris with Giselle? I'm so young, though I feel tired and old and worn out, like my grandfather after a spasm of coughing. Now I was tired the way he had been, walking slowly, slowly through the house, chanting. Nothing I had planned for before the war made sense to me now.

And when I looked deeper into my heart, even I trembled at that darkness there, the voice telling me I could solve everything by getting killed, that I did not have to do anything. Get killed, then it's over, it is over. You do not have to do life.

I realized then how great my wish to die had been, back when I had been given the choice not to fly after my third mission, in June 1944, but had chosen to fly anyway. I had said to myself, I am a Jew, I must do this. How can I retire so soon when my brother is in South Africa fighting Rommel? Is this what I trained for? No, I'm going on, I had told the flight surgeon, who had looked at me. All the surviving crew members had quit shortly after. They had begun to shake at the idea of going back into combat.

Now, so many months later, I was shaking from the force of these memories and thoughts. I could not give in to such despair and hopelessness, now that the war was almost over. I could not.

"Chéri," Giselle said, and I looked at her. She put her slightly chapped hand on mine. I knew she did not like to reveal her hands. She said, "Nothing else matters when it is all said, nothing except love and happiness." I nodded, but now, over fifty years later, I realize that then I did not understand what she meant. She, like Irmgard, was far wiser than I—a quality in both women. She saw something in me that I had no consciousness of then. What did I want? She read my mind.

"You could go to the Sorbonne. We could forge an identity for you today, that would not be difficult. Soon you would speak perfect French, and no one would ever suspect. There would be no problem with money at first, for I have gone quite a way in my job." I said nothing, feeling I had no right to moralize to her—what did I know of her life, except that she had been born in a small village not too far from Paris, and that she had come to Paris to find a life. She had been a salesgirl in a shop, and I knew nothing else. There was no time for that, for elaborate talking, that painstaking talking over the details of one's life. She knew nothing of my life, either.

It was, looking at it today, ridiculous to think that such a venture could have survived. She knew about life because she had lived it. Suffered in it, took her joy in it, made her friends, her enemies, had her lovers and I certainly never asked about them. But she had survived it with a growth of her personality and her loveliness and the optimism for life that her very being expressed. I felt very safe when I was with her, so safe I had thought of staying with her forever, back when I was too shocked, and too saddened, to think of doing life.

Where these bits and pieces of conversation took place is lost. Walking, perhaps, on the Champs-Élysées, Faubourg de St. Honoré, rue de Rivoli, the Tuileries, Bois de Boulogne.

———

To remain in Paris with Giselle: only a few years before—before the war, before Giselle and Paris, and Irmgard, and Karl dying in the bed next to me—I never could have imagined such a day would come, a day when I would consider betraying all that I had ever known. That I would be so far from home that the thought of our Sixth Street row house in South Philadelphia would devastate me, and the thought of my mother could fail to bring me comfort. Only a few years before, before the entire world changed.

At seventeen I would not even have dared imagine myself in Paris with a beautiful woman—and myself there as an air force officer, no less. I thought I was already stretching the limits by thinking of going to Paris at all, by dreaming of the Sorbonne. I could see myself at the lectures, at the library, walking past the landmarks of Paris. I could see breasting the cold and overcoming the heat of Paris, the Seine, the parks, the cafés where adventures might lurk. Could I romance a French girl, maybe? Even that felt a betrayal.

———

It was as if I had seen too much, heard too much, and could not stand anything more, or anything else. Yet at the same time I could not entirely shut my eyes, so I did both. I blurred my vision and I saw as sharply as I could. Giselle couldn't understand how this scarecrow could muster the energy I had. Later I was to pay for it. In the meantime it carried me through the day and the night.

There was a space of time that I had to wait for Giselle. I sat in the small hotel lobby with its several chairs, old and worn. There was a radio on a small table, playing, faintly, "the Marseillaise" from the revelry outside. I sat looking at it: flat on the bottom, then arched, both ends of the arch glued to the bottom piece. The lobby was empty; I thought everyone must have been in the streets but me. I was glad the radio was on.

The small hotel radio and the music of the French anthem were jolts to the memory, and it was a jolt to be surrounded by the people who would suffer years of deprivation after the war. I used to have the idea that all of France was in the resistance movement, though of course this was not true. It was only after the war, when the movie appeared by Marcel Ophüls, *The Sorrow and the Pity*, that I learned what many French people already knew: that many, many French people had collaborated with the Germans and that many of them were later prosecuted. I also did not know that even in May 1945, as I was making love with Giselle and wandering the streets of Paris, heading towards a small café, Nazis were still torturing and killing prisoners. This I read much, much later in one of Janet Flanner's *New Yorker* letters. I had first been in Paris in January 1945 and I had seen and felt what she describes: the coldness in the streets, the coldness in the homes, the scarcity of food everywhere.

It was shocking to learn that many French people did collaborate, but I'm old enough today to know how difficult it is to hold onto a moral position, to hold onto the high ground, whatever the rationale is—to save my life, to save my mother, my father, my husband, my wife, my child. I'm aware of these reasons, but I'm also aware of the consequences of not adhering to the truth, the consequences to one's life, one's heart and soul. Unfortunately, we are creatures for whom there are always consequences.

It was just before my capture that I began to read reports of concentration camps and about the victims in these camps. I no longer remember whether the *Stars and Stripes* printed pictures of them, and I do not recall talking with my friends about them. I think we were still too occupied with our own missions and with our own lives being at risk. We, in our current state of mind, never dreamed that the Germans were doing what they were doing. In war there is a certain form, a de rigueur, that all of us felt existed. Maybe high command knew, having access to the information of resistance fighters who roamed around and observed. Maybe high command within the ETO, the European Theater of Operations, knew. But I understand that even Eisenhower, on inspecting a camp that had fallen to our forces, was shaken by what he saw. These sites, which I later saw myself, were horrifying beyond all belief. So later in Germany, after I had been liberated, when we passed the ragtag line of concentration camp inmates, I had known who they were at once. I was so shocked at the sight of their cadaver-like features, I forgot how thin I was myself. We each had our own particular cell of suffering.

Now, in the restaurant, Giselle was gentle, caressing my hand across the table, holding first one hand and then the other between her own. If this were a movie I would have known what to say, I could have done a crude Leslie Howard, and then it would have been easy, the writer would have put beautiful dialogue into my mouth. She paid the bill, then we walked back to the hotel in the dark, holding hands. We went to her room, undressed, and got into bed. She took out a Gauloise and offered me one, but I did not take it. She smoked, sitting propped against the headboard next to me. Occasionally she kissed me and I her. I was not offended by the taste of the cigarette in her mouth. I had been around the girls of London and Norwich; it seemed all the women had taken to smoking Lucky Strikes or Camels. Americans were generous with everything they had. Her mouth was sweet, and she looked at me with love.

I said finally, "Giselle, I think I have to go back. I could not live here—whatever I might have thought during those days in Nancy. I could not live knowing that my mother knows I am alive and that I have chosen not to come home. I know she would die. Once, when I was a kid, my mother put her hand on my shoulder and said to me, 'Ah, you don't know what it's like to be a mother, you'll never know. Even if her heart lies beside her on the road, a mother will get up, pick up her heart and run to her child if that child needs her.'"

I turned to Giselle and said, "I do not know how I could not feel guilty." She was quiet, and put out her cigarette. She slid down close to me, saying, "Come, hold me, hold me for a little while. I just want to rest in your arms." We stayed this way a long time. Later we made love and afterwards she said, "I understand darling, I understand." We fell asleep and when I woke Giselle was gone.

I found a letter on the table. I opened it and read, "I already knew what you were going to say and do. I think I knew it in my heart from the very first. When you came back I did not dare believe my good luck. In war one tends to guard one's feelings, and certainly I have done that with mine. I want to tell you a dream I used to have as a little girl when I lived with my parents in the village where I was born. I used to dream of whom I would marry and I always had this image of a man's form, but his face would not fill in. I had the feel of the person, never the face. I've known many men, but when you appeared, when I first saw you in January, I knew the man was you. I knew by the feeling. I did not dare let my feelings grow too big. The pain of love is unbearable, the pain of love unmet is simply death. I knew you were in Paris for just a few days, and like men everywhere wanted to have fun. I tried to be fun for you, but it was real for me. I do not say goodbye to you, because I do not want to say goodbye to my dream. You know how important a person's dreams are. Know that I shall grieve your going. I have arranged for Rouget, a friend of mine, to meet you at the hotel at eleven and take you to the train. Trust him, you will be on time."

I felt myself consumed by an inconsolable sense of loss as I put the letter down. My heart pounded with fear and panic, and I got up and rushed downstairs, went out of the hotel. I ran up and down the street, wildly looking for her. I looked at all the women, those farthest away, to see if Giselle was coming back. But she was not in the crowd.

What had I done? Had I made the wrong decision? I did not know that I could stand being abandoned by two exceptional women so quickly, though it was I who'd been forced to leave.

When I returned to the hotel Giselle's friend, a man of Jean Gabin stature, was waiting for me. "Come, m'sieu, it's time for us to go." He knew who I was; I was the only American in the small lounge. He led me to his car, but did not speak with me. I watched him. Her friend, I thought, someone who sees her a lot, someone she trusts. Did he know about Giselle and me? His face revealed nothing. I felt no antagonism coming from him. It was only a job to him, taking me.

I imagined Giselle saying the American has to go; it is not possible for us. I imagined tears forming and spilling down her cheeks. I saw him silent, looking away so as not to embarrass her. And I imagined him thinking, what a shitty world, what a shitty war. I imagined the day when he would sit with Giselle and remember it all. One day she would ask him, what did he look like and how did he feel when you drove him to the station, my young American soldier, and he would tell her, *merde alors*, like a stricken man.

In twenty minutes we were at the station, and I thanked Giselle's friend. "Good luck, m'sieu," he said, and nodded. I went to the track where our train was scheduled to depart to Le Havre and waited for the men to come. Soon they came, by twos and singly, and then everybody was there and finally Wyans was there, too. He grinned and I grinned back. We shook hands.

"Well buddy, how'd it go?"

I said, "As well as I could expect. And you?"

"This is some wonderful town, I saw the Folies Bérgère—now that's something we don't have back home."

I laughed, "We don't have that either, back in Philadelphia," and I thought of the burlesque house on Arch Street, which I never got to see inside.

The soldiers entered the train, and, once again, a compartment was reserved for Wyans and myself. It was almost time to go when a young French girl carrying a violin approached and asked me if she could ride with us, as the rest of the train was full. She was going only a little way outside of Paris, back to her village. I said yes and I helped her up and into the compartment. Wyans did not mind. Soon the train started and the girl began to talk. She was a music student, and was now returning home for a few days. I did not say much. She asked, "Are you unhappy?" I told her that I was. "It's a woman isn't it?" she asked.

We spoke French, and Wyans understood nothing of our talk. I said, "Isn't it always a woman that throws a man into pensive mood? Before I came to Paris I had many thoughts, many hopes to do great things. I think I failed, that I am a coward."

"Oh no, m'sieu, I know you're not a coward. But affairs of the heart are very complicated." I sat quietly for a while. More and more as the train drew further away from Paris, I thought—would I ever come to Paris again? Ever see Giselle again? After an hour of so the train stopped at a small town. The train whistled and the girl waved to me, standing on the platform as the train left. I waved to her; I waved to her and to Giselle, au revoir, au revoir, chérie.

It took me a long time to realize that the Paris I longed for was inside my own heart and mind, as it is for every man and woman who dreams and yearns for freedom.

Now it was over, really over. I was going home. I began again to reflect on my experiences. I tried to slow them down. They were too much, too fast, even blurred, especially with Giselle.

I did not feel guilty about sex with Giselle, though I could have. I think even Irmgard would not have censored me; and one must imagine the sheltered home I had come from, the terrible repressive atmosphere about anything sexual, anything about the body. If one had sex, unmarried, it was furtive and with a sense of transgression, a feeling of guilt, something you could joke about in a veiled way.

Marriage was the only way, which I gathered was why parents wanted their children married young, especially their daughters. Generally mothers felt no girl was ever good enough for their sons. I know mine felt that way.

College was only a little more open, not much. My friends and I knew there was sexual activity—sometimes even an unwanted pregnancy. Comments were of a ribald nature. Serious sex and love were rarely spoken about. Looking back, everyone was so young, so unknowingly false, as the adults—who were the professors who taught us—and we were isolated on the edge of the beautiful town of West Chester, Pennsylvania, farm communities and towns of predominately Pennsylvania Dutch families. I believe I was the only Jew who lived at that school, though there was less than a handful that commuted.

I didn't reminisce about the college years. They were the golden years of my life, opening my eyes to the world. My teachers were very good and made learning fun.

I wrenched myself back to thinking about Giselle, which I did on the train ride to the staging area. Giselle was the romance of my life, an impossible experience to surpass with anyone else at any time, or so I thought at the time. It is as if I knew it at the time and threw myself into the forgetfulness of time. I was at the magical place despite the grim hardships of everyday life.

Paris was reviving. The cafes, the shops and, beneath the misery of years of occupation, the underlying beauty of the city shone for me and it was Giselle who was emblematic of that happiness. I felt the freedom, for a little while, not to think of my obligations, my reality. I had no money and I had no job. It was wonderland. Giselle had lots of money and wanted to share it with me. She wanted to give me the air of Paris as if it were oxygen that I needed for my gasping life.

She understood when I talked more of my love, through my love for my professor Ethel Staley who talked with love and gusto, coat on with scarf, hat on her head askew, and as she talked spittle would come for a distance. French, she would say, is a muscular language. "You can't be lazy Americans who do not move your lips." I loved her and I loved Giselle for what she offered me.

143

I loved Giselle for the openness with which she looked at me, the maturity I felt she had, a maturity deepened by the suffering. I knew the sculpture which she had fashioned of her life, the marks were still there. I loved her voice and her body as it moved through her clothes and her wonderful legs. She was so essentially French, so feminine, at least through my young eyes. I felt despite all my experiences, training in the southern part of America—Mississippi and Louisiana—going north to Spokane, Washington, for further training in the west, then on to Boise, Idaho, and Wendover, Utah, and finally in the northeast at Langley Field, I had covered the country and in each place met the people, met the men and the women of the region. Still it was not the end of my education for there was Labrador and Iceland, Scotland and England, France and Germany.

America was kind to me and gave me what I could never have given myself. In France and Germany, God gave me something precious, unique, painful, and joyful, and finally an aching heart. These times and these people began to fill the blank canvas of my life and soul, giving me the lessons I needed, the terror I needed, the desperation I needed, the fear and relief I needed, chiseling them all into my body and mind and into my skull, still with fragments of iron and the scar tissue beneath the muscles—all part of my lesson that my soul had to have to transform my pain and my disappointment with a few moments of joy.

I felt all the rest of my life I would never have anything like these two women. They were so essentially alike in their love for me, one who would bring me to myself, who defined better than anyone what an analyst is, "Do you want to see yourself, come the far way to my soul, through the pain to my soul and I will show you and I will be able to make it bearable for you to see." Giselle, the physical embodiment of the pure Irmgard, the Madralena of my physical being and I could see better now than ever before how it really was. I could never have stayed with either one of them. There was a pull of greater force than I had ever known. I had to see my mother in "Russia" with her beautiful mother. I would have to go to my mother who made me sad and who gave me joy when she played the mandolin and sang the sad songs. She was the oak root of me that gave me the ability all the rest of my life for all that was to come.

The train continued for several hours, stopping, slowing down and starting again, until finally we were at the station. There was an army truck waiting there for us, and we rode for some thirty minutes before arriving at the gate of our military establishment.

I handed my papers to the officer in charge, who asked me, "Is everybody here?" I said yes. He went out and called out the names on the list. He then assigned us to tents with letters and numbers, and said, "The corporal will show you where to go."

We followed the corporal until a huge tent city unfolded before us. It seemed endless. I could hardly see beyond it and when we got into the actual "streets," the space before the tents was loaded with every conceivable object. All of the men in this vast tent city were ex-prisoners of war, and it seemed that most of them had looted on their way from captivity to freedom. In a way it seemed to balance out, for the German army had looted the houses they overran and taken whatever they wanted. It was like the biggest swap meet I ever saw in my life, except nothing was for sale. Imagine a house with all of its furniture: I saw chairs with velvet covering, lamps, stools, grandfather clocks, Persian carpets of all sizes, German bayonets, German machine guns, and machine guns with rounds of ammunition someone had actually carried I don't know how many miles. I had nothing by comparison: only the colonel's beautiful pistol and its holster, with a clip of ten bullets.

No one laughed at the trophies these men had captured, men toughened by a hard capture, a hard captivity. No one tried to steal anything from anyone. I noticed one thing, however—that those men who had been prisoners for a long time were in the best physical condition. Many of these men were lucky enough to have been assigned to places on German farms where they were well fed. They looked as if they had just come from health farms; by contrast, those who had been taken in the last months of the war looked the worst—gaunt, sickly, and pale. We stayed in this camp for a few days, and then on May 7, 1945, we were loaded onto the ship that was to take us home. Though I was assigned a bunk down below, I was not too anxious to spend the night there; I knew there were still German submarines in Atlantic waters. I spent the night on deck, and even slept there as the boat full of ex-prisoners of war made its way to England. On the morning of May 8 we docked at Southampton, and there the announcement came: the war was over, the Germans had surrendered.

We on the boat did not participate in the wild enthusiasm that swept through the streets of the Western world. I think most of us were too stunned by the rush of events in the past months. The experiences of the men on the boat with me had been more or less like mine, though I did not ask them and they did not ask me anything about them. We were an indrawn group of hundreds of men thinking only, what next? For myself, I thought mostly of Giselle and Irmgard, of the letters Irmgard had written. I slept with my hand on the pocket I kept them in. But my mind was in a jumble, and I was also worried about the U-boats that did not heed the surrender agreement signed by Admiral Doenitz and the other German officers.

The mind is a wonderful thing in what it remembers and what it chooses to forget. Now, looking back, I do not recall much about my time at the staging area. I do not know how these fellows carried their spoils—whether in carts or wheelbarrows or wagons. I do not know how they got their stuff onto the ship. I do not remember what we ate at this time or when or where we bathed in these three or four days. I remember nothing of the daily occurrences on the boat. We must have eaten, shaved, and showered, but I cannot recall a thing.

I do remember sleeping on deck as we crossed the ocean back to America, and staring out at the black glittering water. My apprehensions were great, like those of many of the ex-prisoners who stayed near the deck with life preservers close to hand, worried only about getting across that ocean alive.

I wondered too about my being sent to the Pacific to fly missions upon returning to the States. There was no hint of an end to that war. Maybe the others were occupied with this too—it was sobering and maybe they, like me, were thinking that they just could not do another tour of combat. I thought of Carper, who had flown one more mission after Lou Mazure was killed. On that mission he had simply frozen in the copilot's seat. He had been a hazard to the crew. The flight doctor had grounded him when he got back, and that was the end of the game for him.

I could understand that pitch of terror, the kind that makes you want to scream, but does not allow you even that. The days passed, and the weather was sunny and warm. Many of the fellows shed their shirts, but I was in no mood to relax to that extent.

Finally the day came when we spied land, when we came to the most fabled statue, when we knew we were finally safe. Now I could understand how my mother and father must have felt coming onto this sight, the precious freedom it signaled for my father, and, for my mother, something else. What had she felt as the ship carried her closer to a marriage with a man she did not know, a man whose picture she had seen only once?

We berthed and then were dispatched to trucks. I do not remember much, not even getting off the ship. I never recalled the name of the ship that brought us back to the States. I do not recall anything except sitting on the train headed for Philadelphia. I sat alone making the trip to Philadelphia from the discharge center. I sat by the window, looking at the landscape, not seeing anything, absorbed in the mystery of life (yes, Nelson Eddie singing, "Ah, sweet mystery of life, at last I found thee"). The mystery was dark, a secret which I could not make out then.

It was all unreal. I felt disembodied and unreal. Train rides I had taken from Norwich to London, from Paris to LeHavre, to Stuttgart... was I that person? Alternately with pleasure at the prospect of a hot bath and a show in London, the bars in Piccadilly Circus, along with Jack, tea at the Ritz, , the orchestra playing fox trots, beautiful ladies dancing—some together. The tea carts pushed by the livered waiters with their delicate sandwiches—gone in one gulp—scones with cream and jam. Never again those tastes, those times of pure being, pure physicality where all was right with the world. I was comfortable in my skin watching Jack drink and smile, crack his attractive smile. He knew his charm. "You don't need it with me, Jack." The wheels clicking, my heart growing heavier as we drew near by time, near to goodbye, my fear, my elation, my joy, my love—goodbye to Irmgard as I fingered the brown envelope with her letters—for Giselle a flash of her smile, a picture of her arm through mine as we walked, a moment when we stopped and she encircled my waist, kissed me, "I am so happy, so happy," and kissed me and kissed me.

A movie certainly—it was all a movie. I did not know whether I could get up from my seat. I was too heavy with memories. None would go away. None really wanted to harass me. They simply wanted to be with me maybe forever. And what was I to do?

Now I had a life to make, a life to do. I already felt so weary at the non-life I had already endured. You know one does not live during the war. One suspends time, one holds on—not even wanting to hope—as if death would be an unbearable disappointment. I could bear no more disappointments.

And through it all I knew I may have already lived the highest point in my life. I may have already met the sweet mysteries of my life and I had already let them both go.

I needed to bring something to them that I was not then—an achievement, a worthy accomplishment—that I would be proud to show them, to make them proud. Not a pair of wings that said I knew how to guide a plane and how to kill people. I could not live on that as my achievement. That achievement alone would destroy me. I knew all that in a flash as I was going north to Philadelphia, my Philadelphia.

It would be a long time before I could put the two women in a place of meaning that my heart would accept. It would be a very long time.

The train made its usual noises: the wheels clanked and people talked, their speech buzzing in my ears. People looked at me in my heavy green officer's trousers and my green fur-collared flying jacket. They were curious, but I did not return their stares. I had no luggage to speak of—the colonel's pistol was stuck in my waist belt and covered by my jacket. I entered Thirtieth Street Station a different person; in these three years, I had become a different person. I was divorced from the crowds—they were still the crowds, they were still the winsome girls in those summer dresses, those sexy shoes. They seemed so far away from Giselle and Irmgard, worlds apart.

I felt the distance between these girls and me and wondered if I would ever be able to bridge that chasm, and it was a considerable chasm. Nothing ages you like staring death in the face over and over again. After that you are not living in the same dimension of space and time as those who did not journey with you. I sat silent in the train looking at the same landscape I had seen before, but I looked and did not see it.

It was the end of May. I had been given two months' leave and I was to report to Miami Beach, Florida, at the end of July.

# 7

## The War is Over

*M*y family knew I was coming; I had called them from New York, where I'd boarded the train. They did not know exactly when, but I imagined they were all gathered in the house waiting. I was beginning to feel the density I had feared when I was on the train going from Nancy to Paris. The density of family is a heavy burden; I had been glad to escape to college at West Chester and elated to enlist in the air force. When I left the States in our Liberator, all the vestiges of that heaviness had left me, and inside me was pure spirit, my heart singing freedom.

Now, as I neared home, the old density was coming back. Now I had to endure the tears, the embraces, the kisses, the touches of all these people, and my heart was not light. I told myself, put on a face, do what you are expected to do, you know what they all want, do it, just do it.

The cab drew up to the house. I was able to see the park as the cab passed Wolf Street, but it did not look the same, the entire street did not look the same. I paid the driver and got out. Uncle Harry was at the door and inside I heard my mother sob, "Oh God, oh God, you have given me back my son." I entered the house; my uncle was the first to embrace me. What followed was a blur: my mother who kept holding me and caressing my face and kissing me, and my father standing by my side, awkward as he always was when feelings were in evidence and he had to do the appropriate thing.

My younger brother was there and my cousin George and his wife, Dolly, who had been my closest friend through college. Dolly was buxom blonde farm girl who laughed with gusto the way she did everything else in life. I thought, "Thank God for them, I can relax and talk to them later, maybe go out for dinner." Dolly came over, crying, and she hugged me and hugged me and kissed me, and George stood by her with his big arm and hand on my shoulder and I saw the tears in his eyes. "Cuz, cuz," he kept saying, but I was strangely unmoved by it all. I did not cry. I let them hug me and touch me and kiss me. My farmer cousin Etkis was there; I was told some time later that he had fainted when he heard I was missing in action. He gave me a strong hug. He was an emotional man and his eyes welled up. Uncle Alex and Aunt Eve were not there but called and invited me to come visit them. They were sorry that they could not be with me now. That was fine with me.

There was a buffet, and food of every kind was laid out on the table: chicken, meat, fish, vegetables, lox, bagels, onions, tomatoes, and hard-boiled eggs. Later neighbors came, not only from Sixth Street, but from Marshall Street and Durfor Street, where we had lived most of our lives. I greeted them all. They had never seen a flyer up close, and though I was the same kid they'd seen playing half ball on the streets, they treated me like a movie star.

That entire day people came and went, and still more would enter through the front doors as the afternoon wore on. My mother sat on the couch where she had lain when she heard I was missing in action. People sat next to her, stroking her, congratulating her, and she cried. She'd gotten old, I could see that, and she had lost weight. Is this what V-E Day was like, a mad exhilarated confusion? A joy unconfined? I felt no joy, and no exhilaration, but laughter and voices swirled through the house.

I was tired, and after a few hours I was finally able to go upstairs, take off my shoes, wash my face and lie on my bed, trying to still my mind. I was tired, and I fell asleep. When I woke I saw that I had slept a couple of hours. I could hear the voices downstairs, still pretty loud. I lay awake, trying to think, but my mind was sluggish.

I thought I might get up; I thought about that idea. I heard someone at the door; I could see Dolly peeking in, and she saw that I had my eyes open. She came in and sat on the bed looking at me, just looking at me, and she said, "You're so different." She put her hand on my thigh and stroked it. "We prayed for you every day." I sat up, swung my feet to the floor and put my arms around her, patting her on the shoulder. But I could say nothing to her of my experiences, though my heart was bursting over. I knew she wanted to hear me, but there was no way to reach her; my experiences had plunged to a place in my heart so deep she could not touch them. Would anyone be able to?

We sat this way a while, then I said, "Let me put my shoes on; I'll meet you downstairs. Maybe later we can go out for some dinner."

When Dolly left I lay back a moment and thought, I had changed. I was different from the boy who had felt a special bond to Dolly before. Not that that had changed; it would always be there and as we lived our lives it continued to be there. But I was aware that another level of experience had punched through deep within me, one that made me feel different from anyone else and brought me to a sadness beyond everything. The universe had given me two chances at love but it had not given me the maturity to accept them and prosper with them. As I got up I was aware of this change and the tinge of that sadness which I got to know well in years to come. I shook my head, as if to shake it off.

The evening was just the way the day had been, the house full until after midnight. I was now simply exhausted. I told my parents I just had to go to sleep. I went to my room, took off my clothes and was asleep in an instant.

After a few days at home, after I'd gotten to see everyone who was ever connected to me or the family, I was free to do as I pleased. My mother would not object now that I was safe back home in South Philadelphia. I had my clothes cleaned. I still had only the one uniform, which I wore until I went to Miami Beach. The cleaners did a good job, though faint signs of blood were still visible on the collar. The only thing I did buy was a pair of brown shoes as near to the ones the air force issued as I could find so I would not have to wear the heavy high-top GI shoes. I had picked up a soft hat at the quartermaster's department at the staging area, for I knew if I walked around without a hat I would be stopped by any superior officer. So to avoid a constant nuisance I took this route, though I never liked these soft caps.

I was home ten days or so before Dolly and George came to get me. I stayed with them in Vineland, New Jersey, where I thought I would get some rest, but instead we partied a great deal at the local bar, restaurant, and dance hall—dancing, drinking. We drove to Atlantic City frequently and dined and drank there. Dolly and I did a lot of drinking; George never drank more than a beer. I never told Dolly about Irmgard or Giselle. I felt they were my own precious secrets and that to share them would have been to devitalize them, to degrade them. I was surprised by the vehemence of my feelings; before I would never have dreamed of keeping anything from my Dolly, for there was no one closer to me in the world. It did not matter. These experiences were vacuum-sealed for eternity in my heart. Even after many, many years of analysis my two hermetically sealed romances were to remain untouched. Even my future wives would never know about them or the letters I've now carried in my possession for sixty-two years.

So it was that the days and the nights passed too quickly. Europe seemed far away, Paris, Giselle, far away, Goeppingen and Irmgard, very far away. Even though I had indisputable proof of their existence. I finally went to New York to stay with my Uncle Alex and Aunt Eve. They welcomed me joyously and they were the same; the same gentle mother and father, the same good-natured Moe (my Aunt Eve's brother), the same sweet Dorothy, my girlfriend before the war, more lovely than ever with her white, smooth skin and brown eyes and black hair. She was prettier than I even remembered but she was the same girl I had said goodbye to several years ago, several lifetimes ago. I was not the same person and though we went on our forays to Manhattan to see a show or a movie, eating at Horn & Hardart, my favorite eatery, with pumpkin pie and coffee, it was just not the same and I felt a heaviness in my body and my mind for it would all sound so stupid. Wasn't this why soldiers come back—to find their girlfriends waiting eager to be asked to marry, to begin a life they had held in abeyance, to begin the continuation and regeneration of the family?

I looked at her across the table. What did I like or even think I loved? Suddenly I thought I loved my uncle Alex, the gentlest, smartest of my uncles, and I loved my Aunt Eve, who truly loved my uncle. They had fun with each other, talked with each other, worked together sacrificing for the labor movement, being secret members of the Communist party and knowledgeable about the movement in the States. They sacrificed years of their lives organizing the steel workers union; babies were aborted, and when betrayal came by Stalin, my beloved uncle fell into a deep depression. Sacrifice for what!

And Dorothy—was it a family thing? Were we to be a younger Alex and Eve? Or was she in love with my uncle as I was with her sister, my aunt.

That is what my heart told me. Like a magic wand the knowledge was there with a wave and suddenly I felt she was young, innocent, tender, a wonderful girl, but no one I could possibly marry.

I could not say that to her outright. I felt it would be too cruel or was it that I was too cowardly to just put it on the table.

I could not be a Bogart, cigarette dangling, saying, "It just won't work, baby. Sorry." The movies are the movies but the feeling between us had changed. We walked a little apart, she held my arm though not as closely and there was a distance in feeling which even the family felt, her family and my uncle and aunt. They did not ask me anything. They felt I had changed and I had. I grew distant from everyone. I realized as time went by that the women I met or people who knew women and wanted to introduce them to me were of no interest to me. I was beginning to carry my burden, my deep sorrow, my deeper pain, my ache. I had other things to do. I would do them.

In the mornings Dorothy and I went into Manhattan to see a movie, have lunch, and simply walk among the crowds, enjoying the energy and excitement of the city, so different from the Philadelphia I knew. I enjoyed this precious respite from my family, and Dorothy and I enjoyed being together. Occasionally someone saluted me or I a superior officer. It was special to be alive. I had the feeling the family was expecting an announcement from us, but we had none to make. I would still be eligible to fight after I went to Miami Beach. We held our plans in abeyance, though I'm sure she would have said, "Yes, I'll marry you. I'll wait or I'll come to Miami Beach and be with you." But I could not ask her to marry me; I was already aware that something was wrong, that though I was in this world of time and space, I was in New York, I did not feel a part of the present. I had already had presentiments of this in New Jersey with some of the people there, even with my Dolly, and she was the person I was closest to in America.

Always I felt different, as if I were standing on a different elevation from these people. I looked at everything with different eyes. I think it made me appear withdrawn or stand-offish, but I was never that; I enjoyed comradeship and missed the closeness of my war friends, the crews I flew with, the fellows I bunked with. I can understand the nature of secret societies that demand ritual initiations so that everyone has the experience to the exclusion of all others. One feels one has this special group and that one is special in that sense. Many soldiers who went through similar experiences had the same feeling I did.

But, soon enough, the two months were over and I found myself on the train to Miami Beach with many other soldiers, all ex-prisoners of war. We were met at the train and taken to the hospital. There, while standing in line, I fainted. I opened my eyes and tried to figure out where I was, but I felt only confusion. Finally it came back to me. I lay in a hospital bed utterly exhausted until the nurse came in to take my temperature and pulse, which she recorded the way Irmgard had done in Germany. Later the doctor came and examined me. "Can you walk?," he asked. I said, "Sure."

But when I got up I felt feeble, and so I was wheeled to the laboratory for all kinds of X-rays, blood tests, and then wheeled back. In a couple of days the doctor returned. I had nothing wrong with me except severe combat fatigue. I needed rest. In Miami Beach we were housed in one of the best hotels on the beach. Looking out the window I could see the white sand, the blue ocean, the gentle waves coming up. The beach was not crowded with civilians, for up and down the beach every hotel housed only ex-prisoners of war. A few were on the beach, but the sand did not appeal to me; I was tired.

I rested. There was not much else I could do, and it was almost a week before I could get on my feet and walk. The war had seemed very far away, but now reports came in from the Pacific, where the fighting was intense. I learned that soldiers with a certain amount of points could possibly get an honorable discharge. Counting my own, I realized I had more than enough points to be discharged but I was not sure whether or not that was an option for me.

I was well enough to go out a few nights to a local nightclub, where many girls were around looking for a good time, just as were we. Those well enough could enjoy these pleasures, and the water and sand and sun. A few years later hordes of people were to enjoy these same beautiful hotels for huge sums of money. Now, it was all free, Uncle Sam's thank you to us.

---

The A-bombs were dropped on Hiroshima and Nagasaki, and on August 8, 1945, came the astounding news of Japan's surrender.

The war was over. The relief was profound, the entire country celebrated, but here in Miami there was no jubilation, no great cheers—only a sense of a quiet ending. Instead of relaxing, however, I knew that the real work of my life was about to begin. I had to make my future, I had to get home, go back to school. I had to find out what the requirements for medical school were. I had a tremendous amount of work to do, and I was impatient to get started. I went to the commanding officer and told him I was eligible for discharge, and asked if he could start things going to that end. He said, "We cannot do that here, but we'll send you to a discharge center in Tennessee." He was as good as his word and within a week I had my discharge and was heading home to do the work necessary to fulfill the ambitions of my life. It would not be easy. Military life is easy—someone clothes you, feeds you, finds a roof for you, a bed for you, tells you what to do and how, and they pay you as well.

I knew I would be compelled to begin to do the rest of my life. The war was now just about over. As a child I idealized my uncle Harry, the physician in the family, and was totally aware of the great respect everyone had for him. He wore suits, smoked cigars, had a car, wrote with a big red Waterman fountain pen which held a great fascination for me watching him unscrew the cap slowly, put it on the other part, take out his prescription pad and write in a florid script—a language I did not know—all that was awesome to me as was his doctor's bag with its stethoscope, blood pressure cuff and syringes and solutions of all kinds.

He was the family physician. He saved my mother's life when he diagnosed a tubal pregnancy during his internship in Scranton, Pennsylvania. It was the first time my mother and I were separated; her screeches of pain terrified me. She almost died. Seven years later he delivered my brother Sydney at home and again the pangs of birth, accompanied by the screeches, were terrifying. But he could not save my cousin Fay who had kidney disease and died in a state of kidney shutdown—uremia. I would see cases like this later in my life.

He wasn't God but close. He, too, was a good person dedicated to the class struggle who treated many of the poor free of charge and union members for a pittance. I know because his wife, my aunt, always complained there was no money.

All of my grandfather's sons gave up God to serve mankind. I never saw them put on a yarmulka, the tefillin, or the prayer shawl. Yet in retrospect they had not strayed far away from their father and their ancestors.

But my father was poor and medicine was out of the question for me, so early on I considered being a chemist. Later, I changed my mind, leaving home to go to a state teacher's college, working there studying English and French toward becoming a teacher. And though I enlisted upon graduating and getting my teacher's diploma, I did teach later on after the war. Then the war said "wait a second" to everything I ever thought—my captivity, my experience with Irmgard and with Dr. von Polster and my intimations when I talked with von Polster that this war would not be the last war— and I knew I did not want to be part of the killing, the maiming and the endless pain and suffering especially as I watched as young Karl lay dying, whimpering, gangrene spreading, its smell invading everything and death finally coming in a friendly unconscious moment.

Not for me. I decided to start again if I could. I did not know then that I would be able. There was freedom to gain, America to come back to and there was still a war I would be called upon with my skill to fight. Now in Miami Beach, with the surety of it being over, my heart skipped not with the light but with "Could I?" Could I do all the necessary things I would have to do in order to get that acceptance to medical school?

Could I do it? Could I fly my missions with an uncertain conclusion? If I could do all I did, why not begin this mighty mountain climb?

Once, my analyst asked me did I not know I had traumatic stress syndrome. I said no one had ever told me. It never occurred to me to take any time off. So it was from discharge to classroom almost without perceptible notice except now I was no longer the lead navigator. I was the plodding student among other tough-minded young men ruthless in their intent to knock you off. No mercy in pre-med, no quarter given. In those days, I didn't pray because I had never learned to but I walked endlessly when I wanted to take time off from study. And I thought of Irmgard, my shining angel of light, of hope, of strength. Maybe that was my prayer... reliving scenes and conversations with Irmgard, and sometimes Giselle, for I saw them as the same interchangeable woman who loved me and wanted for me whatever I wanted.

This time there was no fanfare when I returned home. I called my alma mater in West Chester and asked for my transcript, which they sent in a few days. I went to Temple University and spoke with the appropriate person who said if I passed an exam in French they would give me two years' credit for the four I had spent at West Chester. I would then need two years of the basic sciences—physics, physical chemistry, organic chemistry, trigonometry, calculus and so on. And then if my grades were good enough and if I did well enough in the MCATs I would stand a chance.

The competition was strong, with many youngsters competing who had never been in the war. The war service would not count at all here. Well, that was cold turkey, but I had no choice but to agree. But I decided to inquire at the University of Pennsylvania as well, where I got an appointment with a Mr. Duncan. Bringing my transcript with me, I sat at his reception room until the secretary called me. It was now early in September, 1945, and I still did not have civilian clothes. I wore the same green officer's trousers and shirt, with my wings on my shirt and my purple heart under them.

I immediately did not like Mr. Duncan. He was one of those obvious men with a white shirt and a tie up to his collar in a small tight knot. He had an oily smile, and looked to me like a man who feels he's got the world by the balls. I explained that I had just received my discharge a week ago and that I wanted to start school this semester. He looked carefully over the transcript and said essentially the same thing the Temple fellow had said, only adding one more comment:

"That's a lot of work. Why don't you become a rabbi?" He smiled that unctuous smile and spoke with contempt. It was a comment meant to hurt, to destroy the hoping heart. I wish that I had had the greatness of heart then within me to have blessed and forgiven him and gone on my way. But I was too full of rage and trauma that had never been dealt with. The war had left me with scars I had no way of understanding then. I have no doubt that, had I had a gun,

I would have shot him. It would not have mattered to me; nothing would have mattered. It is a dangerous place emotionally for any person to be.

I reddened with anger. This fucking Nazi son-of-a-bitch. I fought in a war to be free to do what I wanted to do and this fucking bastard tells me to be a rabbi.

My cheeks flushed with rage, I stood up and walked over to his desk. Facing him squarely I said, "I just fought in a war so that pricks like you can say things like that." I leaned over the desk, hands on it, and got closer to him. "You cock-sucking son of a bitch. I saved your life today by not bringing my .45." I leaned over more, and grabbing the back part of his tie I pulled hard so that he began to choke and halfway stood up, then I turned and walked out. As I walked through campus, my heart was racing, and my thoughts were racing. I walked quickly, shooting the son of a bitch in his balls and then in his guts, watching him die. "Shit, shit!" I could hardly get the words out, my throat was dry as my arms came up and down with emphasis. "Fuck!" I walked all the way home. It took two hours.

Nothing happened about this incident between Duncan and myself. I think he knew that I would kill him if he did anything to block my way and I just may have.

As I walked, my heart pounding from rage, I turned inward to recall another bitter hopeless time, and then, suddenly, a memory of Irmgard washed over me. I remembered the train I was to have been sent on, my day of pacing and anticipating death. I remembered the words she'd said to me during the night: *I prayed for you all night.* No one had ever prayed for me. It had astonished me, and filled me with wonder. I remembered her whisper in my ear: *I prayed for you all night.* I thought of her eyes glimmering in the faint light, the white of her hands moving in the dark. It surprised me, her coming to me this way, the calming effect she had on my heart. By the time I arrived home my spirits were not so painful, and my rage was gone. I turned my mind to the solution of the problem.

Later in the week I arranged to take the exam, which I passed. I got my two years' credit from West Chester and in the latter part of

September became a premed student at Temple. I was a student again, the war in the distant past. What occupied me for the next several years was my need for success, my ambition to get into an independent position. That was my goal in life for many years.

I rarely thought of the war, except when my copilot Stroble called late at night from New Orleans, always collect, always drunk, wanting to talk over old times, until I could not afford to take the calls anymore. Or when my good friend Jack Wales visited me and we talked long, long hours, him trying to persuade me to join the People's Army in China, to go to China and fly again. He couldn't stand the quietness of his life; he could not stand being the public relations man in his father-in-law's company, where his job was to take clients to lunch or to dinner. He was hugely successful but his drinking also was huge. Finally he quit and got a job flying for some little airline in the area.

And one day coming in for landing, he died. He just cut the switches. No one else was hurt. I think he died doing what he loved. I missed him and the fact that I could never again pick up the phone and talk with him. We had shared campaigns, not unlike soldiers from every army, from any country. We were friends bonded in the most intense experiences of life and death. And what could be more wondrous than that?

# 8

Philadelphia, 1945–1949

*I* did not look forward to life, to a life in which I would be haunted by what had unquestionably been the peak of it: the war, life stripped down, the clear, undemanding truths of Irmgard's flute and Giselle's hand in mine. The world stretched out before me, cold and bleak. It was not easy starting over again, going back to school with young men and women just beginning to explore the world at large. They did not think or speak of the war; it had nothing to do with them, and they had nothing to do with me. I maligned them, perhaps, for I did not know whether they had lost brothers, uncles, family members in the war. If so, I neither saw nor heard any sign. They seemed so much younger than I, and filled with an eagerness I too had felt, a lifetime ago, back when I began my cadet training.

My new classmates were so young, so empty of experience, and those trying for medical school were aggressive, smart, and always out to beat you. There were only so many slots and, on top of that, a quota for Jews. I buckled down to work as I always had, focusing on the job at hand. I did not mix with the others. They had their own cliques with whom they studied in the library and chatted in the cafeteria. I was a loner, not out to beat anybody, only out to do my best. I thought how odd: here I am at twenty-six, starting a new career, employing the same method I always resorted to as a child. Play your own game. Never mind the other guy.

So each morning I walked to the trolley car, changed to the subway up to the university, and passed the same houses I had passed as a child. Once again I was alone. My war experiences were far away, so far that I would sometimes wonder if they had even happened: did I do all those things, did I risk my life so many times, did I parachute out of my bomber two times to save my life, was I ever a prisoner of war? All that time had become like a leaf pressed in a book, the juice squeezed out of it, dry. Leaves I could not touch without them crumbling. I was left aching, and my heart and chest pained me. I felt surrounded by freshness, while I was a flurry of wounds and memories. I had gained nothing, it seemed, for all those days and nights. For all the men and women I had known. London was far away, unreal, and Norwich hardly a blip on the screen. Paris, my January Paris, my May Paris—both were suspended. Goeppingen, a whole other world, one I could not return to, ever. My pain was too great to contemplate that place, now only a shadow on my soul. I thought I dared not open those doors. I was starting over. I had no one who could make it easy. I had no one to share my thoughts, my anxieties, my pain, my despair. I could only taste it, swallow it, and keep my eyes on my goal.

I studied hard. I did not seek out women, though there were many at the university. I felt no pull towards them and felt I had better work. Occasionally I went to a movie. I never asked what the others did. In this time I never prayed to God, for he did not exist for me. My life was gray and though my head was full of the scientific facts I culled from my books night after night, inside I was empty. The lab work I had to do and all that lay in front of me was formidable. The next few years passed quickly—in retrospect, they always do. My South Philadelphia was the same. Summers were hot, and winters seemed colder than they had before.

I forgot. I forgot my college days, my days before the war and my earliest ambitions. That was not me who had once aspired to be a professor of medieval French literature and could now only wonder, "Where would a Jew get a job in that field?" There was only one Jewish professor of English at my college, and he had only reached assistant professor status after many, many years. This professor Fineman introduced me to Gray's "Elegy in a Country Churchyard" and poets like Cowper, Goldsmith, and, best of all, John Milton and his *Paradise Lost* and *Paradise Regained*. Fineman was an expert on Milton and I rejoiced in the language of this poet whose phrases soared and excited me the way the readings from the Old Testament had when I was a child. Yet I had understood nothing. There was no meaning to my life, no happiness, no expectation of anything. I had become the Spartan boy I read about as a child and the stoic I'd read about when a little older. I vowed: I will not cry in pain. I will not cry in pain, though I feel distant from everyone, even my family.

It was easy. I was studying. To my family education was holy. I was a student and I studied at the same desk where my Uncle Harry had studied when he went to medical school. Was there a sign in this? Did it foretell a destiny? I did not think of these things. I worked. Occasionally I saw my beloved Dolly and my cousin George who supported me in every way. They knew how grateful I was to them.

Dolly worried about me. "You don't look well. You are so thin. You look so pale." I merely nodded. Yes, I knew all this and at times a thought would pierce me: suppose you do get into medical school and become a doctor and suppose you are still not happy. What then? But I shut this cold question off, for I dared not think of it.

Living at home again was jarring. I had lived away from the time I was seventeen. But it had its compensations: I did not have to make my bed or cook my meals, or shop or wash my clothes—all the humdrum activities that comprise the essentials of life. I appreciated these burdens removed. I could see that my mother loved taking care of me. Both of my brothers were married, and I was the single remaining son at home. Little by little the discordance split into accordance and a routine was established in our daily living. My father left first in the morning without eating. He loved to have his breakfast near his job, where he could share in the early morning banter of the other blue-collar workers.

I came down next, had two soft-boiled eggs with a glass of skim milk, then went off to school. Evenings there was always the hot meal without much talk amongst us. Afterwards I would go upstairs to study. The weeks and months went by, the monotony dulling all errant strivings. It was as if I had never left the family. I had never been to college. I had never been in the Air Force. I had never.

I did not talk of my war experience because there was no space for it to be talked about. The young students had no war experience. Everyone was bent on their exams and studies and planning for internships and residencies and places to live.

It was as if the war was a forgotten item, a curio one might have found in an antique shop. I found it strange yet it was stranger still that twenty years and more later, young people did not know who Churchill was or Charles DeGaulle and even stranger the young Israelis, according to reports, do not seem interested in the Holocaust.

The feeling was that if you began to talk of the war, everyone in the group would be embarrassed and wonder why you were embarrassing them. As an aside, sixty-one years later when I was given my Distinguished Service Cross and the French Legion of Honor, a dear friend of fifty years was surprised at the things I had done. As young medical students we had shared so much but not this.

I had no wish to talk of the war or my experiences as a prisoner, and I did not. My family and friends knew I had been a prisoner, and nothing more. I told no one of Irmgard, Giselle, or Karl in the bed next to me. How could I have explained it? Today I find it strange that, back then, no one ever asked me about my war experiences. But no one ever did—not my parents, friends, relatives. I can only guess that people, even those closest to me, were afraid to ask me for fear of disturbing me. Not even Dolly, who was the closest person to me and in whom I confided pretty much everything, and in whose house I had had nightmares when I got back from Europe—even she did not ask. I think I would not have known what to say or if I had said anything it would have been so lifeless it would have sounded like something being dragged across the floor. How could I have expressed the measure of it?

Later if people asked I would say, "Yes, I was in the Air Force—yes, in Europe— yes, the 8th Air Force—yes, in bombers," and that would be that. I did not speak about this period during my pre-med or medical years, certainly not afterward. It all seemed to recede, and it seemed impossible to reconcile my life with those events, with those people. They always left me aching, with a void in my heart.

It was a cool autumn evening, a few years after the war had ended, when Jack Wales called for the first time. The phone rang and I said "Hello."

"Bernie!"

"Jack!" I recognized his voice immediately.

"Bernie, for Christ's sake. I thought you were dead. We packed up your things and the quartermaster picked them up. What in hell happened? You flew with that new lead crew."

"Yeah, and it went ok until we got shot up over the target, dropped out of formation and came back alone. We couldn't get any little friends to cover us."

"Then?"

"We were jumped by some ME109s who shot the hell out of us. Everyone was killed except four of us. Got picked up and wound up in a German hospital with the other three guys. One died."

"Were you hurt?"

I said, "Yeah, I've got some stuff in my head and neck."

"Jesus, Jesus Christ," he said, "You are one lucky bastard. Let's make plans for me to come down and see you and you can tell me the whole story. I live up here in northern New Jersey. My wife's family is in pharmaceuticals and I work for the company… that's my father-in-law. I'll tell you about it when I see you. Christ, am I glad to hear your voice. Wowwee, wowwee, like old times in London."

I told him where I lived.

"It's goddamn great to hear your voice," he said, and we spent an hour on the phone, talking and planning for him to come to Philadelphia to visit. He would drive in from northern New Jersey.

Someone you can talk to—maybe as complicated to find as someone to love. Yet, it may happen in an instant and you know this one is right. You know it by looking at the eyes, listening to the voice; the Greeks say that when you lose a friend, you lose a life. Jack was that kind of friend for me.

It was not difficult to reestablish our connection, over the phone. When he asked what had happened, I told him of being shot down. I did not have to say much—he knew the mechanics of missions. Then I spoke of Irmgard, of our eyes meeting during the air raid. I told him of the glass of red wine at night. He listened. I told him of the letters and of her flute. I knew he would understand the depth of my feelings, the situation I was in. I knew he would understand the ineffable in this experience, and he did. There had been no one I could tell, no one I dared tell for fear they would neither understand nor treasure the humanity in this experience. All was locked away, had been locked away, for I dared not risk anybody's cheapening it. I needed to be understood. Later, in my work, I came to understand that to convey to a person correctly what he or she has experienced is to convey to them their truth. It is this expression which evokes love. There is great love in being understood completely and correctly, and the war had come between me and all the others in my life—Dolly and George, my uncles, my mother and father—like an impenetrable stone wall, so that I could not risk it, not even with them.

Finally, Jack said, "You know, what happened to you happens only in the movies. I think you have an angel watching over you."

After that call, I could not study and later that night when I could not sleep, I paced the length of the house downstairs in the dark, much as my grandfather had with his prayer shawl around his shoulders, except I had no shawl and I was not praying. My mind was awake, a kaleidoscope of memories as everything came tumbling down, all that I had willed myself to forget—the war, Giselle, Karl, Irmgard. It was as if the dried, pressed leaves of my past had sprung back to life and were now spread out and glistening. Everything had a vividness that seized me and literally shook me. I trembled, I cried, and for that moment my heart was filled with joy.

---

A few months later I met Jack at a bar on Walnut Street, and he looked just as lean and handsome in his Gary Cooper way as he had when I'd last seen him, back on the base, before my last mission. I remember him there, at the officer's club, drink in hand, smoking cigarettes, talking to some friends, putting his drink down to mimic the trajectory of fighter planes with both hands. I waved at him. He grinned and waved back, holding his thumbs up for good luck.

Now he had a little less hair, but his smile was just as frank and engaging, and his fingers drew out a Lucky Strike with the ease and grace of a movie actor. He cupped his hands and lit his old Zippo lighter.

For a moment the thrill of old times swept through me, and I could hear the planes warming up on the tarmac in the darkness of early morning, feel the pitch of excitement warming up my blood. What would this day bring? Would I come back alive, wounded?

Both of us drank Scotch on the rocks. Jack smoked. I did not. Outside, the streets were wet and sad, shimmering under the rain, and they seemed to reflect something in Jack that I had not seen before, though he was as smooth and charming as always, as if he didn't have a care in the world.

As we talked I noticed Jack had his drink in his hand and I remembered Henry Callahan. Hank and his beautiful Irish wife, who hung around when we were in the States. She was quiet, elegant, never chiding him, never saying "That's enough, Hank," and Hank, handsome, already an alcoholic, maybe twenty-eight or -nine, the good looks going, the teeth a bit yellow from the constant cigarette in his mouth and his drink always in hand, as if left on the table some perverse force would spirit it away. I was fascinated by how he drank, how the glass and mouth were melded and the whiskey slid down easily, naturally, without noise—expert—that drinking only came with practice and now I could see traces of Callahan in Jack. I said nothing to my dear, sweet, love of a friend. Time had made him dear to me and we talked like we used to, never looking at a watch. We were in an endless, eternal space of silence…only him and me and our common memories of joy and nostalgia.

"Everyone thinks I have this great job doing PR for the family business," he said after a while. He crushed out his cigarette. "It used to be fun. It used to remind me of our going to Norwich or London and tanking it up. Back then it was always an adventure, just accepting whatever came our way. There was so much freedom in that, never knowing who we would meet, talk with, drink with, maybe sleep with, never knowing what would happen next.

"The job here had tinges of that, at first. But I've realized it's not real the way flying was real, when we would come back to the base to fly a mission, and that was our business, our job. That was another kind of joy. We were always playing Russian roulette with the stakes always getting higher; and there were always the other fellows to talk with and, of course, you.

"Before, in the war, I was not a drunk like Callahan. Remember him?"

I nodded, letting the memory wash over me. "He was drinking for all of us. Who wants to do something that will get you killed?"

"He had a drink in his hand from morning till night," Jack said. "I think he might have sobered up when he put on his oxygen mask on the plane, but I'm not even sure about that. Remember how pleasant he was, always talking about what he was going to do after the war? I knew guys like that. They all became drunks. Callahan was a nice one. We all liked him and his wife, that nice Irish-American girl, remember her? The fact is I've become a drunk and I don't like it and I don't want to do it anymore—the job, drinking—anymore."

"I've lost my purpose," Jack continued. "The war was my purpose for a long while. I loved the nobility of what we were doing.

Nothing makes a man feel as good as when he is morally in the right place, and we were. I envy you—you have another vision, one that will take you to the end of your life. Damn, how I long for that. Now what do I do?"

I didn't answer. I could not answer. What could I have said?

"I keep asking you," he said, "Let's go to China. We can have a purpose. There's no one I would rather be in China with than you. We're a perfect team—I do the piloting and you do the navigating."

Then, after a silence, he asked, "Do you ever think of Paris?"

"Yes, I think of it," I said, "especially when you call or I'm with you like now. That's all I think about, sometimes." It was such a relief to talk about this with Jack, to unburden myself, finally, after all the long nights of studying alone at my Uncle Harry's desk.

Jack said, "I recall Giselle. Later that night I met Martine and we had a little something. Funny about those two women. Maybe the war, the fear, their being alone….and I felt that they were loners…. made them stronger. The way she looked at me, right in the eye, her look was like giving you her heart. I never knew whether it was something she did with everyone. I didn't really care. We talked a lot during the night. I drank a lot. It wasn't like so many of the English girls, nice but simple. With them it was as if the bed was not wrinkled. With Martine, the creases had character. Hard to explain beyond that. We talked a lot, smoked, made love and talked some more until almost dawn when she fell asleep like a child. Her face was innocent. I thought of smuggling her onto the plane but what would I do even if I could. I think Giselle was even more than that to you. I could feel it in the short time between you and her that night. You were lucky to meet Giselle, if luck had anything to do with it. I don't understand the world and the way things work. That girl, that woman, was different in everything from how she dressed and stood and how she talked. Her voice had layers to it, like lives upon lives and eyes that took you in and in maybe because we were friends.

"To be given that, to have to leave that, I don't know what kind of life you could have in store for you. And now your life is on hold." He was quiet, more smoking, more drinking. "As for Irmgard, I can only imagine from what you say, she was an angel."

As he talked I had began to cry and by the time we were done with Giselle and Irmgard, I had wiped away my tears again and again. Was this why it was raining…one of those steady, gray, rainy days in Philly when a good place to be is in a bar. This was a great one—dark, expensive wood, a few groups at tables talking quietly, a solitary drinker here and there at the bar and each of us, Jack and I, reliving a piece of our lives, a piece of our loves and a piece of our deep affection for each other.

What are memories for anyway? It's all alive for me today just as when it was all happening….when we were reminiscing, when I was crying with relief and grateful that I could…the crying a child does deep within his heart, crying then sleeping then waking refreshed as if the world were new again and full of hope.

"I think I made a mistake, Jack, a bad one," I said. "I don't want to think too much about it. It's where this life is so different from that one. The mistakes you might make off base in towns or cities are trivial in wartime. The only important mistakes you can make are in that airplane. Then it may cost you your life, but in this life, now, it's really hard. Already I think not going back for Giselle was a bad, bad mistake so I don't think about it. It's too late now; I had this one moment, just one, and then the world changed. So now I do my work. I study hard and long. These young kids are out to beat your ass. It's like being at cadet school in a way."

He said, "Women like that, you can't find them over here. We don't have the wine or the espresso."

I said, "You know you are the only one I have ever talked to about Irmgard. That experience has a sacredness about it to me. It's so different from what people say about the Nazis. I know she was not a Nazi, but she was German. I'm afraid to speak of it lest people think I'm excusing the Nazis for what they did, and so I don't talk about it. I feel almost embarrassed about this experience, as if I did not suffer enough. As if it was not enough to be worn down to a bag of bones. Why didn't they torture me? But they didn't. They helped me and tried to help Karl. They really tried. What do I do with that?"

He said, "I can see why you, a Jew, might not want to tell them about it." He was quiet, then said, "You know I think you're the luckiest of men and I think you are going to be the most bereft of men. I wish I could help you, but I understand why you work so hard. I don't think you're ever going to find women like those two ever again."

"I try not to think about it," I said. "I'm preparing my life to be hard without that kind of companion, without that kind of lover. I guess we're just a couple of sad bums. But I do think of China, being in that adventure once more. All I know about the Chinese is this: just two blocks up from our house on Sixth Street was this house turned into a shop, a Chinese laundry shop where I'd bring my grandfather's collars. I remember the Chinese man sitting behind the counter, and he was the first Chinese person I had seen in my life. I could not explain my feelings then between the smell of laundry, the heavy iron on the board, the clean heat that hung in the air. Beside the man were always two little children, a boy and a girl, with the brightest eyes I had ever seen. I knew China, had studied it in school. I knew the Yangtze River, Peking—and, because of a movie, I knew Shanghai and the movie star Anna May Wong. Her name was like a bell chiming, and she was beautiful to me. She touched my heart."

He listened and then said, "You know there's something great going on in China now, and I think we should be part of it."

I heard Jack's words and my being trembled at going there, joining the millions on the march, but I was silent, feeling too tired, too weak for another great adventure.

"I might have to sit this one out," I said finally, and he nodded slowly. "I feel like getting drunk," I said.

"Even that's not going to help. I've gotten drunk for far less."

"No, you help, Jack. Talking to you helps. We are soldiers together. We were soldiers together, like two pieces of gold joined by the melt of silver, our Giselle in Paris. Can China ever enhance that?" What

I meant was: could China ever have enhanced what was already indelible in our memory, and in our bones?

---

Jack had been right: I had another vision, one that could extend past the war and into the rest of my life. I was caught, suspended by two great feelings: the longing for freedom and danger of the war years, and the fantasy of being a doctor, a fantasy I had not forgotten even in the war, in all the days and nights.

---

In 1949 Jack's wife called me and told me he was dead. I said the conventional things to her, then I left the house and began to walk. I did what I had done as a child. I walked and thought. I played scenes over and over in my mind. I played conversations over. I knew I had not only lost Jack, but also a link to the great past which had haunted us both.

No more a him and a me, and a past that gave meaning to my life. And to him, as he told me, his. No more plans to go to China—to fly and fight for the people, to drink and entertain the girls, to share in a final, magnificent adventure. No more breathtaking views from the cockpit of a bomber. No more deep silences that held us heart by heart in that noble feeling of friendship born of danger, of imminent death. Never again would we sit in a café, drink a scotch, and talk, or lapse into the quietness which is also part of the structure of love.

My heart turned to the past I felt Jack had taken with him, to that last morning with Giselle—getting up to find her gone, the note on the table. I knew it completely. I could write it now. Suddenly I felt an unbearable pain in my chest. How could I have left her?

I tried to bring her back with all her beauty. I sought her as if on the screen of my mind. January and March—hallowed months and cursed months and now I was bereft. With Jack gone, the link broken, it was as if she had died in my arms.

Hours—hours later—I felt I had been emptied out. I did not want to feel anything for the pain would have killed me. Now I knew what Giselle meant, "The pain of love is unbearable." True, even more, the pain of love lost is unbearable. It is true, as I was to discover later, that one can die if one loses one's love. The doctors can say cerebral hemorrhage or cardiovascular accident or cancer, but when love is lost, one chooses how he is to die. There are many ways.

Now I was in double jeopardy. Not one woman did I let go for what later in my life would seem ridiculous—my ambition—it was love that was important and only love. Did Jack die of a broken heart living a life that brought him no joy and promised an empty future? Jack and Giselle were there in my memory, and Irmgard. They were a reality. Memories do not bring back realities. I can see why reality is cruel. It is being lived and if it is not used, it goes away forever, like Giselle, like Irmgard. It seemed to me they were both alike. They were a reality. Maybe Irmgard now even more so because I had nothing left except the fragile tissue of memory but I did have the yellowing papers of Irmgard—all of her letters, her handwriting. There was a reality to that. There was a torture to it as well because I was aware of the kind of love I could have had all my life and now there was none and I had no knowledge there ever would be one.

Giving up love so far had brought me nothing but pain. I had yet to see what ambition would bring. Could it ever be big enough, deep enough, the fruits of it to do away with the pain of the real thing? So I was plagued by doubts, by fears of an ambition but there was no purpose. Ambition stood like an empty box. Ambition for what and how and when. I was tired of being lost.

Still walking the streets in the very late Philadelphia afternoon, the furious autumn leaves dropping on all sides of me, I thought back once more to Irmgard.

I knew fear, and the pain of looking into the future and seeing nothing, trying to think and getting only a blur. I knew how the heart sank, and I knew what it was to be dried up. I knew what hopelessness felt like, how to long for a quick death. I could not, I felt, endure the panic rising in me. I had lost a best friend, and two women who had deeply touched my life. The losses had happened so quickly—anybody would have thought: only two months, five days, four nights, only a moment out of all the moments of one's life. Yet in the quick-moving days and nights of war, roots are not planted, do not reach into the marrow. There's no time to plant one's feet and hold on. Yet there is something in us, in me, that could not forget. If I live to be one hundred, their memory will still be found in me. Were I to be cut open like a tree, the ring would be there.

Now I could no longer feel my legs or my feet. I felt that some spirit must be moving me, for I had no energy left. I thought of the wine beside my bed, the slight touch to awaken me. I thought how good it was to have no feelings. If there were any left, I surely would collapse and die as I walked. I do not remember coming home. I remember nothing until the next morning when I had to go to school.

I made no resolutions about Jack or Giselle or Irmgard. For me Jack had always been hope for a new adventure. I did not realize how much I missed the old one and how I wanted another chance, another choice. Now there was nothing left but longing and, what was worse, now there was no one left to talk to.

# 9

## The Future Begins

When we first imagine a goal, it possesses us. There's almost nothing in our lives with meaning aside from this thing that drives us—we cannot imagine a life without it, or, if we do, it is a life without value. There is no possibility of pleasure in that view, for we would not have gotten our heart's desire. We believe that if we can reach our goal, the world will open itself to us entirely; our spirits will be lifted, and there will be never-ending happiness, like the promise of a movie ending when the two stars kiss. Personally, I always wanted the movie to begin there.

I earned my medical degree in 1952. I was satisfied, even a little encouraged, by the achievement. But not too much, for I realized there was another hill to climb and, beyond that, still another. I felt old, for the cost had not been inconsiderable to have come this far, and I could still see around me my young peers—energetic, keen-eyed, all smiles, nothing but victory in view.

There was another story, too, which I did not share with anyone. I recalled my class with Fineman and Gray's elegiac line "many a gem is born to blush unseen." I recalled the fear that had grasped me, the way I had been so lost about everything back then, after the war. I did not know about medical school, whether I even had a chance of getting in. I did not have an alternate plan. I was not able to see any other kind of life before me, only the one I was starting now with this rolled up piece of paper in my hand. It had only been a few years before.

How do we measure time—not by the calendar, but by our goals, our achievements, our failures, our lovers. Those years of aspiration, of devotion to an ideal, were uncertain for me. I had no mission to fly, no orders to carry out, no airplane waiting on the tarmac. I held my breath for years. Who would have understood how I perceived the world? Our lives, so fragile, in the hands of people who could destroy us in a moment, over whose whims and whose pressures we have no control. I was many years away from knowing the tortuous path to the foot of the mountain. I knew I was trying to capture a little foothill, that was all. It would take years more for me to understand the suffering, and to endure it on the way to the top, until I could say with honesty and despair, "Please, Lord, give me a heading, as you did over the North Atlantic."

I knew the wait would be long; residency would not bring me sufficient knowledge, not the kind I yearned for. It would have to be something else, something more to calm my complexity, my restlessness, my ignorance; the more I studied, the more I realized I was learning all the outer clothing of the human being. In a way it was like learning to be a mechanic or shoemaker.

It was why, I realized, I could not work with my Uncle Harry as a general practitioner, though he invited me several times to share his office in Strawberry Mansion, near Fairmount Park. If I did that I would never know what the inside was like, what made a person who he was. Though I might know his blood pressure, his cardiovascular state, the nature of his blood panel, and his cholesterol level, these could not add up to what I needed to know: who this person was, and how he got to be the way he was. What made him function well, or not at all.

It was on the last day of medical school that I realized I would become a analyst. I sat alone in the library reading an article on psychoanalysis, and when I closed the book, one phrase kept repeating itself, "Neurotics suffer from reminiscences." I was not defensive about that term. I already knew everyone was in some way neurotic but the phrase caught my imagination, in the way a child might become fascinated by a red balloon on a vendor's stick, coming back to it again and again.

The fact was I was full of reminiscences, and I was immediately brought back to Irmgard calling me arrogant. I recalled my surprise, my chagrin, at being so identified. I had been confused. I did not know whether I liked being called arrogant, or whether I should be ashamed, as if she were saying I still sucked my thumb or wet my pants. My confusion betrayed my mixing these two feelings, and I had to think a while before I would determine whether I could agree with her, and argue the point, or whether I would deny it ferociously. I finally agreed with it, and recalled how it led to a sequence of thoughts and feelings that exhilarated me at the time, my captivity notwithstanding.

I reminisced. I reminisced over my days of captivity for so long that my legs fell asleep from not moving. The pins and needles woke me from the reverie, but did not shake it loose entirely.

In those moments I knew I would become a psychiatrist and a psychoanalyst. What could be more thrilling than to discover yourself, the way Irmgard had led me to discover myself. It was to take years before I could put these fragments into a proper, more fully formed perspective.

I needed to discover what my future patients would not know themselves, and could not possibly know. During my last year of medical school I had read Freud; his words offered an entirely new world to me, the possibility of knowing all I had ever longed to know. Even more, they offered the possibility of everything that I wanted and needed to know about myself. The roots of all the answers to my questions, I realized, lay in the unconscious and could only yield to the correct method of interpretation, which was analysis.

For though I could sit and write an essay detailing my life, I would be unable to say how I became what I am, or why I did what I did—all the information that I would later learn was locked in my unconscious mind. I was not aware then how difficult this information was to access.

And as I left the library I felt I had achieved another victory: going to college was one, for I never thought I could have afforded it. Getting my wings was another, for I never thought I could compete with the finest young men in the country and win my place. I survived the war and I survived the loss of two wonderful women whose like I had not come across since. And now I had become a doctor.

I wanted to show her, I wanted to show Irmgard, especially her: Look, look what I have done. And I have further ambitions which I am too embarrassed to tell even you, to whom I would tell everything, for I feel my heart would be safe with you. I did not realize then that I was making a fundamentally spiritual decision, and that it was she who had made it possible.

During my internship year, I made inquiries about residencies and psychoanalytic training in New York and Los Angeles. I had determined to leave Philadelphia. I could not stand the oppressiveness I felt, much like modern Italian artists in Florence feel, haunted by the past at every step. I went to New York in the fall of 1952 to be interviewed by two prestigious psychiatric residency institutions, and was assured that I would be accepted.

Friends told me about Los Angeles, a city that especially appealed to me because of the weather. I was finding the winters hard to get through. I had been frostbitten during the war once when my electric flying suit went out. After that, it seemed I could never get warm enough, and winters were difficult for me to endure. Colds and the flu were pretty constant companions , and now that I had a chance to fly south, I decided to do so. I followed through on this lead, and found that I could get a residency in psychiatry at the Veteran's Administration Hospital in Brentwood, California.

There were two psychoanalytic institutes in Los Angeles. Both were members in good standing with the central body—the American Psychoanalytic Association, based in New York. I knew what I had to do; the outer structure of the next few years of my life would be mapped out between residency and psychoanalytic training, during which time I would receive the treatment I would be able to give in a few years. This treatment was to lessen any neurotic tendencies in my personality, to help me understand the nature of my life, to experience the course of a psychoanalysis, and to enable me, finally, to love and to work—the desirable end of any analysis, according to Freud.

No one liked my decision. My family, especially my mother, was against it. How could I leave her, after all that had happened, and why? I told her simply: I have to do it.

I decided to make a clean break with my past, even leaving behind the girl I was seeing then—a dark-haired nurse with a full, glossy mouth.

The end of my internship came, and, in the summer of 1953, I, with three male friends, drove off to Los Angeles in my new Pontiac Chieftain with the Indian insignia on the front hood. In this way I got to see, once again, the greatness and beauty of America, which I had once—it seemed so long ago now—surveyed from the skies above. The cornfields of the Midwest, the flat, spooky expanse of Montana, the miraculous Colorado Rockies.

And then finally, we came to the end of the land, to Los Angeles, which seemed strangely flimsy and unreal. No matter: I would come to feel at home in the city, and I have returned to Philadelphia only four times since, the third time to attend my father's funeral, and the last in 1980 to say goodbye to my brother Paul as he lay dying. Though I had no way of knowing it back then, I really had said goodbye.

---

As I moved into my life in Los Angeles, into my residency, into my analytic training, I was confident that I could quickly learn to unlock the secrets hidden behind my eyes in the mirror on the kitchen wall. It would take a war, it would take being a flyer, it would take misfortune to let me begin to know, many, many years later, what I was asking to know as a youngster, looking at the mirror on the wall. For years I had dreamed of the secret wisdom being revealed to me. Before, from my reading, I thought I would have to go to unknown centers of the East or Middle East where small communities lived outside the noise of civilization—sacred places inhabited by monks and priests. Now, all of sudden, it seemed I was to learn everything right here in Los Angeles.

My analysis was conducted five times a week, as all at that time were. I lay on the couch and related my dreams, gave my associations, and talked about whatever came into my mind. At the end of the fifty minutes, or any time in between, my analyst would make a comment on the material and interpret the dreams, revealing a knowledge to me that I was unaware of. Most times this unawareness was detrimental to my everyday functioning. Sometimes the dream revealed progress and a clearing up of an issue, but, then, there were always other issues to clear.

I did not learn quickly. Studying analysis was not easy and being in analysis was not easy. I slowed down, telling myself that patience would yield everything. I did learn a lot, and a few things about myself; I became more tolerant of everything, and of everyone.

Yet my doubts, my fears, my war neurosis did not yield. The war played almost no part in analysis, despite the good faith, the honesty of my analyst. He was a straight shooter, tough, real. Many thought he was rough. I did not. I liked his bluntness. He was Dutch and had obviously had a hard life, and accomplished much. I appreciated him.

I had no particular symptoms I brought to analysis the way a married person might bring problems with a husband, wife or children. I was an ideal analysand, single with no burden from prior marriages, none of the usual baggage even single people come to analysis to help. It became clear that I was or I had a character problem, so to speak, high functioning, quick student, enthusiastic about analysis. Indeed, little by little, I marveled at the information my dream life, therefore everyone's dream life, held. I was lucky to have an analyst who loved dreams and put much stock in them.

Though intellectual knowledge came and more appreciation of the development of the field and the greatness of the Freudian invention—the discovery of a dynamic unconscious—I believed as did Freud that the dream was his greatest discovery.

Inside me there was still a stoicism that I felt, a pessimism about my life, for I had no great liking for the women I met along the way or in these years of my training. No one made my heart tremble.

I had forgotten about the war. I had forgotten about Irmgard and Giselle. I forgot the letters. They were always somewhere in the various places I lived. Incredible but it was so. The mind can do anything, really everything, to protect the person from pain. It was this that remained unchanged from beginning to end of my training analysis.

I realized that in analysis one can learn everything there is to know intellectually, and still have no change in the personality. It became clear that most aspirants did exactly this: they were rewarded for being good, clever students, and did well.

Nonetheless, I advanced—I graduated and began to teach at the institute. I was a good teacher. I taught everything, every course in the curriculum, but loved most the course about dreams—for me the foundation of analysis, and I agreed with Freud that his work on dreams was his most valuable legacy. But in the end I was depressed at the little inward progress I had made. Hardly any secrets had yielded. I spoke of my dreams, my preoccupations, my problems, my family, the war—yet nothing happened, nothing changed.

In the meantime I was living my life. One evening, while I was having supper at a café, a friend of mine came in with a glamorous blonde woman. They sat a few tables down from me, in the same line of red banquettes. I was curious about her and her relationship to my friend, who had recently married. At one point, the woman dropped her napkin and looked back at me, covertly and quickly. I did not miss it.

Later I got her phone number from our mutual friend and learned she was an analyst from Philadelphia who had just moved here and who had a little girl from a previous marriage.

I had seen a lot of women by now for shorter or longer times. I was in my late thirties, no longer young, and I was eager to be married and settled. I called one evening not long after the sighting in the restaurant. We spoke for a while about Jim, our mutual friend. We talked about Philadelphia; I asked her if the Academy of Music was still there, and she laughed at me. I felt that it was destiny, for her to have come from my hometown. Luckily she was, and still is, a generous talker. She could talk about anything. We talked about psychoanalysis a lot and then after the heady experience of several conversations, I asked her out so we could speak face to face.

I picked her up at her apartment. She lived on a good street. The little girl was ten years old and thin, with straight blonde hair, precocious eyes and a quiet manner—a child who knew how to be alone. The babysitter arrived and we left for the restaurant. Frascati's is no longer there on Wilshire Boulevard near Rodeo Drive, which was a sleepy street then, but back then the restaurant was glamorous the way she was, my future wife, and we ate veal piccata and veal milanase and were surrounded by movie stars. I will always remember the magic of that night. Yes, Carolyn was beautiful. She had a wonderful laugh. We married six weeks later and remained married for twenty-five years.

My life in Los Angeles was a happy one. I was in love, newly married, living the kind of life I had always wanted to live, one filled with art and operas and symphonies, weekend trips, parties and endless, passionate discussions over coffee and plates of fish or veal. My wife and I ate out frequently, at places like La Scala or Frascati's, with its soft lights, its French paintings, its red curtains that gave everything the feeling of the old world—a hushed, dark world where one could talk for hours. It was the closest thing we could have had to a life in the cafés of Paris; we were full of passion for our work, our lives, this world that was, for me, entirely new.

Yet it was familiar; I began to collect art, to spend Sunday afternoons at the museums or with my stepdaughter and her friends, driving up the coast to Malibu or Santa Barbara, and I slipped into this life effortlessly. It seemed I never slept. This was the kind of life my wife was used to, having come from a wealthy oil family in Texas; she was at home in this luxurious, sparkling world of Los Angeles. Once in a while—a long while, only rarely—I would think back to Philadelphia, my mother crying as I begged her for a penny with which to buy candy, and it was startling to me that I could shed my past so quickly. Could this be me? I would wonder. Could this really be me?

Los Angeles is a lush city, one of wide-open spaces, lemon trees and dangling bougainvillea—so different from where I grew up, in a house flanked by many more houses, and nothing but houses up and down the street. Not one tree or flower had lived on that street made of black pitch and whatever else they put into it to harden it. I was only a young child when the city decided to modernize its streets and sidewalks, but I recall how the workers pried up the uneven cobblestones that had been there at least one hundred years, how they pried them out and carted them away. I remember the big steamroller tamping down the ground, leveling it, and the men without shirts who worked both on the machine and beside it, tamping down the newly poured pitch. The texture, the patina of the neighborhood changed forever when the coarse black pitch replaced the cobblestones. I remember how beautifully the cobblestones had glinted under the rain, how magical they had seemed to me as a child.

But we exhausted ourselves, my wife and I, and there was not much time for memories. And still my ambition was not satisfied— not yet. My passion for analysis consumed me, my need to understand how it all works, to find a way to encompass it; I wanted it to be my servant, not my master. What could I do? Write articles illustrating some point Freud had made, firming that point? I saw no use or value in that, and never attempted to do it. At this time, I did not know what it was that would fulfill me; this too was to take a very long time. I did not understand then not to measure time by the calendar, which has nothing to do with how the events of one's life are lived. It took me over thirty years to learn that our lives are indeed our responsibility, that our choices are consequential, and that we will pay for every wrong choice we make. I knew cursorily about this. Later, I was to discover how injuring, how deep in the precepts of life this law is, the law of karma.

When I practiced my craft, at which I had studied very long and very diligently, I suffered my own ignorance, and I often felt I could not help my patients. I could only offer them banal interpretations, all from a great grab bag of bones every candidate learns in his analytic studies. And when I was in despair many times along the way I would think of my Irmgard writing to me in one of her letters, "I hear my patients cry in pain. They are in great pain, and I cannot help them." At these moments our souls met, for I knew what she meant in a way I never could have as a young man of twenty-four, lying wounded in a hospital bed.

And over the distance of time, I would wonder about the young nurse, only nineteen years old back then, who had written me the crinkled letters I've kept with me all these years. I knew that someone who could write such things to a stranger could not have been a Nazi, though that possibility was there. Of course, there were so many things I did not know about her. I never told her I was a Jew. I did not tear off my dog tags and throw them away as I came down to German earth, already stained with American blood, in order to tell her or anyone else that I was a Jew. And what if I had told her, what if I had not thrown away my dog tags? What would have been my fate then? When I came down in my parachute, bleeding and stunned, I knew that I had to get rid of that piece of tag around my neck. Has anyone ever found it, in these sixty-two years?

Yet, despite all this, I believed and do believe I could have felt the Nazi in her if it had been there. I could feel it in the officers I met at the other station hospital, who were friendly to me as a fellow officer and who shared a drink with me. I could feel the Nazi in them the way I felt the Nazi in Duncan, the official at the University of Pennsylvania, the man who asked me why I didn't become a rabbi.

Today I hear Irmgard's words as they lie written on yellowed sheets: "My patients are in pain and I have nothing to give them." I hear her words as a prophetic statement that extends to the guilt of the German people, to their great pain. I see it as her despair, that she had no medicine for them, for she knew only confession would do—and remorse and mourning, for the loss of God's humanity.

Working all these years in analysis I have come to see, and to understand, that psychoanalysis is a spiritual discipline. That rightly used it can purge people of the pain that has so encumbered them all their lives—to make them cleaner, purer, and more childlike in their maturity, more spiritual in their way of life. Their dreams begin to envisage the incomparable beauty of the divine in his manifest form.

But back then, in my first years as an analyst, living in Los Angeles with my beautiful young wife and my stepdaughter, going to the theater and fine restaurants, I did not think of things like God and faith. I was not aware of any religious calling. I had no wish to join a temple. I was aware only of the insistent call within me to find a way to ease the psychic pain of my patients. There is no question as to whether psychic pain exists, and I took Descartes as the model: it exists in me, therefore it is.

Looking back—and it is only by looking back that we can trace the course of thought or of actions—I was calling on the God within and above to help me, to tell me in some way the direction to go, and how to avoid the pitfalls that lay all around me, especially those of cleverness—for the intellect can fabricate almost anything. I was never an intellectual person. That was the greatest asset I brought to the problem. Let me feel the truth, and I would know if I felt it, the way you know Bach or Beethoven is the truth, or a sculpture by Michelangelo or Rodin—that feeling would be my guide. Flashes of Irmgard's letters, her references to spirituality, came to me, but never fully, only in intimations that would later flower.

# 10

Family

*I* think we have to live in a country for maybe hundreds of years to feel so wedded to it that there is no doubt about what our identities are. Perhaps it was this thought that had struck me when I first saw Pagnol's *Marseilles Trilogy* a few years after returning from the war. The films "Marius," "Fanny," and "Cesar" were thrilling to me because they told real stories about real feelings in situations true and real. Real people. I knew what the problem was with American films. We seem to be able to get only to the skin, whereas these films easily cut through the superficial. One was immediately at the heart of people's lives, deep in their conflicts: the youth, the girl, the love, the sex, the boy aching to sail away, the father, the suffering. They knew who they were in the Trilogy and would go on from there.

We, immigrants, the children of immigrants, did not even feel welcome in this most welcoming country of the world. I never heard my parents talk with the clearness, the openness, and directness of the actors in the stories and it was that heft that I had missed in my family and all the families I knew. Yet, I knew something was there, but where? I knew they had not been open with each other, my mother and my father, let alone honest with themselves—or so I felt.

When I saw the Trilogy, I was brought back to memories of Giselle, for I was achingly familiar with that simplicity, with that directness of joining a relationship that was foreign to me by training. I had not been ready for what she gave me, and I left what I have since worked my entire life to find. I knew only how my parents lived a life together, and this had permeated my entire system. When I thought of Giselle after the war, I knew I had missed my chance. Giselle was of another time—another me, hardly ensconced in the reality of everyday life as I was, now, with Carolyn. There was more, for Giselle did not come from her head. She was primarily a feeling woman, whereas my wife was primarily an intellectual one. It took that other time of being in love, still etched with the grace of Irmgard, to reassure myself that life was still there, from the exaltation to the desperation. This was branded into my blood and bones, never to be forgotten. Sadly, I thought no one woman could ever satisfy this insistent longing. And all of this lay buried in me. No matter what, I felt there was something important, very urgent to me, that I needed and did not have.

Walking with Giselle, in the café with her, in the chilly bedroom with her, in that precious intimacy of familiarity where everything was right, everything had been easy. Always Giselle brought me back to Irmgard and, as time went on, I did not know what to think and feel about her. Feeling, touching Giselle had given me a reality imprinted in my memory; the flesh gives it an enduring quality ever after. But then the letters gave me a more enduring sense of Irmgard. I could never touch Giselle again, but I could read Irmgard's letters, which could at once put me into a reverie of sweetness, nostalgia, and evocation. So it went year after year; no resolution between these two, both memories giving me a sense of desolation that I had already lived the most important part of my life.

I did not quite understand the intense hold these two women had on my mind and heart—through my years of schooling, the years of my marriage, and even now, as I write, sixty-two years after the last goodbyes. There could not be one for me without the other. It is so in the mind. It is how memories are laid down, the connections the mind makes. The dying Karl would always be a part of this circle, along with von Polster, Woluski and Radek, the German colonel who ran the hospital. Any one of these images could bring the others into life.

I staked a lot on analysis. I felt there was a way to understand all this and to be free. Early infantile conflicts ranged alongside later ones and though I could delineate them as I do now, in the actual doing it is not as clear—much like any mission can seem to be simple, yet, in one moment, can turn into a nightmare.

It was not my experience to have the war experience resolved by analysis. What is unbelievable to me now, as I look back on it, is how years of analysis never brought the experience of Irmgard and Giselle to light. I never discussed them, nor thought to do so. I do not know why, but I am aware that such an omission never consciously practiced by me is staggering.

Had I tucked these experiences so close in time, so opposite in expression, in some deep crevice, in some underground mountain? If so, why? I was puzzled. I am puzzled.

By the time I was writing this memoir years after my divorce I no longer agonized over the schism I had previously felt and voiced between Irmgard and Giselle. I had perhaps through a trick of the mind combined them, interdigitated them so that they were one, and though I felt the loss deeply I had come to know another profound loss that shook me and stayed with me for a long time….the loss of my first child, the most beautifully formed infant with a face chiseled by heaven; and this picture of her in the morgue will be with me forever.

I was quite old when she came. I had probably an unrealistic expectation of this child and I used to think maybe she felt she could not live up to these expectations and chose to die. I thought and felt all kinds of terrible things—rage, sorrow, to murder the doctor. Had he done his job correctly? It was living in hell for a long time.

Later when I came to my theories about the importance of imprinting, no analysis could have unlocked the material which is so bound in great emotional shock and distress and pain and fear—all of which are locked up. All analyses at that time, in my opinion, were fundamentally of a cerebral kind. The emphasis still seems to be on theory and it would seem that since dreams and their analyses have fallen away, there is no chance that deeper, more vital layers of the personality can be accessed and released. In my view, at this time, no analysis can be complete unless the mother's imprint, whatever it may be, is uncovered and worked through and mastered.

In science we are taught that formulating the right question is paramount. If we ask or are asked the right question, we can focus on ways to devise the answer. To construct the proper experiment, one must ask the proper question. In analysis—at least as I have performed it and continue to perform it—it is crucial that the analyst ask the right question, not so much to get specific answers, but to stimulate the free associations that will, in their indirect way, bring the right answer. When someone says, "You have just asked a great question, the fascinating question," a vibration goes on in that person's psyche, impelling the mind to come forward with the information that will lead, eventually, toward healing.

If the answer does not come at that time, however, I do not worry, for things have been set in motion so that the dreams that follow will reveal this person's past, forgotten experiences, which lie buried in his or her cellular memory. It is as if the cell is being massaged to release the information. People are not born ill; they are born whole and are compelled to illness or to what will become illness as they grow. But always there is a longing to return to an earlier state of oneness, of singularity, of unity. That spark always lies waiting to hear the right question. To which we may respond to with joy, "Maybe now I can reassert my original self." My own analyses never did formulate the question.

---

"How arrogant you are," Irmgard had said, and my immediate thought had been to negate her. My feelings rose up with some anger, but remained unexpressed. Then I wondered what I had said or what kind of tone I had used that lead to her remark.

In a flash I had known she was right. It was as if she had made an interpretation to me that was so right at that moment that it was like a bombshell throwing me into a whole new way of thinking and being, one I was unaware of before that moment. She had become an analyst of high order. Today I know it is not easy to make interpretations that summarize and characterize a person's state of mind and being at a particular moment. An entire false structure falls. A lie falls, lies that maintain a state of mindlessness which will attempt to destroy the truth in every way they can.

She saw that I agreed with her and her eyes lit up. I think I was everything she intuited I was, and a rent had been made in my structure. A crack was formed during my weeks of captivity—between our speaking, her flute playing, her letters to me, and the letters I scribbled in the bathroom, alone, forced to condense my ideas and feelings on the page or two of paper I was allowed. I knew the torrent that she raised in me, my quickness of expression and reply. It was a strange paradox: in my time as a prisoner, I was liberated.

Much later, when I mused on these events, the unlikelihood of these circumstances—a plane shot out of the sky, a few survivors, a young fellow American who would die of gangrene, a beautiful, intelligent nurse who would call me to attention—I would understand that these events were the beginning of my serious quest, not only for self-knowledge, but for knowledge of the many mysteries that lay all about me.

When I consider these two women now, Giselle and Irmgard, I realize my experience was of three: Giselle, Irmgard, and Giselle again. Giselle was the bread—good, strong, dark bread of sensuality and practicality. Indeed, this meal was one of pure liberation because there was no ancient tradition it had adhered to. I came to feel that Irmgard was my soul and on either side were two angels protecting the fragile gossamer.

It is clear today that had I chosen to remain missing in action to stay with either one of these enchanting women—to remain with Giselle, or to seek out Irmgard, somehow—I would not have been able to sustain an idea, a possibility that lay ahead of me. Indeed I knew nothing of these potentialities then, when they were still potentialities lying, the way all the secrets of the universe lie, waiting for discovery.

The universe is prodigal with its secrets. Every despair, every hopeless moment has to be endured as the descent is down and down to enlightenment. There is a paradox here. We do not go up for enlightenment, but down into layers upon layers, brushing past veils, one only yielding to another, until one is near a knowledge that can elicit the wild surmise of Keats on seeing the Pacific Ocean, feeling like a "watcher of the skies when a new planet swims into his ken." Every person has this possibility, or should have it.

I had made my choices. I was married to a wonderful woman, and anxious to have a family. My wife and I wanted children together desperately, but, as the years passed, our hopes were dashed again and again. My wife had several miscarriages. Finally, she sought consultation with a highly reputable obstetrician in the best part of town. He had a superlative reputation. I met him and liked his professionalism. His manner was that of an eastern physician. He was always distant, though Carolyn and I were physicians also, and still a friendliness shone through. He knew how important it was to both of us.

Then, with a wish of luck from him, we were off counting the days and months like any two young kids, even though she had been through this before.

She became pregnant. We were both sobered by the thought of this new being about to enter our lives; I was over 40, and had waited a long time for this promise. One weekend, about a week before the baby was due, my wife felt something was wrong. The baby was not moving. We got to the ER and the doctor examined my wife. I was not in the room. He came out and looked grim. My wife was taken upstairs. He said to me, "There may be no good news. Please wait in the corridor." Carolyn was taken to the OR, and had begun to have contractions. The baby, a little girl, was born dead, strangled by the cord.

I waited until Carolyn got back to the room. I sat with her for a long time. She was pale, drawn. She cried. I held her hand, quietly patting her shoulder, caressing her hair. Her hair lay dank on her skull.

The doctor appeared, and spoke his words of regret, "Sorry, very sorry. It happens. Very, very sorry." I heard him from a distance. I could feel a deep, deep pain inside me, then a rage that scared me. I could have destroyed the hospital and everyone in it. After all the years of waiting, waiting, to be left was unconscionable, incomprehensible.

The doctor felt uncomfortable, sensing my rage, and left the room after telling me that if I wanted to see the baby, she was in the morgue. He gave me directions. I nodded. After a long while I disengaged my hand from Carolyn's. I told her I was going to see our child now. She nodded, still crying quietly. She had no strength to sob; I could see that.

The morgue was empty except for one newborn lying on her back, eyes closed. There was no attendant; no one had wrapped my daughter in a blanket or towel. I approached her, lying there alone on a table, and looked upon my desire and my hope. I kept wiping away the tears so I could see this loveliness—even in death. Her body seemed perfect to me, with limbs that seemed sculpted by Praxiteles, and a long, perfectly shaped torso. The face was unmarked, her skin smooth, and her pointed little nose aristocratic and chiseled. She was a miniature Greta Garbo. I touched her arms, her chest, her face, and could only sob, the way a child sobs when it cannot get its heart's desire, deep and full.

No one had come in. I heard no one about, only silence, only my heart beating for the two of us, as it has continued to do all these years.

The next morning Carolyn still looked thin, drawn, gray. We talked intermittently in dead voices, and did not look at each other. Though I knew it was not her fault, I felt rage towards her that I could not control. I said I would be back later. I got into my car and drove to the ocean up the Pacific Coast Highway and stopped where there were no cars, no people, and I got out and walked on the beach, up north and back south again. I did what I had done as a child when I was upset or overwhelmed, when I would walk through the city for hours at a time.

What does one do with grief when there is no lap to put oneself in? I sat on a rock on the beach, looking out on the green water of the Pacific, the whitecaps twinkling rhythmically as they folded forward. The seagulls were circling, sometimes high, sometimes low. And the horizon, somewhere in the future.

But I could not think of a future. All of me was enveloped by my suffering until there was no time and no thought. I felt my entire being was heart and I ached with the loss of my child. Soon I did not hear the waves, or smell the crisp air.

I could not understand why God had done this to me. I who had waited and waited to do everything right, to choose rightly, to live as rightly as I could. And suddenly I recalled my tonsillectomy, when my mother told me she could not be there with me because that day she had to get her mother and father, just come to Ellis Island from Russia. I had begun to cry, and she had taken out a toy, a present she had bought for me to play with after the operation: a little wooden cannon that actually shot a ball. Look, she had said. But I had not wanted it. I clung to her, sobbing. I had never had my mother away from me, and I did not understand. She held me as I whimpered, and rocked me. It was not comfortable because her belly was big with a baby to come.

I had fallen asleep whimpering and awoke with a whimper, holding onto my mother's finger with one hand, and the neckline of her dress with the other. When she brought me to the hospital and left me with a nurse, she followed herself, crying, which renewed my tears. In a room with several beds I held onto my toy and sat upright, my legs folded under me, wailing. No one could stop me. Finally I was exhausted and fell asleep. I remember nothing until the next day when I woke with my throat sore. It was painful to cry. My chest heaved. I held my toy cannon as tears fell down my cheeks without a sound. I was desolate.

I sat on the beach, rocking slightly, and I found my cheeks wet with tears. I had a pain in my throat and chest. My tears, my sobs, would never bring my child back, and I asked, as so many others have, why had this happened to us? What sin did I commit? If this were God, this sand, this water, this sky—why would He take note of me? I was as unimportant as any one of the billions of grains of sand on the beach.

Suddenly Irmgard was brought to my mind. "My soldiers are in pain and I have nothing to give them," she had said. There she was in my mind, as I have always seen her. My heart was saying, I need to creep into your presence, and if I were not ashamed I would crawl into your lap and sob away my torn heart.

And my thoughts turned to the past—had I lost my chance? This great hope seemed to have been denied me, and the sorrow was more bitter than any I have known. What if I had stayed in Paris, I thought, as a young man of twenty-four. What if I had married Giselle? Would this have happened then? People have babies without a thought. They find they're going to have a baby and then it comes and then it is here.

Such thoughts could not encompass my tears and my rage. Why had I waited so long? Suddenly as I sat rocking and moaning for my baby, I thought with a surge of guilt sweeping through me, "What have I done, asking Irmgard to wait for me? Did she just use up her life waiting or did she finally give up?" I was mortified at having done so cruel a thing; was this an equal punishment? Finally I went home and I went to bed, exhausted with pain. I fell asleep instantaneously, curled up as I did as a child.

Carolyn was home in a few days, and we got a nurse for her until she could get on her feet again. Our conversations were constrained. "How are you today? Have you eaten?" My stepdaughter was at school and, in the evenings, doing her homework, she was silent. She had been ashamed that her mother was pregnant. I could understand that. Sexuality is always a problem for us Americans. "I'm sorry," I said to her, "that there is so much sadness in the house, that we are all suffering so much." Friends came to visit. They brought flowers, stayed to chat, then left. At the end of the month, Carolyn went back to work.

———

When the babies finally did come, Mary Elizabeth and seventeen months later, Matthew Miller, starting the next year, the maids came, and the staff to run the household while we were at work. Little by little there was a thaw inside me as I watched the wonder of babies, the magic of unseen growth, the usual parental delight, the first word, the first tooth, the first uncertain step, the beauty and the innocence of them. They swept my heart away.

My wife was wonderful at managing the house and every morning she would dress while the main maid attended her, writing down the duties for the day with pad and pencil: what to feed the children, what to shop for, and what to make for dinners.

Carolyn was not a maternal woman. I think she would have been surprised if I had said that to her. She was very proud of being a physician, an analyst, self-sufficient enough to be able to do exactly what she wanted. Carolyn had all that careless swagger of someone who had always been rich, who has always been the prettiest girl, the most desirable girl.

It was all true. She was pretty and desirable, but she was not maternal—only natural, for her mother had not been a maternal woman either. Carolyn was in the same mold. Her mother had worked in the oil and gas business, while Carolyn worked in the doctor business. Carolyn's family would traffic with the Murchisons of Dallas. The joke about the group of oil multi-millionaires was that they went all over the world, everywhere in Europe, but the men never left their hotel suites, where they played poker and drank. I didn't think Carolyn could understand my background, my early travails; she had been born into wealth, and could trace her roots to the Mayflower. My world had been so far removed from hers.

———

I had thought marriage would quiet the surges of restlessness I had all my life felt, even as a child, and the insatiable curiosity that filled my being. In the early times of my life, I always went to bed with the thought, "What would tomorrow be or bring or how, how different?"

During the years of war, of schooling, and of working as an analyst, it was the same. As an analyst, sitting perfectly quiet, at times not even breathing, just listening, sometimes closing my eyes to see a pattern emerge, I just had to be patient. I was patient. I could wait. I had trained myself against the impatience that I had always felt, the friskiness of a young dog, tirelessly running about. All that was inward and remained inward.

I never spoke of this to my wife. It seemed to be something essentially me. After those first few years Carolyn and I lived our lives quietly, occupied with what schools to send the children to, taking pleasure in their achievements. It was a pleasure to see them skate or swim or ride horseback. It was a great pleasure for me to take them to ride ponies or ride a miniature train with them at an amusement park. The children were inseparable when young, and would leave the house hand in hand. My wife and I would laugh, "They will never find anyone like the other to marry."

The seasons passed. The years passed. We took our children on trips across the country, to places like Washington and Monticello. As I watched their faces in these historic places, I used to think— will they ever know what it means to be poor? To never even imagine seeing places like these? At one point I took my children to Philadelphia to see where I was born and raised, as well as to West Chester, where I went to school. We stopped at Levitt's, the hot dog stand on Sixth Street below South. But as I looked and stepped inside, I saw that it had lost its magic. My children, teenagers then, had an ice, but they were not impressed. My growing up was not theirs, and in a way I felt sorry for them, for they did not have memories of a neighborhood in a grim depression and a neighborhood in transit to more prosperous times. Our old-fashioned ethnic neighborhood, its first-generation children scrambling ever upwards—that's why their parents had come, to give their children, born and unborn, a better chance.

Later we took them to Europe—England, France, Italy, and down south to Portugal and Spain—even across the water to Northern Africa, Tangiers, and Morocco. I remember how, in Marrakech, our kids rode camels and we visited the Souk. Everyone stayed close as we walked through from tiny shop to tiny shop, all carved into caves. Here my senses reeled. The smells were of such fragrances that I was overcome and struck by the similarity of the moving stands to the ones on my Seventh Street in South Philadelphia.

Except here there were more people, more natives, more smells, the smell of urine permeating throughout, and a thousand years of spices and herbs and whatever anyone might want. The guide said, "They hold an auction every Tuesday. You can buy whatever woman you want." I asked, "Where do they come from?" He shrugged his shoulder. "Sir," he said, "no one asks or cares." One evening in Rabat we saw a belly dancer whose body alone could transport you to crowded bazaars: Arabs traders, merchants, horses, smoke-filled hashish rooms, clothes, costumes, a million colors, as she quivered from toe to thigh, from thigh to belly, and from belly to hip.

Always it was a deep joy for us to be able to do these things as a family. We traveled well. We stayed in fine hotels. We did not spare money for anything that was worthwhile to do or see in these great foreign countries. I could not help but contrast my young life with my children's and I wondered—was it all too easy, too rich? Would they have the fiber to go higher when their turn came to fly away? I wanted them to be able to fly away and fly higher than their mother and I ever had, else what's heaven for?

In those times the wartime past seemed far away from me. My children had driven Giselle and Irmgard away, except for a moment in Paris, as we ate near the Café Des Deux Magots, when I briefly thought of Giselle, but I struck that away. I did not want to make comparisons between her and my very American wife, or between the life I might have had, and the life I had chosen.

# 11

## Yet Another Fight

*I*n linear time we set ourselves schedules and pathways. We have to meet at specific moments and in specific places, marking time by the calendar and clock. I had my goals set up, one by one: graduate from college, earn a medical degree, become a resident in psychiatry, an analyst, a father. Ever since I was a child in South Philadelphia, I had been filled with a fierce desire to make something of my life, something better, and I had allowed myself to be governed, almost always, by the future goal.

Circular time is allowing yourself to flow in your life experiences, knowing you will come to the right intersection without great effort, not allowing yourself to miss opportunities. We have goals that we set on straight or linear paths; yet when the pathway is allowed to expand outward, to flow, twist or turn, the enchantment of life will be present, available in the present moment and not four years, five years, ten years down the road. In one instant, when your whole mind is open to receiving it, you can intersect with the right opportunity—not looking at the world in terms of what must be, but how you will allow it to be.

Why didn't I ever return, in the fifty years following the war, to find my Irmgard or my Giselle? I wanted to be a doctor and I went into my linear time. Had I understood circularity, I could have gone back to my nurse or to Giselle and I still would not have lost my capability to become a doctor. I could have lived both the lives I seemed destined to live, had I understood.

The life I had chosen, my life as an analyst, was stressful and miraculous and consuming. Being an analyst is different from being a specialist in any other type of medicine—except, perhaps, from being a pathologist, whose patient is a corpse. Or perhaps it is not so different from being a radiologist, one who speaks to an X-ray and listens as it speaks back.

Day after day there are the ruin of problems, all before you: physical illness with large psychological components; self-destructiveness in a job or in relationships with spouses, or bosses, or boyfriends or girlfriends; the accidents and the depressions with no apparent reason behind them. You hear of new boyfriends, new girlfriends— the great thrills on finding them, and the great despair, often, on finding that it cannot work, that this particular love or this friendship can lead only to unhappiness. And always I, sitting there, day after day, teasing out the subtle element that leads inexorably to the family as source, to the mother and to the father, the brothers and sisters. Every day there is one more piece to the puzzle. The analyst has to be patient, for secrets do not yield easily. He must be a person capable of silence, and one who can provide a culture of warm silence—a silence that is comfortable, always inviting speech—in which the process is planted and developed.

Every day there is, before you, the ubiquitous masochism of people, the refusal to take advantage of the wonderful life that can be lived if only something inside will permit it. Common are those who insist on flying into the face of their own unconscious, or who mistake the analyst for them or for a member of their family—a mistake known as transference, one of the great discoveries of Freud.

These are some of the problems the analyst faces every day, every hour, but there is rich pleasure in the unraveling of the mysteries that are presented—and every session is a mystery. The analyst must illuminate the daily anxieties with honesty and respect so that the patient is always thrust forward; he must teach the patient a whole new way to do his life. The job is intense and serious, for there is a life at stake, a life already partly used up. As an analyst, one is aware constantly of this huge responsibility: just one life is all that matters in this room, for this person who has come for another chance to find the true path of his life. And it is the analyst's job to say the right thing every time, for the patient has already spent a lifetime listening to the things that are wrong.

I had my tools. I had my own experience lying on a couch, and I had the experience of the war, when my life and the lives of so many airmen had depended on my navigation. Back then, everyone expected my words to be exactly right, for in the air there is no such thing as being more or less on course. The navigator's reading either is or is not correct—a little more or a little less than on course and you were certainly dead, you and everyone who depended on you.

I remembered flying my first mission with fear, and the apprehension that had accompanied me in my bowels. I recalled my admiration for the warriors I had seen at prior stations before being assigned to mine. Such awe I had felt upon seeing these men and their war ribbons that told of wounds and trials by fire. I was envious because they had that appearance of seasoning, that gaze that spoke of a death they had almost touched. Another dimension was added to all of them. We were all young; they, in their youth, were different. They knew. They had battled and survived. I had hoped to become one of them: experience may change a man; great experience has a better chance.

Back then I had wanted to fly, and becoming a flyer was a great adventure. There were the women, the drinking, the great, great fun. One could do almost anything then, with one's youth and strength and willingness to take the risk that made life altogether enchanting. The other life, one's life before, was temporarily on hold—that is, if one survived at all. We had left all that we had ever known, and we had done so to enter into this great human experience. We were nations in turmoil, nations uprooted, nations fighting on the right side and nations fighting on the wrong side, but when we stepped into our planes and brought them to the line, gunning the engines and taking them to the skies in spectacular formation, when we fought for our lives and for the lives of the oppressed everywhere, then we were the high warriors of mythic times, formed from a mythic mold.

Psychoanalysis was a new warfare, but war and death are the same to the soldier on the ground, in the chariot, or in a tank: the drinking is forgotten, the women are forgotten, and only the task is kept in mind with a sharpness of focus that would be unthinkable in any ordinary situation.

No matter how vivid the imagination, no one can know what battle is like without having been in it, on the ground, on the sea, or in the air; the paradox is that a soldier can never convey those moments of raging battle except to those who have shared similar moments, and to them you do not have to talk. They know already. This was my connection with Jack.

It was not quite the same in analysis, for one sits in a comfortable chair in a comfortable room and listens and talks, and, listening, attempts to discern what specific issues are bedeviling each specific patient. It does not look like much, but there is something serious going on here in this great room, in this quiet room between these people. A life will be made or unmade as a result of these discussions—and here too a battle is raging.

In no other treatment does the patient know less of what is really going on than in this one. In no other discipline can a treatment be deleterious with neither the doctor nor the patient knowing consciously that it is so. If in the end there is a bad result, it is too easy for the analyst to see the patient as recalcitrant or unsuitable, or as a bad person—without looking at the real issues, or at the analyst's own inability to provide a heading.

Though I did not know it then, there is a way to know the proper heading, always: one has to understand how to solve the riddle of dreams. Dreams are essential, for they not only detail one's truth as one is living it, or one's lie at the moment, but they can tell us of the past—the origins of the lie or the reason for the lying, and the manner in which one has been imprinted to live the life one has and is living. The dream is the true compass to one's life, and it never lies.

Back then I did not understand how important the dream was—not the way I do now.

And in all this time, in all these years of struggling for the answers that could end my suffering and the suffering of my patients, of dancing with and teasing the unconscious mind as if it were a lover, I only rarely thought of Irmgard or Giselle. Occupied by my work and by my family, I let these phantasms of the past remain as such—in the past, except for one momentary reflection about Giselle when we were in Paris. I thought I had done with them, though not with bitterness or anger; there was no reason to be angry with them. I recalled Jack Wales's remark to me about being the luckiest of men, and the most bereft. I had suffered this feeling of loss for a long time, and when it was time to put it away I did, with a deep sigh.

I had not reckoned on how unwilling the mind is to give up anything. It is amazing how quickly we enliven the past with a vividness that is almost unreal. No detail is ever lost. We human beings are reluctant to give almost anything up in the realm of human experience, good or bad, and our capacity for human experience, the capacity to let someone touch us, our capacity for vulnerability, is endless.

But in those years in Los Angeles, my love for psychoanalysis and my passion and my joy in it—all of these consumed me. I felt the joy of a child called outside to play with his friends—baseball or handball or marbles or soccer—the joy of using your muscles and speed, though you never think of it that way then. It is just going out to play. It is going to sleep, knowing tomorrow is more play, more fun, more joy—the purest, most clean joy in this world.

It is that feeling that drove me every day to the office, wondering what beautiful and puzzling things about people I would find there. I remember the excitement of analysis back then, always accompanied by the slight apprehension: could I understand it and say the correct thing to afford these precious people some relief, some hope that they could in some great measure take control of their lives, maybe for the first time?

And that would be an even greater thrill. Watch a child begin to walk, the first steps reluctant and hard, the child swaying back and forth, falling, then picking himself up again—and so it is with a patient just beginning to control his life. It may be only a feeling he's never had before, a speaking up he has never done before, a sudden urge to do something new. Little by little the confidence grows. We as analysts have to be patient, always ready to deal with a fall and the reasons for it, and always ready to encourage, once again, the slow steps toward achievement and evolution. There is great joy in seeing the efflorescence of the personality, which will be evident in the patient's dreams long before it is in the outside world.

Outside of my work, I spent as much time as I could with my family. Weekends were especially for the children: taking them to the carnival at the corner of Beverly and La Cienega, long since gone but once a magical place for them, with ponies, a Ferris wheel, and the usual carnival rides; taking them to the museum on Wilshire, where we'd go through one exhibit, usually, before playing ball in the park behind the museum; or just spending hours at home, around the pool, in the garden, or sprawled out on the living room floor.

Our house in Beverly Hills was the perfect setting for these lazy afternoons with the family; we had moved there a few years after the children were born, from a small house in the mountains. This house was our dream home, one with a white picket fence surrounding the bright green lawn, giant flowerbeds out back, and a hanging lantern by the path that led to the front door. Behind the garden in the backyard—a garden we'd designed ourselves, with every kind of flower—was a row of ficus trees and, beyond that, a gleaming blue pool surrounded by lounge chairs and an umbrella-covered table. We would spend hours at a time by that pool, the kids diving and flopping around in the water, Carolyn and I reading, talking, lying in the sun.

From the pool we could see and smell the flowers—the overwhelming scent, the reds and pinks and purples and whites. We could see that array of color from almost everywhere in the house as well; the French doors and the yawning windows looked out upon it from almost all the rooms in the house. I used to spend hours out there alone, painting the curves of the petals, the arch of the stems.

Years went by in this manner. My past was almost forgotten; there was no reason and no time to think of the war, my fleeting love affairs, or the brick row house in South Philadelphia. The past had been unstable, unsure, while my life now was a secure, safe life, but always an adventurous one; it was a blissful time, one I hoped could last forever.

But things started changing in Los Angeles in the world of psychoanalysis. New ideas had come to the city—ideas from an English analyst named Melanie Klein that were original, workable, and, as it turned out, highly controversial. Along with a small group of other analysts, Carolyn and I were ecstatic at first to find that, with these new ideas, we could help our patients in ways we hadn't been able to before. We had discovered a whole new way of looking at things; a different world had opened up to us, and the results were thrilling.

Yet others, who preferred the old ways of seeing things, balked at these ideas. Infighting followed at the Institute, which was the focus of all the teaching work I was doing, and I found myself on the side of those who went against the traditional thinking of the Institute. At one point the leaders attempted to prevent me from teaching a course I was slated to teach, on the basis that I would be poisoning the minds of the young with these new ideas. The atmosphere was such that anyone associated with Melanie Klein was blacklisted, and when the situation escalated, I chose to fight for academic freedom—a fight I felt I could not back down from. For four years, then, there were endless meetings, and suddenly I felt as if I was fighting World War II all over again, but that now the enemy was not so clearly marked. He looked like me, and had the same degree and title—but he was from another world.

One evening before one of the Institute's many meetings to discuss what to do about the "Kleinian" situation, Dr. Q., representing the majority faction who had removed me from teaching on account, said that I was corrupting the young. To my mind there was no Kleinian situation since there were only two declared Kleinians who were known to be such and they were not singled out. I instituted a lawsuit against the Los Angeles Institute, against the American Psychoanalytic Institute which supported the leadership, and the International Psychoanalytical Association (the IPA), which was apparently controlled by the American Institute.

I sued them all on the grounds that there was no due process given me, and I kept the lawsuit going for four years.

On this occasion, before the weekly meeting, Dr. Q. said, "Why don't you drop the lawsuit, and let's talk it over."

"No, why subject myself to the tyranny of a stupid majority? And a paranoid one at that."

"The report said you were out of the mainstream of American traditional psychoanalysis."

"Please define that for me." (I never could get anyone to do that in Los Angeles or New York).

"Well, it wasn't us but them, the authorities in New York," said Dr. Q.

"But you agreed and you instigated this brouhaha because their report said in fact that you, as chairman of the education committee, failed and abysmally failed."

Dr. Q., a man about my age (then fifty-three), educated in an Ivy League school, spoke with a tight voice and an accent apropos to that region. "I don't know about that."

"You know I am not a Kleinian and Drs. C. and D. are. Why was I removed and they were not?"

Dr. Q. replied, "The American felt you were the important person."

"How would they know me or what I do? None are from here. What they know is what you have told them. When people used to attack psychoanalysis as a doctrine, as a fanatic religion, I would get mad. They didn't know. Now I think they were right. It is unbelievable that a group of analysts are telling others what to think and saying they know what the right kind of analysis is that should be taught."

Dr. Q. said, "You are not in the mainstream."

"Are you a talking puppet? Do you know what nonsense you are saying? It is hard to imagine a more discourteous group of people—not inviting a former president of the British Psychoanalytic Association to speak. Dr. Bion is a man known to the psychoanalytic world. Are you not ashamed of your boorishness?"

"He doesn't fit in," Dr. Q. said stubbornly.

"New ideas don't fit in. They upset you. Where else but in the church are the people told what to read and what not than in the Los Angeles Institute? Are you not goddamned ashamed?"

"No, we know what is best to train our candidates," insisted Dr. Q.

"You know best how to close minds," I replied. "I thought psychoanalysis is about opening minds. I guess I was wrong. And by the way, I loved you placing me alongside Socrates. I would rather be with him than those who condemned him. But be aware I don't intend to poison myself."

"You are all alone. Don't you mind that? Can't you hear that the majority is mad that you have paralyzed the Institute?"

"I don't mind, especially when I hear distinguished Jewish analysts say, 'Let's throw them out, let's kill them.' Jewish analysts—are you not appalled? Jews talking like Nazis. Isn't the American appalled, and the IPA? I guess not, since they're not telling you to shut up. You and your 'elite sixteen,' which makes me laugh. Show me somebody who says 'we are the elite' and I will show you a fascist bastard."

"You can't win this."

I replied, "Neither can you, and we will go to trial and we will see who wins. You are all dishonest, corrupt and no better than con men selling snake oil. If you can do this, talk this way, you are all poisoning the minds of all you touch, and the fact that the membership hasn't arisen en masse and voiced its angry displeasure tells me the whole organization is corrupt. What you sell is corruption. What you preach is 'power is best and control is necessary and no minority is required or wanted.'"

"Why are you this way?" Dr. Q. asked. "Why don't you make life easy? Don't you want to hold office?"

I replied, "Hell, no, not in this stink hole."

And we broke off to go into the meeting where everybody was quiet. The auditorium was not full; there were some fifty to sixty people in the room. I slipped my tape recorder out and put it on the floor to get the blasphemers onto tape and later onto paper, which I did.

One night several weeks later, I met Dr. Q. again before going into the meeting. He must have been waiting for me for again he assailed me, asking how much longer was I going to hold this lawsuit over his head.

I said, "As long as it takes to get a fair shake. What I heard from the meeting last week did not give me much hope."

"What did you hear? The majority wants Kleinians out of the Institute."

The judge, formerly the lawyer who wrote the constitution for the organization, had said, as he presided over all the meetings, "It comes down to this: Do you want the analytic institute to be a private club? If so, you can have in it who you want. Or is this going to be an organization whose central authority is in New York and it is an educational institution?"

There were cries of "Kick the bums out, kill them," I heard Dr. D. say, and again I was shocked. I said to Dr. Q., "I never thought a Jew would call for the ouster of a colleague or his murder. What kind of fascist thinking is that, and from a man who supposedly had some analysis from Freud himself?"

Dr. Q. was quiet. "He didn't really mean it. It was the heat of the moment."

I said, "Are you a fucking analyst or not? I know you are not, none of you are—here, in New York, at the American or the IPA. All of you are fascist bastards, morally bankrupt and just exerting your power over a lot of weak confused people who think they are analysts or who think they are learning to be. If they really were, there would be an uprising against all of you, heard around the world. All of you are just miserable sons of bitches, lacking guts in great numbers."

Dr. Q. said, "You got it all wrong."

"Have I?" I said. "You want to get rid of the Kleinians. There are two declared and known ones and I am not one of them, and those two are the friends of some of your friends. Why don't you kick them out? You have always known who they were. Why did you pick on me?"

Dr. Q. said, "You are a Kleinian."

I said, "Is this the McCarthy era over again? I thought we were done with that bullshit. Are you his reincarnation? You are one stupid, cynical, frightened asshole and so is everyone associated with you here, in New York and in the IPA, and you can go to hell, all of you."

That was the last time I talked with Dr. Q. This was all a long time ago, in the 1970s, but I remember it as clearly as if it were yesterday. Aside from my run-in with Mr. Duncan at the University of Pennsylvania, this was the most vivid display of disregard for the freedom of expression and choice I have ever witnessed. To this day I am appalled that members of a profession seemingly engaged in the pursuit of truth can actually engage in dogmatizing such truth. For once truth becomes dogma it turns into a lie. It no longer sets you free. And I could not stand imprisonment any more. I was determined to fight this to the end.

---

Again everything changed, and slowly, ever so slowly, over those four years that led to my biggest battle, the idyllic life I had built for myself and my family in Los Angeles—the life that now, looking back, seems to me to have been emblematized by the many-colored flower garden that stretched behind our family home—eroded into ruins. Carolyn and I had no time and no energy to lie around the pool with the children, or to take drives up the Pacific Coast Highway or to the carnival or museum. The fight drained us in every way. My wife and I did not see our children at all some evenings; they were often in bed by the time we returned home at night.

I am not likely to forget what this fight cost us and our children. Conversation between Carolyn and me was now mostly confined to this struggle, and to the children. Our relationship had become dull: wars of attrition do not enhance anyone's beauty or buoy up anyone's personality. Altogether, those three or four years were desperate; they were depleting, and they had begun to bleed the marriage.

Finally, in 1977, the issue was taken to the highest channel for psychoanalysis, the Congress of the International Psychoanalytic Association, held every two years and held that year in Jerusalem.

Carolyn and I prepared for the trip. I thought how wonderful that this moral dilemma, and the greatest fight of my life, was to be decided in the Holy Land. Politicians never think of the truth as holy, or of lies as having consequences. All is expediency, all is "can we do in the weaker party, leave him with no recourse, no friends, no power." But they do not count on how the universe works. On the way to Jerusalem we stopped in London, where a leading Kleinian analyst—one whom we supported and trusted, and one associated with the ideas, from Melanie Klein, we were so thrilled by—urged us to drop the fight. The betrayal we felt was immense.

The children were too young to really know of the political events in our lives. For them, our trip was fun. We had been to London, then to France, to Italy and now Jerusalem. Jerusalem: my people, my God, my truth. On the plane to Israel I looked at my children, my blonde-haired son and brown-haired daughter, their sturdy bodies playing away at their puzzles and games, and there was our older daughter reading a book. How innocent, such joyful hearts.

But, suddenly, I knew what would happen. The Kleinians too would betray us. They wanted nothing to happen in Los Angeles for fear of losing their preeminence, their power, and their money in London, where most of them practiced. I knew it in my guts, and, looking at my beautiful children, my heart searing with pain, I said to my wife, "They are going to betray us."

And I thought, was I flying my last mission to Ingolstadt again, waiting to be shot down again? My feelings were an admixture of happiness, to see the Jerusalem of my people, and of sadness for the history of my people, and the resolve to do what I would have to do, whatever the outcome. I was determined to survive.

# 12

Jerusalem, 1977

*I*t was in Jerusalem that I found Irmgard and Giselle again, in the midst of my most bitter disappointment. I had held so high an opinion of psychoanalysis, about what it could do. I still believe it can do what I had imagined, that it can solve the problems that plague mankind.

Today I understand that the betrayal I felt had literally shaken me as if I had flown through the sound barrier. My passion and my love for this one raft of the human mind had been betrayed, the one and only lifeline we as human beings have: the truth. I understand now that psychoanalysis stands or falls by this one principle. In the end it is the quiet insistence by the analyst to look at the facts, to face the meaning of the facts as they are laid out plainly, that will heal the patient who suffers. The wise men, the great spiritual leaders and poets, have always known this intuitively. Psychoanalysis confirms it: it is ultimately the truth that cures, the truth that melts away the lies the patient is filled with from the beginning of life, the false perceptions he or she is asked to believe, the prejudices which fill the mind and heart. And it is all in the truth, mankind's only mooring to the divine, and to one's own soul. Whether there will be satisfaction and peace in an individual's life depends solely upon the truth of that life. And only we can carry that burden or that gift for ourselves.

To give up the truth is to give up every decent chance, every worthwhile thing on earth. Truth is beauty, the poet wrote, and there, in Jerusalem, I thought that now I could understand what poets understood already, without the benefits of science. All scientific advances will be meaningless if there is no attention to the mind, to the feelings of a single human being. Psychoanalysis can save lives; it can salve tortured minds, and it can save families and children. The deepest truths by which people live, the internal laws by which people live, can all be derived from analysis.

I view psychoanalysis now as the supreme gift of God; to sully it is a profound desecration, and this is what I felt as I walked the streets of Jerusalem, or the hallways of the congress.

And somewhere in the silence of the auditorium, in the small rooms where people gathered, in the lobbies where members of the analytic societies stood and talked, I felt a tugging, a stray memory, and suddenly I became aware that I was thinking of Irmgard, and with her came a host of other memories. It was not the first time Irmgard had appeared to me in a moment of distress.

I went to a quiet place in the hotel, in a corner, and sat down. I sat quietly, leaning back, closing my eyes, shutting out the noise that had become a steady blare. And there was stillness within me. Memories have such a wondrous quality to them, the way they seem to burst upon the inward screen for no sensible reason—though I know, as an analyst, that this is never true. There is always a sensibility to any strong thought and feeling.

Sitting there, Irmgard so close I felt I could have reached out and felt her crisp uniform, I consciously went over the war for the first time in years—my initial Atlantic crossing, my third mission, and my last mission, which led me to Irmgard. The coming into Iceland, a white jewel before us, and the black thread of runway, our salvation.

I remembered that trip as if it had happened the day before. It was January, 1944, and on our way to Europe we had been stuck for a week in Goose Bay, after an equally long, snowbound week in Presque Isle. We were young men eager to fight a great war, and by the time we left Goose Bay we were almost at our wit's end—I even more so than the rest, due to a great tragedy I had suffered there.

One thing all flying officers pride themselves on is their cap. I had gotten mine in August, 1943, and I had toiled to fashion it, to shape it, to break it in exactly as I fancied it should be. I had been at this for almost six months. One evening we all wore our coats and caps to mess. The place was filled with airmen, and the air was fantastic. Youthful libido unleashed, youthful appetite and vigor, and all were officers and gentlemen.

After supper we hung around the club drinking, playing cards, listening to the jukebox, when at one point the announcement came over the loudspeaker that all flights had been cancelled, the snow was falling too heavily. Visibility was too poor. We went to get our coats and caps and, to my consternation, I found that my cap was missing. Some ill-formed and ugly cap was there in its stead, the only one. Someone, having taken mine, had left his for me in turn. May he rot in hell. I seethed, threw this cap on the ground, stepped on it, spit on it, I almost pissed on it. My pilots, Skufca and Stroble, stopped me. They were laughing now.

I never wore that cap; I wore only my soft hat from then on. Officers and gentlemen, shit! Even today in the finest restaurants I insist on taking my coat to my seat. If the U.S. Air Force cannot be trusted, why should any restaurant be?

For the next week I was morose, between the constant snowing and my great loss. The thief was clever, for though I checked caps at every meal, I never saw mine again. So, when we were told we could leave Goose Bay for Iceland, it was not soon enough for me.

Early that January morning we had been briefed about a terrible storm with winds of over a hundred miles per hour, some three hours out. We were to be careful not to run into it, to go above or around it instead. We took off and after some circling and climbing, Skufca asked for a heading and I gave him one, taking account of the wind that would bring us to Iceland. This was to be radio silent. The ocean was infested with our submarines, German submarines and vessels of all sorts.

We must have been out less than an hour and a half, flying at thirty-three thousand feet, when suddenly the plane lurched. We had flown directly into the storm. I could hear Skufca saying there was ice on the wings and they began doing whatever they needed to break the ice—otherwise the plane would fall into the ocean.

I was watching the compass because Skufca, trying to break the ice, was not following the course. When I finally looked up at the cockpit, I saw that Stroble had slumped over. I punched Vassey, the chief engineer, and he quickly found that Stroble had lost his oxygen connection and fainted. Vassey put the mask on Stroble's face and checked his line. Stroble regained his senses, and now both pilots were doing whatever they could to save the aircraft.

No word from the intercom. My heart sank. In this gale, they're pointing the nose down, diving to twenty thousand feet to break the ice, pulling out. The compass veered crazily and finally all was calm. They'd broken the ice on the wings. Both pilots were at the controls, awake, shaken, and after a bit they turned to me, asking me for a heading.

What the fuck was I, a magician? To go through all that and then expect me to say twenty degrees? Yes, they did expect me to give them a heading, and I did, and I crossed my fingers and prayed. So, we descended slowly and as dawn appeared we were flying the heading that I had given them.

The sea shone dark and fearsome. The sky at this level was gray and cold. Inside, Skufca tried to contact the field at Iceland. He tried over half an hour and kept on trying. At this point Vassey told us we only had one hour's fuel left. Now I began to sweat. The crew in the back was unaware of what was going on. For them the plane had simply veered and waggled and righted itself. Everything was ok in the hands of their pilots and navigator. So we watched the minutes go by, the clock ticking. I said, hold the course, and they did. They kept trying to get through to Iceland, no answer. We kept flying. Vassey's face was grim and gray—he did not fancy an ocean ditching at this time.

Then, suddenly, above the horizon we saw a dot. Now I was standing between the two pilots and we all saw a dot, which grew and grew. We yelled, all of us, "Iceland, Iceland ahead!" Since we could not contact the tower, we just headed straight in, we just landed. When the plane rolled to a stop, we got out, kissed the ground, kissed each other. Both pilots looked at me as if I were a genius, but I knew I had not done it. I would not have known how to do that. Later my good friend H. O. Irwin told me that I was chalk white when he saw me and that I remained white for hours after. And that was our Iceland.

And within me now, here in Jerusalem, I felt a sudden love for that plane, for the two men who flew it, and the engineer—those in the cockpit who shared the fearful knowledge and who shared their courage, who shared their faith in me. They set the plane down in a quick burst of beauty, and waves and waves of quiet exultation rolled over me. These were men I could trust forever. I could turn my back and know they would protect me, as I would them.

And then I knew why I had these thoughts. How different from where I was, and what had led to my being there.

There was no one in this entire assembly of psychoanalysts whom I would call my friend. No one with whom I could share that brotherhood of fire. Not one would pass the test. Yet each one called himself a navigator of the soul. I did not believe it, and had not for some time, so I never thought about it in this context.

An analyst is a navigator, I am convinced now. A lost soul comes to the door imploring help, asking for a heading. Not only one, but a thousand times; and a thousand times a thousand. And the analyst has to be there to give it to him, or to her.

The pity of it is that, sitting in that room, you cannot truly know, without the dream, whether the heading is correct, for the unconscious is as vast as the universe and without boundaries— infinite and awesome. With his intellectual theories the analyst can spin fantasies for the patient, fantasies that might never help the patient beyond his suffering. That's as cold as the infinite heaven, for there is only one thing that can say, beyond all doubt, that the course to safe harbor is right, and that one thing is the dream, which reveals the intricacies of one's life in one unfolding pattern.

So these analysts who could so easily trample on the foundation of analysis, the truth—these analysts could never be navigators, in the simplest, truest sense of the word. They could never realize a soul; they could only give false testimony, and lose themselves in the many veils of deception that are about us.

I thought of all this in a flash, as we are wont to do in dreams or fantasies, when whole stories come back to the mind, and for a moment I relived the entire Iceland episode from our landing to our leaving, all of us having shared an unforgettable adventure, all of us having known for a little while an unforgettable love. And then the song came back to me: "I Can't Get Started With You." On our second day in Iceland, someone had found a Victrola and the only record in the entire place. For the next five days all we heard was Bunny Berigan's plaintive, rasping ballad, "I Can't Get Started with You." The song came over me now, the sounds of the busy hotel lobby fading out, the wail of the music transporting me back, back to another world. We had all learned the lyrics to the song; the more we had heard it, the more we had wanted to hear it. We never tired of it.

I remembered how one night the announcement came that there were winds of 150 miles per hour, so when we went to the mess hall, we had to crawl, holding onto each other for fear of being blown away. Skufca and Stroble put me in between them to make sure I was secure. Bill said, "That little wind might take this little son of a bitch out in the wild blue yonder, or is it the wild black yonder?" Well, we bent low, hugging the ground, and we held hands and followed the leader. It was that dark.

Inside we took our seats in the large dining room, which had many long picnic tables with place settings starting about ten rows in from one end. The many unset tables at the other end were clearly not meant for us. One was a rectangular table ten feet long. And suddenly, from that end, three people appeared: the colonel, or commanding officer; a lieutenant colonel, probably second in command; and a breathtaking blonde with a nurse's insignia on her tunic. Every eye in the place was on her.

She did not look back; I imagined this was old hat for her and for them. All the men looked at them, thinking some variation of "That fuckin' son of a bitchin' ground pounder keeping that little o' lady to himself." We were all thinking the same thoughts. It was a case of "eat your heart out, buster, no one is going to get near this little pretty, who is all mine, anytime." That was the longest dinner hour we ever spent. We all watched her and dinner got cold and we did not care, there was always breakfast tomorrow morning. Later, back at the barracks, Bunny turning out his love song would seem so appropriate, maybe even sadistic. That colonel fucker could have done that himself, put this Victrola here to torment us, while he laughed all the way to get his target, the nurse. All ground officers hated flying officers, who showed their contempt openly in turn.

"Hey, listen to the words," I said that night. "That colonel fucker put that record here for us to eat out hearts out, listen."

*I'm the glum one*
*It's explainable*
*I met someone unattainable.*

"Isn't that all of us?" I said to Bill. "Think of it, flashing this beautiful floating island before us, so our tongues hang down to our crotch."

Bill said, "You little ol' fucker, I think you're right."

*I've been around the world in a plane*
*Designed the latest IBM brain*
*But lately*
*I'm so downhearted*
*'Cause I can't get started with you.*

Bill hummed along with the rest of the words and finished with "I can't get started with you." He said, "You little bastard, that's why we keep you around, just to tell us why we can't get any nookie." So we laughed and began to talk about what Prestwick might be like— the girls I mean.

Bill stood up and announced, in his Louisiana drawl, "Listen here, all you little ol' fuckers, I don't want to hear any whacking off

221

tonight, y'all hear?!" and everyone laughed. We watched this drama for the remaining days; we all came to eat, the colonel came with his lady, and we all stared. They talked and ate but we all wondered—what did they have to talk about being stuck here day after day? What could they possibly have to say that was so intriguing? Of course maybe it did not matter at all. As one fellow put it, "Who talks? Just stick your dick in that sweet pie."

"No," someone said, "pie and ice cream."

Bill said, "Pecan pie and ice cream, and that's enough for you fuckers."

I will never forget that song, the piping tone of the coronet as Bunny played, the melody evoking feelings of dejection and rejection; one doesn't even have to listen to the lyrics. There are plenty of lyrics in one's own life that can easily fall into place:

*I've been around the world in a plane*
*Designed the latest IBM brain*
*But lately*
*I'm so downhearted*
*'Cause I can't get started with you.*

I smiled, thinking of the beautiful nurse none of us could get started with. As the sage says, "We can't win them all."

Now I felt a great sadness. The frustration of the song, its hurt desire, brought me back to my situation now, here in Jerusalem. I could not get started with analysis, not with these people and not with their kind of analysis. And, moreover, if this is what their kind of analysis could prompt them to do, I did not want to get started with them.

I suddenly realized why this memory had come to my mind. On the simplest, most carnal level the story of the colonel and his lady was about envy, but here now I felt there was a deeper meaning, as if this autocrat of his base was one of the officers of the analytic

222

organization, wanting to keep the beautiful woman—psycho-analysis, the unconscious—to himself. This beautiful woman will love you and give you everything if you do not shackle her; she is no one's to enchain, only a woman for whom you must be grateful, for you are one of her lovers.

The psychoanalytic association had begun to resemble the church, masquerading as worldliness, the very institution Freud had so abominated—here was the irony, and more so that they did not understand it. Rumi's lines came to me, Rumi who lived just a desert away: "You must marry your soul. That wedding is the way. Union with the world is sickness."

---

I once again reflected upon the miracles I had witnessed in the war. I recalled my terror as the bomber lost its direction, gyrating, twisting, diving, all but shuddering to shake the ice off the wings, and the black sky that revealed no stars, nothing except fear and the prospect of a violent death. The pilot's voice had come: "Give me a heading." I thought he was crazy to expect me to be able to do that. No one could. No one. No one. But I had; I had followed the gyrations of the compass and was foolhardy enough to believe I could more or less do that. It was crazy, but I did. I did that. The plane settled into its course, the engines roaring away, the darkness beginning to lift; the ocean more menacing than ever. We could not contact Iceland. The chief engineer said "We only have one hour's worth of gas," in his soft Tennessee drawl. One hour to oblivion. I had no idea how far we were from Iceland, or whether we were on the right course. Strike it, a dot on the ocean.

It was not I who traced the wildly pitching compass, nor I who designed the heading.

I thought of us carrying Karl, and resting in the bomb-shattered train station in Stuttgart, the angry muttering crowd. I recalled my kneeling to comfort Karl. Suddenly this resonant voice, the voice of authority shouted a command in German. The crowd dispersed. I rose to salute a Luftwaffe officer, immaculate and handsome in his uniform. "Thanks," I said. He nodded. I could be grateful for his having saved our lives. That was not hard for me to do. Where he came from, where he went, I do not know, but he was there. The hand of God had not forsaken me.

And I thought of my third mission with my pilot dead, the colonel with his foot blown off and the pilot-less plane, a bomber gliding without effort, all engines off. It had been a swan going downward in a soft descent. Moments of silence, moments of quick action saved a stranger's life. The calmness in that plane despite it being ravaged and dangerous—the calmness. What blessed force kept that plane up long enough for a proper conclusion? The two of us got out alive. Still, the hand had been with me. For though the colonel had been frozen, he had survived, miraculously. After I had bailed out, he had gotten into the cockpit and succeeded in putting the plane down in the Channel. The impact had blown him clear of the plane. He had been picked up quickly and given immediate medical attention.

And last I thought of Ingolstadt, our plane riddled with machine gun fire, which killed the pilots and five more, allowing me once again to plummet to captivity, but alive, gratefully alive but scared of what lay before me.

And there I had found Irmgard.

I no longer remember exactly where it was in Jerusalem that Irmgard came to my mind, but she did not come back suddenly or directly; there were tuggings, something out there on the margin, something I didn't even see at first. After, there was a perceptible movement that frightened me, for I was not expecting anything to move on the fringe; my eyes were in front, watching the road.

I could not say how long the jacket-tugging had gone on. I had to work backwards, and it reminded me of the many dreams I had had where I would awaken suddenly with only a thread of them left; I would have to lie in bed quietly, not even breathing, for fear the breath would pull the dream back into my lungs, or blow it back into the air. There I would lie, waiting for the reversal to begin: what had happened before this, and where was I, or who was I, or who was it I had seen? What had I been I watching and what did I feel? Slowly, go slowly, tread softly: dreams are one of the fragile creations of the mind, and one of the most important. Little by little, if I am lucky, I can retrieve the text, and once I feel I have enough to go on I can relax and breathe, sure the creation will not go away. It was so with Irmgard. If I spoke in that idiom, I'd say the angels were pulling me in that direction. The truth is today I am positive they are. Today I feel sure about so many things I had not even thought about then.

Here in Jerusalem, wandering around in the crowds, hearing the buzz of conversations in the hotel lobbies, or walking around alone in the streets, once paths of my forefathers, I knew there was only one important issue, that of freedom; once academic freedom falls, everything else begins to collapse. Not even the few analysts of great repute raised their voices; no analyst in any of the societies raised a voice of protest. I was stunned by the fact that liberal Jews could and did take this arbitrary position.

How is it, I thought, that analysts traditionally liberal in spirit, generous in hand, open in heart, could be so treacherous, so devoid of principle to their own craft—for being a psychoanalyst means to be open to new ideas. Every patient is a new idea. Did these people not understand what they were doing? I don't expect analysts to believe in such sweeps of movement as karma, but I believe the universe does work like that and that analytic work must take into account the individual's karmic status: where in his life's cycle is he? And analysts have to reckon that everyone has to suffer the consequences of his or her actions; there is no immunity for this and there is no plea bargaining. Of course I myself had no idea about karma then; it's not what institutes teach.

Then I thought of psychoanalysis as like a political party, and obviously it is. Oh Joseph, I thought, no one here would want your dream interpretations; I thought it would all be gone, all the discoveries of psychoanalysis, hardly one hundred years old and already worm-eaten from within. When I could not listen to the papers being presented, which I did not believe—if you can't believe the men how can you believe what they say—I wandered about the hotel or outside, walking ,walking, thinking, and ever Irmgard now was with me, and Giselle.

This city, this Jerusalem could only have awakened the memory of these two profound experiences in my life—my life, too raw and unaccomplished to identify and recognize the meaning of what the universe had brought me. I longed for the authenticity of Giselle. I longed for the open willingness of this woman ready to devote her life to me. The face of psychoanalysis was a mask; the mask spoke the words but the words had no heft.

And I longed to be a prisoner again; I longed for that truth; I longed for that glass of red wine, for that fleeting touch of Irmgard's hand, for that softening of her eyes as she glanced at me. I longed for the P-47s to fly over the town. I longed for the air raid shelter, and to be at the beginning with this wonderful woman, and how she was then—shy, delicate, slim, attentive, blushing. I longed for it to start all over again. I longed to hear the flute again and her voice saying, "I want to play for you. It makes you neither a German or an American, just a man who is moved by the music as I am." I longed for the illness again so that I could touch her hand, if only for an instant, and feel her lingering.

I even longed for the end of our journey, for I knew, even more, how deep her feelings were for me, and mine for her. And now I felt how wretched was this place and this time, here in Jerusalem—how far from the nobility of those tender, evanescent moments.

So I swung like a pendulum from the one to the other and always I returned to Irmgard in this Jerusalem, this city of divine spirit, where the spirit of our people is the strongest of all the world. The body dies, but the spirit, the soul, never. Psychoanalysis will never die, though at one time I thought it might.

# 13

## Coming Home

*I*t was in Jerusalem, then, that the miracle of the past came to me—the gifts I had been given, the chances I had won, the beauty of a German nurse playing her flute for me while a man lay dying and the bombs dropped outside. It was in Jerusalem that Irmgard and Giselle returned to me, haunting me like the press of kisses already given, a tingling in the lips and down the neck. "But where are the snows of yesteryear?" the poet had asked, with the wistful feeling that something irretrievable had been lost, a feeling I knew all too well.

And it was in Jerusalem, this city of my people, that the promise of Irmgard was finally realized—after all those years without her. For it was Irmgard who had begun the movement of my soul during those six weeks of captivity in 1945, back when I was still a young man. Now in Jerusalem I had grown old, and I faced the biggest disappointment, the most heart-wrenching betrayal of my life; yet it was in Jerusalem that I returned, finally, to my God. Irmgard had begun a flowering of my soul, and now, in Jerusalem, the petals began to open.

---

We had been met at the airport by our guide, a colonel from the '67 War. Before and after the meetings of the congress, my family and I toured Israel with him; it would be our last trip together as a family, a brief respite for all of us after these years of pain and fighting.

I understand now that those days had the wistfulness of an ending, a finality I did not perceive then.

The colonel was a tall amiable man, and he narrated the story of Israel's past as he took us to places like the kibbutz where we spent a few days, the one in which Ben-Gurion, Israel's first Prime Minister, had lived. I remember one supper in the kibbutz, how we had St. Peter's fish, a tasty but bone-laden fish that required careful eating, and how I imagined the fish to be emblematic of the Israelis; they were not a people who could easily be eaten, as indeed the world knows. We traveled through many towns—towns like Bethlehem, Ashkelon, and Gaza—and, through it all, the colonel cautioned us to be careful; there were angry feelings lurking, but he took care to shepherd us. It was not a surprise; if there is such desperate fighting among analysts, how many more reasons there are for these people to continue old feuds over land, over money, over power, over religion and religious sites.

In the course of the week, we visited the Dead Sea. The children tried to bathe in it, and my wife and I bought salt from it as a souvenir. It was very hot, as all Israel baked in the summer. We went to the battle lines where the Israelis were fighting Lebanon. The colonel was able to get us close enough to hear the mortar fire quite clearly, as if it were coming from the next hill, not too far away. We visited the Golan Heights and on the way, by the roadside, there were tanks left from the '67 War. My children climbed atop them, and I took their picture.

Later, one noontime, we stopped out of the city at an Arab restaurant; it was a simple affair, no one there except us, and we ate delicious food, dish after dish, that I had never seen before. The colonel had a good friendship with these people; everywhere we went there was an affectionate greeting between him and those we met, and I had the impression he must be known throughout Israel. Travel with him was as comfortable as his air-conditioned car could make it, and he smoothed all bumps in the road.

We stopped in an area where there were no houses—nothing as far as I could see. A large meadow, clumps of bushes, some trees in the distance. The meadow was flat, the grass green. We exited and followed him, and as we gathered around him he said, "This is where David slew Goliath." He told the children the story and as he did I was bewitched by the feeling of "Oh," by waves of "oh"—for it was unbelievable to me that my childhood Bible had now become a reality. Our journey throughout this land was over and over again streaked with history I had heard or read about years before.

I remember it vividly: the expanse of smooth grass, the low-lying bushes, the serenity of the place, the quiet. No one else was there. As I stood apart from my family, I turned, imagining Goliath there, almost as if he were a part of the committee soon to convene in Jerusalem to decide the fate of psychoanalysis. It felt that way to me then, betrayed and alone, fighting long past the point when others had dropped their swords.

Later in the week we stood looking down on the Wailing Wall. I said to the colonel, "I'm going down." The scene was fantastic: the long, ancient wall filled with cracks and crevices, each of them, seemingly, stuck through with folded prayers, little jutting notes, a lone daisy or peony. People were everywhere, crying or praying or swaying back and forth with their heads leaning back. And I too wrote a little note, *God of my people, help me. You know who I am.* I did not sign my name.

And I felt it then: I do not have to sign my name; you know who I am. It came to me as I stood by this ancient monument, relic of a second temple, fought over and won by the Maccabees. I felt as my grandfather, whom I had watched so many times as he put on his phylacteries, his tefillin, and his shawl, and then, thus altered, book in hand, slowly walked the length of the dining room and prayed. I heard a mutter of words I did not understand. Now as I stood in that hot sun, people all around, with the noise of pain all around and the blur of two thousand years, I understood my grandfather Jacob as I never had as a child. At this wall, looking to the sky above, I understood my grandfather's faith in God; he did not need the world's affairs, for he knew that God was the great constant. In the end, it is only the Lord who remains—and all is just, and all is as it should be.

I had never asked Jacob about his life. Many times I'd sit in the kitchen with my grandmother. She would make tea for us and put out a plate of cookies. She would drink her tea from a thin glass with a cube of sugar between her teeth. As I ate and sipped from a teacup, I would watch him walking with that beautiful silk shawl draped around him in folds and falling to his knees. He looked like Abraham Lincoln to me, with his week's growth of beard, his salt and pepper hair, and his brown eyes. I never saw him angry. I never asked him what he thought of, or what he said as he paced back and forth.

What did he think, as he paced up and down, of his four sons, one of whom was my father? What did he think of his educated sons who denied God and became Communists, members secretly of the party? Did he think of his firstborn, a daughter, who died before she was one year old?

I never asked my grandmother what he said as he prayed. In fact, I never asked her what she said as she performed her Friday night weekly prayer over the candles at sunset. She would have bathed, washed her hair, and combed it severely back with a part in the middle. Her face would gleam cleanliness.

I was never taught to pray. Having been taught to be a Communist, I did not believe in God. Usually there was only the job to be done, and I let nothing else come into my mind. Yet in those rare moments— over the target, attacked by fighters, lost over the Atlantic—I immersed myself in the stillness of my soul, though I could never have identified it as that then. How did this man cling to his prayers, murmuring, intoning? What else came to his mind? I used to be better at exclusion. Now it is hard to keep strange, irrelevant thoughts away, and today I follow them with another part of myself. They give me clues as to what my heart is saying, what my body is needing, indeed what my soul is declaring.

It has taken a lifetime to come back to the Gods of old, my Gods, of Joseph, of Judah Maccabee, of Saul and David and Solomon. Of them all, Joseph entranced me the most, because he was the one who could read dreams. He could spare a people and save a nation. Without realizing it before now, and after all the moments and years, I was slowly becoming a believer. Though I never learned the prayers my grandfather muttered while pacing back and forth, and back and forth again across the dining room floor, I too felt I could place that shawl over my shoulders and give myself over to the chant of the prayer. What is truly hard about God and God believers is faith. Do I believe my grandfather was with me on that plane over the Atlantic, or at the Wailing Wall? Now I believe. Then I was just beginning.

---

On the last day of his service to us the colonel brought us to Vad Yashem, a museum dedicated to the Holocaust. My wife and children went one way while I took my solitary route amongst the cases. I stopped at one filled with the remnants of someone's life; I saw a tattered prayer book in the case, a pair of glasses, a cigarette holder, a purple velvet bag with a prayer shawl neatly folded inside, its tassels showing. My own captivity came over me once more. I could see Colonel Prilippi, von Polster, Irmgard, none of whom had changed. They were ghosts standing alongside me, along with the ghost of myself. The two men looked grim. Tears came down Irmgard's face. "Lord, forgive us," she whispered. The men were silent, looking down to the floor.

I saw the white-haired prisoner in the Paris May Day Parade with his accusing eyes that withered the crowd.

And suddenly I began to cry. I tried to be quiet, but the cry had already come from me. I turned my head, leaned my forehead on the case, and sobbed. I could see the colonel look around the corner and withdraw, leaving me alone, until I was through.

What prayers could I have said? Are there any written to match the immensity of human degradation? I was unprepared for this feeling, and it ruptured into my soul. Now, in one moment, I could understand that picture of my mother's father recovering from his near death—lying in bed, gaunt, a bandage around his head where he had been struck with the stock of a Cossack rifle. I had seen the picture as a little boy and had tried to understand the story. It was beyond me then, because of the cruelty and inhumanity it suggested. But these had only been words to me then, and no word could match the single deep feeling of despair that covered me now.

As I looked from case to case with their heartbreaking, ghostly contents, it was not hard to see how the soldiers who gathered these items might have seen them as so much flotsam, the way my broken chronometer must have appeared, hanging by one nail from a wall in a room. That had been just an ordinary room in a makeshift hospital, in a little town called Goeppingen, about forty minutes from Stuttgart. Yet in that room a young soldier had died, a life had been changed forever, and a love had been given, a love I have carried in my heart for over sixty years. Someone must have entered that room after I left it, after I left Irmgard forever, and someone must have taken that broken chronometer from the wall and tossed it away. How insignificant an item it would have seemed.

Yet it, like the pairs of spectacles in the cases before me, or the booties a child had worn once, held the bonds of remembrance, of love and need. And what had to overwhelm anyone who gazed upon these piles of booties and spectacles and bags and buttons was the way that they, so vividly and startlingly, became heaps of unfulfilled need, of torn away love, of ripped away remembrance—everything that makes for the adhesion between two people, among a family, in a neighborhood. A man had once worn these spectacles as he sat down to read; a mother had placed these shoes gently around her child's tiny foot. They were now a heap of objects, open to any viewer.

The ovens had burned and the German people had smelled the suffocating smell of lives burned away, of human disintegration— the flesh burned away but the soul alive and vibrant, even then. What were they thinking, those men and women who stood silently on the sidelines? And the executioners, the men and women going home to their wives and husbands—what were they thinking? I knew a little of that desperate time, waiting to die by a bullet or a knife or a rope. I had known my odds as a flyer, the likelihood of never returning home to that brick row house in South Philadelphia, where my mother was knitting and my father sat reading the paper. And in my fear my heart had chilled to slowness. I vowed I would not let my captors have any satisfaction by my death. I looked through them, by them. I looked through them, into eternity.

Back then, during my captivity, I did not know the extent of the atrocities. The full measure was only revealed later, after my freedom. I was as shocked as the rest of the world was, and one day, in Miami Beach, I sat in my room looking over the quiet beach and the ocean, the waves quietly rising and receding. And I thought of Irmgard. Had she known? I took out Irmgard's letters and read them. I did not see a Nazi in her, and I did not see an impostor. There had been men in the hospital who would have killed me on sight. Still, I saw no Nazis. I saw an Air Force German officer who saved our lives. I saw Germans who could be Nazis as they were whipping themselves up to a killing frenzy as Goebbels spoke.

I was a different person after my experience at Vad Yashem. Seeing Irmgard had awakened a force in me, an intensity I had not believed possible. A universe had shifted; a strange new frightening feeling swam inside me. Later, in the hotel room, I felt a powerful estrangement, like the feelings I had had when I saw the Etruscan paintings deep in the earth, when the red burned like a fever in my body. In those pictures, in the Etruscan graves not far from Rome, a death was happening; you could feel the dread of it, the inevitable press of it; but now something new could come into existence in me.

I attended the last meetings of the Psychoanalytical Society in Jerusalem, but I no longer heard what was being said, for I was doing my days, my nights with Irmgard again. The cafés in Jerusalem reminded me of Paris and Giselle—the gaiety, the noise, the people, the energy. But finally it was too much noise, and I chose to be in quieter placer. In Tel Aviv we visited an art gallery and we bought some ancient pieces; one was the face of a woman that was so like Irmgard I bought it immediately. It came with papers authenticating it as first century piece. To me it did not matter.

The betrayal I had girded for came one night at dinner; the destruction of academic freedom was condoned to the tune of page after page of doublespeak, the same language that politicians use. Analytic politicians are no different from those in my country or any country. Nothing matters but staying in power, accumulating more power. They forget one thing: they do not control the universe, the universal law. I thought of these colleagues no longer as such; they seemed to me like the Roman legions besieging Masada—except I knew they would not have the satisfaction of victory, not in the end; even for the Romans it was a Pyrrhic victory.

After this Irmgard was on my mind constantly for a long time. My wife asked me what was wrong. I said nothing. I felt I could not explain, or perhaps I did not want to.

---

Several years went by. We resumed our lives, our work, now undermined by the shattering disappointment with psychoanalysis. I understood how my Uncle Alex had felt when the ideals he believed in so fervently were destroyed by the viciousness and lies of Joseph Stalin. It had taken him years to reconcile that betrayal and loss....

---

Things at home had been strained enough already—before, during and after our time in Jerusalem. One day, years later, as I sat in my office listening to a patient, the thought came to me as a free association, in response to the patient's associations. It came simply and quietly: I no longer loved my wife.

By the time the children reached their early teens, I decided to leave. There was no other woman that captured my heart. There was only the feeling that I could not endure this placidity. The marriage had become dull, my life gray. Only work and the fearful challenge that was alive and desperate for me. And in these hours and desolate states of mind I could talk to no one. It was my own journey. I might have chosen this quiet path and gone into old age that way, except I could not. Perhaps it was not the dream I dreamt. It wasn't. I let it come into me fully.

The house was no longer filled with love the way it had been before; the pool lay unused, day after day, and I no longer felt that our garden—this dream garden with every flower in the world in it, or so it seemed—was a place of solace for me. To leave was a heartbreaking decision, one that breaks my heart still. Carolyn knew there was nothing she could do. There was nothing anyone could do. The children would be all right; it was better for them to be living in the truth of the situation than to be living the lie of Carolyn and I pretending to be married. By that time I had learned enough from my work to know that holding a marriage together only for the children's sake is wrong. It teaches the children to live unhappily and to endure suffering. And, more than anything, I had my eye upon the mountain. No woman could have competed with that.

I left without great fuss, and after our divorce, my wife and I maintained a good relationship. I think we respect each other. I thought simply, I have married and loved a gentile woman, and had children with her. I have also divorced this woman. Mine was the first divorce in the family. I did not ask my parents about the first issue and I did not ask them about the second. My mother did not question me about either—my mother, who had seen her son go through so many things. I recalled my mother as she was that wintry day in 1938 during my first visit home from college. I sat in our living room watching the snow drop onto the trees outside as she knit a sweater for me, looking up at me from time to time, knitting a sweater I knew would cover me with all the love that went into the making of it, every stitch. I was her hope for everything in this new land to which she came with anxiety and fear. I was her hope.

---

When I drove back to my office after hearing the judge declare me divorced, I cried. I think later I was crying my wife's tears and my tears and my children's tears. I cried for my wife and for me. I cried for the end of things, as I used to cry when my mother did not have a penny to give me. That had been the end of things, seemingly the end of hope. I had felt the same way when Jack died, and when I said goodbye to Irmgard and to Giselle. Now another childhood dream was gone.

So I rented an apartment in Santa Monica and came home to that, feeling old and tired. Another combat fatigue had overcome me. I had to begin again and I was no longer young. I had lost my wife and my faith in the discipline I had trained for, had spent years practicing. No, my mind was not sluggish. I went over it carefully. No, I had not lost faith in psychoanalysis, but I had lost faith in the men practicing this discipline. They could all have been shoemakers. They had merely plastered a superficial imago of the analyst, their analyst, on top of everything. It did not work. I had a series of dreams that helped me over these terrible moments of distress. These were little stabs of pain which pricked at me endlessly. In my dream I was thinking, can I go on? Will I? Must I?

A voice said in my ear, "Allow yourself time to rest. You will find the true answer. The divine flows through you. You are not complete on this earth. There is much sharing to come through you and to be given back unto you. Relax within yourself, find yourself important enough. What will occur? The divine in you will flow freely. Put all of those things on individual lives."

There was no one to tell the dream to. I wrote it down and kept it to look at from time to time as a manna, as substance, as a miracle such as I had been part of during the war. I could not distinguish the voice. Was it a man or a woman? Was it Irmgard coming to help me as she once had?

The dream, beyond the strength and wisdom, the dream is the greatest of gifts. It was Joseph who used this gift wisely, who forgave his brothers, who reigned wisely and benignly, caring for all the people. It was Joseph who left the seed in my heart. I understand now that that seed was nurtured by a German nurse who had a love of justice in her heart. I understand too that if we do not heed the great information given to us through dreams, we shall forego the opportunity to wrest new knowledge from our hearts and minds. As in the past, all of mankind's riches have come from his unconscious. There can be no doubt that psychoanalysis is the true discipline of spirituality. No one who has worked with dreams can fail to see the wondrous symmetry, the wondrous knowledge that lies in the unconscious, as well as the unconscious fear to become acquainted with that knowledge and use it. That fear is also wondrous.

And then, after so many years, I was finally able to see the meaning of my two women: Irmgard as the beauty of my soul, wanting eternally to do service, to love the poor and the suffering, and Giselle as the body, prized and enjoyed, for she carried the vitality of life, the physical joy of life. They were partners who nourished me ever and always and will continue to do so, replenishing my heart, my physical being with vibrancy and health. Both are what God has sent to me in this lifetime to encourage my faith, to test my patience, to sustain my hope, to increase my charity. These were not accidents. There are no accidents.

# 14

Hamburg, Germany, 1985

*I* went back to find Irmgard when I was sixty-five years old. It had been forty years since those nights in the hospital room when she took my pulse in the dark, when her eyes glimmered in the glow of the flashlight as she passed through the room. At sixty-five a great deal in my life had been cleaned up and simplified. I was no longer the callow youngster I had been during the war. I no longer had the wild impulses that had possessed me then. Life had sorted many things out for me, and I had long ago given up the idea of the intensity of love I had felt for the German nurse. I was divorced from my wife, but we remained friendly. I saw my children, and had wonderful times with them. And I worked, feeling alone in my profession, as if all the old models had failed me, forcing me to forge my own way to a vision of the unconscious that included the idea of a soul.

It was in this respite that one day my thoughts were stirred to Irmgard, and I took down the letters which I kept in the library, in plain view of everyone, in a simple folder. There they lay untouched by anyone except myself, the only one for whom they could possibly have any meaning. It was she, I knew, who had given me the life I had chosen. It was she who had led me to think, once more, of things like soul and God and love.

I touched the letters, slipped one out of the envelope, and read the small neat handwriting on the lined paper. Suddenly the words meant more than I had imagined, and I seriously turned my attention to one letter and then the others. Who was this woman who had spoken to me so simply, and who had begun a movement of my soul that would lead me to have the life I did? This beautiful girl who had shown me something of the heart of the German people, and who had shown me something of what is possible in this world, even in the most dire of circumstances? And I knew, suddenly, that I had to find her again, after all these years—not because I wanted to consummate an aborted love, but because my curiosity raged within me and drew me on. I longed to know something of her life. I longed to know again that sharing of heart and soul.

---

I returned again and again to Irmgard's letters. It had always been difficult for me to read them, even when she first wrote them to me. Then, I had had to sit alone in the bathroom, reading slowly, carefully. But by now I had almost memorized the letters; I knew the topics, I knew the phrases, so charming in their syntactical errors, and I could always see her in front of me, as if not even one day had passed, though the envelopes had become dryer and the writing on the pages paler.

So, when the announcement came in March 1985 that the International Psychoanalytic Association was to hold its meeting in Hamburg, Germany, in the last week of July and first days of August, I realized that this was my chance. Hamburg was Irmgard's city. She had come from Hamburg, and I thought she might have returned to her family or whatever was left for her after the war.

Was Irmgard still alive now, forty years later? What had become of her? I reasoned that she would most likely be alive, as she was younger than I. I enlisted the aid of a German friend, who helped me place an announcement in one of the German newspapers. I thought that perhaps Irmgard, or at least one of her friends or family members, might see this. I included a picture of myself taken in 1945 in my officer's uniform, and also a more current one.

I received nothing, except many phone calls from reporters who wanted to know which famous Hollywood stars I was analyzing. When

I had no comments, these calls soon stopped. I enlisted the help of another friend of German descent whose immediate family had come from Hamburg. I'm very grateful to these friends, for there were leads, and their friends in Hamburg were able to follow up on them. I discovered that von Polster lived in the area, and that the members of that hospital unit still met yearly to celebrate their old comradeship. This extended to the wives and, I imagined, to the children.

I was impatient to get to Hamburg, and soon enough I was there, staying at a very fine hotel across from the Alster, a beautiful lake large enough to have a boat circling it, and beside the lake a park. I met with the friends, who were excited because they were about to get the phone number of Mrs. von Polster. There was also news from another woman who had either been a nurse or an administrator at that hospital. Finally, through my friend, I was able to speak on the phone with Mrs. von Polster, who at first only asked, what does he want? But then she said her husband had died only a month before, that he had been a highly regarded physician, and a kind and generous man.

I said I was very sorry, and that, too, was my experience of him when I was a prisoner; that I had wanted merely to see and talk with him. I was extremely saddened by von Polster's death, but his widow seemed fearful that I might bring charges against her husband even at this late date. She did not believe I had come in friendship, and so was not willing to meet with me in person. The most she was willing to do was send a woman to meet me at the hotel lobby, and to give me some documents. This woman had been associated with the Goeppingen group but she did not know me, though she had known of me. Nothing could change Mrs. von Polster's mind.

All of this happened during the pre-congress meetings attended by training analysts. I attended some of these meetings, but my mind and heart were elsewhere. I took walks in the park, I rode the boat around the lake, deeply lost in nostalgia and sadness. Why could von Polster not have lived one month more? Everything might have been different if he had, and surely he would have known of Irmgard. So far I had heard nothing of her at all. The meetings had ceased to have any interest for me. The congress arranges tours in conjunction with the meetings, and so I toured Hamburg, and I liked its vigor. On one trip we drove by the ocean. On another tour we passed the great houses of the wealthy businessmen who live on the Alster. These houses exuded comfort and security, orderliness. Indeed, in many ways Hamburg itself was a city of order, and lacked the slight edge of shamble that Los Angeles has.

---

I spent the rest of the days at my hotel, constantly checking my mailbox for messages. I did not know what to think: why did I get no response? Surely a friend or family member or even Irmgard herself had to have seen my ad. Surely they would have let her know about it, if she herself did not read the papers—I thought that it would be strange for her not to read them, however, because she had been so knowledgeable. The sort of person who would keep up with events. Moreover, the entire city knew about the convention. Not that Irmgard would have known that I had become a psychoanalyst, but the campaign I waged was enough in the public eye.

Daily I grew more despairing and more bewildered. It helped that the woman sent by Mrs. von Polster appeared and handed me a list of names I might try contacting—but she offered nothing more. I became morose. Soon my stay in Hamburg would be over.

One morning there was a knock on the door, and the bellboy handed a packet to me. I tipped him and sat down to open the manila envelope, which was wider than long. It seemed to be a sketchbook, and as I flipped through the pages that small hospital in Goeppingen once again came to life before my eyes: the nurses walking in groups down the road in their aprons and blue dresses, the wounded soldiers with bandaged arms and missing legs and crutches, the shaded portico I had been just able to see from my window above, the tree branches dangling over it.

I turned page after page. As I turned the last page, I saw a trio on a stage. Piano, bass, and a woman standing with a flute in her hand. *Irmgard.*

There was no name or address on the envelope, and when I inquired at the front desk, the concierge said only that a woman had left it. He could not describe the woman, and she had left no name with him, nor address, nor phone number. To this day I know nothing more than that.

I took this to be a sign. A sign that I have kept within me for all these years and turned into a memoir so that it will be there for everyone to see. Again and again I returned to this page. I feared that if I left the book in the room, it would be thrown away by a zealous maid. I hid the book, only to take it out and review it again and again, turning each page to see what her life at the hospital had been like. It was a different world from the one I had seen from my window. I could see her in the garden the artist had drawn. Had she ever played her flute there? Had she ever thought of me while staring at the bright flowers, the slim trees? I could see her on the front steps, talking with a group of young nurses, or in the hospital rooms, folding bandages, or sewing. I could see her in front of me, as if not one day had passed. It was her world in the pictures, and I felt the pain and the loss of all the things I never knew.

I closed my eyes and I could see Irmgard again, and hear the piping sounds of her flute. Was she close by me, even then? Had she played the flute even as an old woman, in those quiet hours of the afternoon? I remembered my touching her hands, and I replayed all those ancient scenes which left me immersed in nostalgia, in sadness and sweetness. It was the beauty of a rose pressed between the sheets of a beloved book, the petals now dry and flaking with just a wisp of smell left, the smell of a love never consummated and never lost.

---

I returned to Hamburg a few years later, alone, to the Kenpiski Atlantic; I had no wish to stay at any other hotel. The unprepossessing entrance from the side street led to the front desk, and beyond that was the most comfortable lobby in the world for me. The lobby was relatively quiet, filled with leather chairs and settees with little tables by their sides; everything was comfort. The light was just right, and we could read or sit with a drink or a cigar or cigarette. The help was attentive and especially polite, but not aggressive. I usually sat early in the morning to read the newspaper. There seems to be an especial pleasure in reading the Herald Tribune away from the States, and I had read it in nearly all the big cities of Europe. After Hamburg, I most enjoyed reading the paper in Florence, Italy, in an outside café in the sunlight, enjoying a coffee and croissant. Here, however, at the opposite end of Europe, I enjoyed the morning thusly. One of the great attractions for me was the Alster across the street, and I spent many hours sitting on the benches in front of it, and walking. Sometimes I would take the white boat for a trip around the lake.

This was an endless pleasure for me, looking at the park or the city skyline or the rich, comfortable houses the shipping tycoons had built years before. The rich always have it in their means to be comfortable, and there's always a difference between countries in how they do it or how they enjoy it. I could imagine that the Hamburg gentry were very different from the Tuscan gentry; the sun mellows everything, and here in the north it remained cool even in summer, never sweltering the way it does in the Tuscan valley or in the French or Italian city. That alone was a great comfort to me, for the heat always enervated me.

Here in Hamburg I was energized. It seemed the smell of the ocean was always in the air and here on the shores of the Alster I took out my letters from Irmgard once again—sometimes one at a time, sometimes two—and sat reading them, afterwards folding them carefully and putting them back in their small packet. I imagined every word she wrote, and I brought to mind the moment I first saw her in the air raid shelter: slim, dark-haired, with red-tinted cheeks, indrawn but strong. She was one of those women who appear slight yet from them comes an extraordinary fullness and firmness. I imagined the exchange with Resi, the attractive blonde nurse of whom Irmgard disapproved. I savored in my mind that first look from Irmgard, the recognition between souls—for I have been told that when this occurs it portends shared past lives. Of course I have no memory of such, but I like that meaning and I feel there is no harm in believing this. How else can one explain the way strangers can meet and feel at home with each other at once?

I re-read her lines, "You smiled at me, I had a deep joy and why should I not tell it to you," and stopped reading; after a while I realized I was smiling at her again. Luckily no one was there to contemplate this odd American. And she repeats it, I filled her heart with joy.

I would sometimes read Irmgard's letters under the arcade looking out at the Rathaus. I admired the Gothic columns and, beyond them, a wide expanse. In front of me and in back were rows of small tables for two, a custom long entertained here as it is elsewhere in Europe, so that people can come together and talk. All of this has come late to America, but then we are a young country and a young people and we are exuberant with our opportunities. Here and elsewhere many people have already triumphed and left behind legacies of their struggles. The race is long and because they have realized this they pace themselves better than we do. And always I thought of Irmgard, and her writing down to the best of her memory, "They also serve who only stand and wait."

There was a strangeness in my feeling, being in her city over forty years after the war, without her. I do not doubt that she, too, had been to the Alster or to the Rathaus, where I ate dinner with a friend of my German friend in Los Angeles. Or to the canals in the area and the arcade, which reminded me of Venice with its many shops.

I do not doubt it at all: I know she walked these stones, put her hands on the iron bridge over the water, and shopped in the arcade before sitting to have some cake or sweet with tea or coffee. That was also a great joy to me, sitting there in the coffee shop with its smell of fresh baked goods. I would sit and watch the ladies, mostly ladies naturally, middle-aged women much like the kind who frequent the coffee shops at Neiman-Marcus, meeting their friends or their daughters.

Not too many young women here; I imagined they had their favorite rendezvous elsewhere, for there were many "elsewheres" in this rich old city that did not bustle the way New York or Tokyo did. Here at least there was a hint of decorum. I could see Irmgard in this coffee shop; it would have suited her. I liked the water everywhere; it gave me a feeling of cleanliness, everything clean and everything smelling so fresh. I imagined that Irmgard had been one of those people who, even on the Russian front, with mud everywhere, was always crisp. Somehow these people seem to have a secret.

And sitting in that coffee shop one afternoon, I noticed a woman enter. There was something about her carriage that struck me, something about her proud bearing that made me sit up and stare. It was hard to tell her age, but she was probably in her fifties or sixties. Her hair was thick and black, with only a hint of gray, and she had a matronly slimness that betokened children but also spoke of a woman who prized her appearance. Her eyes were dark. Her olive skin had a rosy tint to it. My heart beat faster. She had not quite looked at me— no reason for that. My eyes followed her as she ordered her coffee and cake. She sat down. I did not wish to stare, so I looked at her casually from time to time, but I was careful to show myself to her.

She sat down and sipped her coffee slowly. If this were Irmgard, she would not fail to recognize me, I thought, and I waited for her to look up. I imagined this woman was a mother, indeed a grandmother, and perhaps the wife of a well-to-do person, maybe a doctor. This seemed a woman who lived her life in great order, in comfort and in pleasure, and I watched the way she bit into her cake, enjoying each bite. How good life can be, she seemed to be saying; for now that I have overcome all the mountains, and all the storms, I have earned this one simple joy.

When my eyes met hers there was no recognition, no startle, just a look of interest at this foreigner quietly pursuing his day. I did not feel too badly. Perhaps, after everything, it was enough just to be here in her city, learning more of her life with every step.

Still, I watched the woman finish her coffee, and then after a few moments, get up and leave. Perhaps she was going home to prepare dinner; perhaps there was a husband, and children and grandchildren, waiting for her to return. Perhaps she liked to drink coffee on some afternoons when she had a moment to herself, and remember all those who had loved her, throughout her life. I was happy to think this, and it pleased me to find myself here, exploiting my taste buds and eyes and nose and ears—all my senses were enhanced, for I felt I was breathing air that Irmgard also breathed, somewhere in this handsome city, near the parks, near the ocean, or near the beautiful Alster with its Thomas Mann burgher houses running around one side of it.

The air was invigorating, as if it were touched by Irmgard, touched by love and its life-giving impulse, ever refreshing the body and the soul.

I wandered her city. I took out a letter and read, "If you wish to see yourself, you must go far away to yourself through my soul." And I thought that I had gone far away to her soul, to her city. I spent my days, which passed quickly, trying to come to some equanimity about her, whether I was on the white boat circling the lake or in the arcades or on the benches surrounded by trees, grass, flowers, and the water dotted with white sailboats that reminded me of the paintings that Raoul Dufy would create in the south of France. Were we dreaming in the midst of this terrible war, from which terrible secrets would issue? The feeling had been known only to her and to me. She said *it is wonderful to go somewhere in the darkness and as slowly it grows light, your foot finds more and more little place to go on. Is this not how it is when one heart explores another and finds firmer places to step?*

I imagined our standing by the bridge over the canal and I wished to encircle her—yet I'm not sure she would have been comfortable with this, though she may have yearned for it—and to look into her face, ignoring those strolling by. I was not aware of the young couples doing exactly that on the bridge, drinking each other in as, it seems, only the young and the smitten can do. I was no longer young but that did not stop me from going off with my arm around her waist or her hand in mine. "I wish to be pure and innocent for the man I love," she had said.

How odd a juxtaposition: the people around me laughing, unaware of me, my feelings and thoughts, and I reminiscing with a legend, for to me, Irmgard, you have become that and will always be that. And I recalled your saying, "I have just read precious poems of love and I wish that you might know these poems." Out of all the men you had met, all you had taken care of, I was the one you gave your heart to and you betrayed that in the ways you touched me, in the way you played your flute for me, in the way your eyes filled and softened when you saw me, and I have no doubt that mine did the same.

I grew accustomed to the park; I had no wish to see other parts of Hamburg. I enjoyed the pathways, the sidewalks and the long walks in the late afternoon—walking, walking in the sunlight, in the shade, in the dank places where the sun could not penetrate the smell of earth, of trees, of leaves, of flowers, all there in one heady flush of aroma, and there, out on the lake, one could see a few sailboats enjoying one last turn before heading in.

And I too was enjoying one last turn, trying to set my heart at rest, thinking that I had made a mistake in not coming back sooner to find her.

I do not know if I shall ever return to Hamburg. It does not matter. I do not have to read Irmgard's letters anymore. They are in my heart.

# 15

Los Angeles, 1990

"Can I sit down there?"

The young man pointed to an empty seat. I nodded. I was attending a gift show at the convention center, supporting a friend who had recently opened a business. The young man sat down. I was drinking a cup of coffee from a paper cup, slowly, resting. There were so many people about, and I felt tired. I could feel his eyes on me, assessing me. He wore a badge indicating he was an exhibitor.

I was silent, then he said, "You look like you've seen everything."

"I've seen a few things," I agreed.

"Have you ever been in a war?"

I wondered at this turn of conversation, but simply nodded.

"Oh yeah? Which one?"

"World War Two."

"Was that in 1946?"

"No," I said, "1941."

"When did it end?"

"1945."

"Oh, my father was born in 1946. Is that the war when the Japanese bombed Pearl Harbor?"

I nodded.

"And what did you do?"

I said, "I flew in bombers in Europe."

"Oh, the Hitler guy?"

"Yeah," I said, "him."

"Did you bomb people?"

"I'm afraid I did."

"Did you see them, the people, men and women and children?"

"No," I said, "I did not see them."

"Did you think about it? Did you think about it in the past? Are you thinking about it now?"

"There's no way not to think about it now." As I was saying this, his partner came up and called him. He got up and left.

But I sat there thinking a long time. I did kill men and women and children. The Nazis killed Jewish people and gypsies and homosexuals and communists and whoever they felt got in the way or would get in their way. The fact remained: I killed people. What was the difference? Is there a difference?

I felt sick; I wanted to vomit. It's not that I had not thought about this before, but I had never come to a satisfactory answer. Could not Irmgard have said, You too have killed innocent people? No, she would not have said that. And it was not the same. The Nazis had started their purging, now called crimes against the people, ethnic cleansing. They had made gods of themselves, deciding who should live and who should die. No, it was not the same. Still, I felt the shame and the guilt more deeply than ever before. Perhaps because I have become less defended, more vulnerable.

And how would the story have turned out if Hitler had had a mother who loved him? Or Goebbels, Himmler, Goering, and all the rest? But that is what our job is in this time, in this new age; it is this that makes the transition to the twenty-first century so exciting, because all things must change.

Around this time I had a dream. I see a superhero who disposes of evil men and their images. These evil men have full plates. The superhero has an almost empty plate. At a certain signal the plates are emptied, and the evil men are vanquished. And I thought: I will leave my fears at the doorway of the past. Yes, I will step forward, knowing that what I am sharing here is, above all, the wisdom of the divine. Therefore, I will be able to set it out in this world, and it will be utilized by the divine essence of all people, and God will see to it that the right thing happens.

I thought about this dream for a very long time. There was no one to tell it to, and I had no wish to do that. No analyst thought or was thinking the way I was beginning to think, and though I was in the deepest of darkness, there was also coming in the veriest bit of light—in flashes, and instants.

I remembered Joseph. I remembered all the kings and emperors and their soothsayers, and the oracle in Delphi—all capable of looking into the future, predicting the future with great accuracy. I remembered the king, deciding whether to invade Carthage, being told by the soothsayer—Freud relates the story—"Tyre shall be thine." And so the city fell to the invading king. I thought of my life, the wonder of it, and I felt a falling away of fear, of dread.

# 16

## Closure: China, 1995

*I*n 1995 I went to China. I had never been there. I knew the Fu Man Chu movies, Anna May Wong with whom I fell in love at the age of eight. I knew later about the Japanese invasion and their massacre of the Chinese people, later still the revolution and General Claire Chennault. I always remember Jack's plea, "Let's go to China and fly and fight for the people." Jack was a good guy at heart despite his life with very well-to-do circumstances.

Many years had passed since Jack's death, so when my friend Tom suggested I go to China, that it was important for me to go, I decided to do so. Tom was a Chinese man who I had met at a party, a journalist for the local Chinese newspaper. He said he was a Buddhist and followed the way of the Buddha.

Since I had no obligations except my practice, I decided to take six weeks to spend in China. Tom arranged a guide, a man in Beijing who met me at the airport. He spoke English tolerably well. I spoke no Chinese. I trusted my friend who said, "Don't worry. Zhu will take care of everything." And this Zhu did. So I saw the Great Wall, the Emperor's summer palace, Wushi, Shanghai, Xian, the Erme mountains with the many monkeys that are friendly and perch upon your head. We ate with a monk in a temple and I was privileged to see the huge golden Buddha kept in a special prayer room.

Xian was spectacular with its soldiers and horses made of clay, silent witnesses to a time we in the West know little about. All was astonishing, especially the incredible amount of people in Beijing and Shanghai, day and night, like unceasing waves of the ocean coming at you and over you.

At the end he took me to see the Buddhist who was the leader of the people in Beijing and perhaps elsewhere. We went to a nondescript house, walked to the third floor, and seemed to traverse a number of houses making turns. I followed closely for I knew I would never find my way out alone. The Buddhist leader, the Abbot, a man who looked about sixty, sat in a room decorated with Chinese scrolls, candles and statues. He was dressed simply in pants, shirt, a saffron robe and a red sash that ran diagonally across his body. He looked comfortable.

I sat next to him. He looked at me and I at him. I wondered why my friend Tom felt I needed to be here. After a long silence, the Abbot looked at my face intently and picked up my left hand, which he turned over to look at the palm and then let go. My guide interpreted the Abbot's words.

"You were poor when young."

I nodded.

"You worked hard all your life."

I nodded.

"You have been in a great war."

Again, I nodded.

"You are a hero."

I said "Yes," and thought, "So he's a psychic."

Zhu translated, "You are not with a woman, you are divorced and have two children, a girl and a boy."

I nodded and thought, "How the hell can he know all that?"

The guide continued: "He says you have a lot of work to do. You have not yet found the way. You will."

I shrugged my shoulders. Zhu went on translating.

"Much has been done against you unfairly. It is all complicated but it will pass. You think about two women. They are both dead now. They are from the war. You still feel bad. You do not understand."

I said, "Yes, true, how does he know this? No one knows this."

Zhu shrugged his shoulders. "He just knows that, and he is doing Tom a favor to see you." Zhu continued to translate the holy man's words.

"You meet people that's arranged long ago before you came here. Each woman helped you. That did not mean you had a future with them. It is what they promised, although you do not recall. Your recalling is not important. They're helping you with your karma. They were paying you back for past lives, for past things you had done for them. Now you are in balance. Nothing more to do. Later if you want and they want you will meet again. That is not your concern now. It is finished."

The Abbott paused and then went on, Zhu translating. "Be careful. There is an accident in your future. Wear this," and the Abbott gave me a talisman strung on a red string to wear on my wrist. We were silent. There was nothing else to say or ask. It seemed he summed up my life.

I asked Zhu, "One thing before we leave, ask him will there be another woman in my life?"

The Abbot answered almost immediately, all this in Chinese. "Yes, later, a Chinese woman."

And that was all. Maybe that was why Tom felt it was so important for me to go to China to see the Abbot.

*A few years later I did have an accident that almost killed me. I did not think it was because I stopped wearing the bracelet. I wore it for about a year and then like most things I no longer used, I did not put it on. Do I think my accident occurred because I stopped wearing the bracelet? I don't know. Maybe and maybe not. The bracelet lay for a number of years in my bureau with many other trinkets I had gathered.*

*Less than ten years later I did get remarried, astonishingly to a traditional and gracious Chinese woman whose family roots go back to Xian, home of the first Chinese Dynasty.*

*I found out later that the Abbot was the Abbot of Fang Zhong monastery in Chifang, Mongolia. His name was Dan Jiong.*

The information the Abbot had given me was unsettling. There was no time to ask more questions. That was clear. He had told me what I needed to know and that with brevity so when he stood up, we did, and he clasped his hands like Chinese do, one hand enclosed with the other meaning "my good wishes to you."

When I began to ask Zhu about the information he said, "Look, all I can do is repeat what he said. I have no ideas any more deeply. I hope you do in the light of your life and what you know of your life." I saw there was no point in badgering him for information he did not have. We went on to do other things and finally it was time to go back to Los Angeles.

On the flight back I thought about the idea of karma. Americans are not really acquainted with these ideas, though we know the word. The meaning it has for us, I thought, was shallow if meaningful at all in contrast to what it might mean to an Asian or an Indian.

Past lives? How does one get information about that? Certainly not in the Library of Congress or the *Encyclopedia Britannica*, although there might be erudite articles written about the concept. But what use is that if you want to know about you? The thought came to me as the plane flew effortlessly through the sky, maybe it was what I was trying to ascertain when I looked into the mirror as a boy of twelve and asked who was I and where is that essence to be found.

What the Abbot said made everything more complex and more understandable. Past lives meant with other people, maybe with other cultures and what was the use of all this? I know some people think you just live and die. There is no meaning to life or death except you do not exist. If that were true, why are humans trying to extract the meaning of most everything in the sensible world and people of spirituality trying to sort out the immaterial world?

And how does a person like the Abbot attain this knowledge of someone not Chinese? It was all too confusing, and to add to the confusion was this prediction of a Chinese wife. Why? My circle of friends were almost all Caucasian. Another mystery.

I did recall that when I was first enveloped by Beijing in what seemed to be a hundred thousand people on the street and ten thousand bicycles moving, I felt quite at home. I should have been overwhelmed.

But I could go no further with these questions. Later I thought I would ask my friend Tom to help me. I knew he would since he had known I should see the Abbot and had arranged it for me. There was a lot more to him than I imagined. He was a friendly Chinese newspaper man who introduced me to many Chinese restaurants in Monterey Park, Alhambra, San Gabriel…all of which I liked and frequented. That would be my game plan, to talk to Tom.

There was still Irmgard and Giselle, still a little disquiet after fifty years, after a marriage and divorce, children, after a professional life with less life ahead than behind me. I was not worried about dying. My health was relatively good. After the war, death was never a fear for me.

What I wanted was to be at peace with those two women. Could I believe the Abbot? To believe was to come to realize an eternal continuation of what we call spirit or soul, for certainly the body ages and weakens. The diminishments come with surprise and yet with an "Oh, so that's what it's like." No longer to have that wonderful balance, to have instead a neuroma in your foot. I have two of them that makes walking difficult. Unfair. I loved walking all my life.

Could I believe that in some prior incarnation….there, I said it to myself….I helped these two women? Were they both in my life at the same time, different times? Were they Chinese? Was I?

My mind went to the sudden appearance of the German air force officer when we were being taken as prisoners of war. That was a miracle. Was he repaying me for what I had once done for him in a forgotten human past? I know people might say, "Coincidence." Was it a coincidence that the absolutely true heading came to me so that we could land in Iceland? Who put that number into my mind?

There was only one answer left. There must be a soul, and everyone must have a soul, and someplace beyond their knowing there is a tally; else why would the Abbot say of the two women, "They promise to help you in this lifetime"? Who did they promise? Me directly, or something on earth called the divine?

It seems to be man's proclivity to decimate everything, to degrade everything, to make everything meaningless by blowing things up or misusing them; yet even those maneuvers have not diminished the luminescence of the concept that there is a force that coheres, that regenerates, that promotes love, that is unknowable in our human form and only known indirectly by our unconscious minds. Yes, I could buy that, because I have analyzed many dreams of patients whose development brought them to this deeper knowing; and also, I know this from my own dreams.

Flying back from China I felt I could lay to rest the disquiet that had been there a long time and I wondered why, if there was a prediction of work for me to do which said surely I would be alive to do it, why did I need to suffer so much? Why suffer at the hands of mean and jealous people who wanted to hurt me? Through a war, fighting from an airplane where you could get maimed or killed, and your body was prematurely aged by the constant barrage of hormones needed to keep going at your level best, because your life depended on it?

I could not answer this question and many others, not yet. I did fall asleep on the flight and I slept deeply.

# 17

Los Angeles, June 2002

*I*t's been fifty-seven years since the war ended, since I knew Giselle, and Irmgard, since I began my medical training that long-ago September. It all happened a lifetime ago, but these moments, all of these moments, stay with me and have a presence and clarity that sometimes take me aback, still. My days are peaceful now; I long ago rid myself of the rage that tormented me when I returned from Europe, when I might have killed a man for offending me with his words. At times I sit in the garden outside my house, in quietness, and I look out at the colorful banks of flowers: impatiens, begonias, roses, and the western sycamore, which always reminds me of the ones I loved while growing up. The park across from my grandmother's house in South Philadelphia was filled with sycamores. The park that contained so much history: my brothers, his friends, my friends, the card playing, the joking. I can see and hear all of it. Young faces, hopeful.

The small, graceful fountain shoots up its arc of water and deposits the drops into a pool that ripples endlessly.

Now, in this quiet time, in this bursting garden with the floss silk tree, the Chinese magnolia shrub that flowers purple and white, the ficus and coral trees, the birch—the beautiful slender birch with its flaking white bark, standing in threes, standing alone, aloof, ever a beauty to the eye—all of this is very far from where I have come, from the impoverishment, the noisy streets, the smells of hot knishes, freshly baked challa bread, and red borscht simmering on the stove.

Here in Los Angeles, a star-filled city, I conjure up Seventh Street and wonder: what could ever equal that glamour? There watching the women and their children, and their talking, which gave one suddenly the idea: this is what it means to be a person. This is what it means to be grown up.

See! Look at their faces, their stances. And look at my mother— the most entrancing woman there, both in body and beauty and stance. I know I have had the best, the finest, the truest.

---

The quiet hangs like a lace curtain on a front window. There is no wind today. The sun is not hot. The drops that fall into the pool, splashing and tinkling, give me the impression of musical notes. A perfect Los Angeles day.

Sometimes, even now, I try to do what I used to do as a child on my cousin Etkis's farm, lying under a tree to lose myself, extending my arms and legs, melting into the ground, the grass and the wind. Until there is no me left. I can hear my mother's mandolin. I can hear the notes of the flute, crisp, running swiftly as water runs in a swift flowing brook. And when I enter this vibration of music I could be with Irmgard again in this ineffable state, as once we were together, for one brief moment when our hearts pulsed with love.

---

There seems to be a plan, masterful in design, to teach us that we are fundamentally physical beings—the species must be preserved, and the primacy of the physical has to be established. And since we are more than just physical entities, we add our minds, our perceptions, our capacities to consider the other. Is this the one I want to have children with, the one I enjoy being with, the one I want to make love with and talk with and be with all the rest of my days? That's a hard call, but we make it and we make it with other unconscious factors playing the primary and usually unknown role. And then, it makes sense. Body and mind, mind and body at work. Choosing and being thrilled by the choice. Every trial and error is to bring experience—sometimes happiness, sometimes darkness—but all in all we are to finally learn from all our encounters.

Considering all, there is no doubt of a greater force in the lives of us all. If we can go to a quiet place, if we can sit and reflect, if we can consider the possibility of there being a thing and an everything and a no thing, we can face the ineffable divine, for all of these are in it. So now, fifty-seven years after returning from the war, I can sit and see before me the many marks, the many long pauses, the many rests in the music that makes up a life. I am aware that now, this time, is a period within the rest. I am waiting for the next note of the music to begin. And I'm blessed with my knowledge of the mandolin and the flute.

Our minds are prisoners of our pleasures, which we want to repeat over and over again. We are like children telling their parents, "Read me the story again." So it is with Irmgard. From the first sight. From the first touch, when she took my pulse in the dark. When I put my hand on hers. My noting how sure were her hands. When I looked at her feet and noted how gracefully she walked. Though her uniform hid her form, I always tried to discern the feminine within her, by the gait, the stance, the way she played the flute—once as close to me as this fountain is now. The fingers that took up their stations were sure and nimble. The music evoked happiness in me, and I knew that she, too, was happy.

Irmgard told me how she worried about her wounded soldiers. I could imagine her distress at not being able to help: no more than a touch, a soft word, a prayer. I could imagine her aloneness amidst all these women. She knew she was different from them.

I can see her finally coming toward me, erect and slender, the letters in her hand. She extends her hand, touches my hand as she puts the coffee-colored envelope within. In place of a kiss that couldn't have happened in our circumstances, in our lives—then or ever. There is only this: to know that, in some way, never stopped talking, never stopped wanting to be with each other. When I think of her, I have brought her to life again, and she is as real to me as anyone I might have seen and talked to an hour ago. So Irmgard and I have never stopped being together: she can call me from her being and I can call her forth. We never tire of each other. I know she is my spirit.

261

# IRMGARD'S LETTERS

These are Irmgard's letters to me from March and April, 1945. She kept the letters I wrote her in 1945. I have written these letters to her over the years; this is what I would say to her now, if I could. And I am sure she would understand now, even as she did then.

*I know that it is not allowed to give you this, my conscious. However, it is quiet and I would not do anything bad. You smiled at me, and I had a deep joy, and why should I not tell it to you. But, you must promise to destroy the paper, it would not be difficult for you. You must really promise it, or do you believe that you need not do anything you have promised an enemy?*

*You do not speak well about women, if it really were, and I don't believe your opinion, you also must have bad thoughts about love. I just have read precious poems of love and I wish that you might know these poems. For when a man tells such fine things to or of a woman, the woman must be worth of it, and naturally the man must be too. And when there are such fine thoughts of love, love must be a very precious treasure and nothing we take and throw in the mud.*

*I am not able to translate you the poems for I have lack of the right words. I will only try to translate one, and when you understand the meaning you will guess the high opinion we have of love. You will see its beauty in spite of my bad language.*

*This is the poem:*

*All thoughts which you don't say I know them from you*
*all the pains of which you don't speak, they weep in me*
*long words which painfully listen to say your shy mouth*
*are like the wishes which you sincerely have dreamed*
*strangely known by me.*
*you are living within me with such a great love*
*do you wish to see yourself?*
*You must go to the far away to yourself through my soul.*

*I believe that love is something holy but that one must not speak much about it, one must only feel it. And now in our days it often will be thrown into the mud. I will write of the book I held this morning. The French lady must choose between the German officer's death and the grave danger for her and her country. For when she does not betray him, he will reach his lines in order to shoot upon her castle for military reasons. She talks with a French officer, "You are Frenchman, Claudel." Suppose you love a German woman you have met and have the deepest feeling for, you live from this feeling and war is coming. You belong to the nation, you are obliged to it, you sacrifice your feeling. I would blindly sacrifice it but it is stronger. There is nothing which is stronger than the nation, you are right. There is nothing which might be stronger, only but this one, and so she lets the officer escape. Then I know two little French songs, which I will tell you, are they pretty?*

*You call me your life, you call me your soul*
*I want a word from you that lasts more than one day*
*Life is ephemeral, just a breath blows out its flame*
*But its soul is immortal*
*Just as is love.*

*When one loses through sad occurrence one's hope and gaiety*
*The remedy against melancholia is music and beauty*
*Which obliges more and is more able to put on a good face*

*Than an armband*
*And nothing is better then to hear a soft and tender tune*
*Loved long ago.*

Irmgard, you entrusted to me your innermost thoughts, your heart, which I already knew was a precious gift I had to take care of. I did not have to destroy your words, I gave them back to you, for you to hold. I knew you would. I would have not have dared to say then, when I read the story of the French woman, that you loved me. But if I spoke badly of women then, I can only say I believe I have changed.

Today, when I read the poem you quote, I am more deeply moved and understand better than when I first read the beautiful words. I wonder who is this poet who knew the human heart and mind so well. There is great psychological knowing in this little verse, great wisdom. Each lover says, "Do you wish to see yourself? You must go far away to yourself through my soul." Your two little songs invoke in me a nostalgia that makes me put down my pen.

*I did not understand all of your letter, I must read it again and again to know all you have written. But all I have understood filled my heart with joy. Therefore, I beg your pardon when I not yet give back your letter. At first, I must study it long enough to know, all right? But is it not so that they never would look at my things and find the letters while they perhaps would find it by yours? Why would you have it back? Naturally I should give it to you, but later you must return it, please.*

*I will answer you, you are right, and many things in your letter, but I cannot do it in this night for I cannot be quite absorbed in writing. The soldiers cry with pain and I must hear it without helping and this does not admit me to write quietly. So I only wish to give you a little answer to or how you that I think of the present enemy and understand his longing for freedom and many of his others thoughts, but we all must bear a little bit of the great faith of our country. One more, one less and I believe it to be the same in yours. You must not be sorry that I have had conflicts. I am stupid that I told you of my struggle, nor will I finish talking. I only don't wish to come into the wrong light by letters.*

*Naturally I did not talk when I knew that it caused no joy for you, for I never speak to a man who is bored at the speech who does not like it. I would be ashamed of this running after someone, and please don't forget what you wish to keep you must put under your pillow in the bed. When an alarm begins, then I shall take it out. What you don't wish to keep, you must once do it again, you promise it?*

*Did I keep this poem right in my mind?*

*When I consider how my light it is spent,*
*and half my days in this dark world and wide,*
*and that one talent, which is death to hide lodge with me useless,*
*though my soul more bent to serve there with my maker*
*and present my truth—lest he returning chide, does God exact day labor?*
*Light denied, I fondly asked. Put patience to prevent that murmur soon replies,*
*God does not need either man's work or his own gift.*
 *Who best bear this mild yoke they serve him best, he's kingly.*
*Thousands at his bidding speed and post or land and ocean without rest.*
*They also serve who only stand and wait.*

Dear Irmgard, I must acknowledge today that I no longer recall when I smiled at you, though I think it was in the basement during the air raid, the first day I saw you. In that dim light I felt your call to me and turned to face you and I smiled. I smiled at you because it was a moment that had to be.

Through my captivity I had a glow, an inner one, which might have been visible on my face. You might have seen it. This spiritual love sustained me. I always knew you were there. Men have been sustained by less.

Of all the other matters you write about, I could say the same and I understood now as then what it meant for you to risk writing to me. It told me there was no one among your people to whom you could say these things; you already knew my companions were not people I would share my deepest feelings with.

You quote Milton's sonnet. I might wonder why this poem came to your mind, I might say that Milton was a greatly spiritual man, and earlier, Dante: two great poets of the soul, each drawing his vision of the upper realms and the lower ones.

*The only reason why I'm writing you an essay, you do not do it, maybe that I must think too long to translate my opinions, but it is a very little reason. Sometimes it seems to me that I must be very little proud I doing so, but really it is not truth. And I make vanish these thoughts, but if I knew that you would smile at my efforts and my strange manner I would be deeply hurt. I often try to explain you the reason of which I'm talking with you and I don't know with which intent you wish to talk to me. You have said for personal reason you don't wish to do away my letters and this I cannot explain. I only will tell you what reasons orders me to ask you for doing them away. At first, you know, that it is forbidden and I am sure you never would do it in my situation. Second, I do not speak about these questions to all people, I know I'm different from them, with all my soul, I am by somewhat obliged to speak to you about these things, but I often think if it has a use (if it's useful to do it) for you too are quite different from me. You may not understand my wishes, my striving, you may be sarcastic at them. Perhaps you may anyway later tell with other Americans from the German woman. You may show them my letters, you all will laugh at them or discuss about them. I would freeze in thinking of it when you did not have anything written by me it would be better, when you could not speak about me to other people, at least not in this distinct manner. Therefore, I fear your personal reasons. I believe that I've never written fifteen times the same, but this night is dreadful. My wounded soldiers cry and I cannot help them.*

*Yesterday, you asked me something I know. What I have told about light and shade you think that one also must know the bad side of love (I believe that you know it, and of this reason I said in the morning that you also must speak sometimes that meaning ugly things). In spite of that you never would tell them to me.*

*But, I think in the following way, some other peoples I know, the bad side of love for I have eyes and ears. One time I even nearly happened to know it by myself, but I was not guilty. I'm ashamed of thinking of it, I have the great wish never to know it like the lash, I wish to stay pure and innocent. Did I speak right? To a once and great deep love fills my heart, I will be worth of this love. You must not think that this opinion, if given to me by my spirit and that I must make big efforts to fulfill it. No, it is born with me and it's quite impossible for me to be otherwise.*

Dear Irmgard, I will probably say again and again I do not recall the exact day you wrote this or what I might have said to prompt you to write this letter. You were writing this on duty and were distracted by the wounded soldiers. I suppose they needed antibiotics and pain medication, but there was nothing you could do.

Though we often think of love as a province reserved for the young, I think now that it takes much experience, great joys and great sorrows, to know about love, and it takes the wisdom of maturation to think about it and more to write about it sensibly. I rather think that what I may have said was callow and I apologize for that. Besides all this, I have come to another understanding about love.

Wherever you are, you know that you never had to fear I would misuse your letters to me. You see, it is the opposite of ridiculing you. I never did and I never would. I will never forget when you came and told me, "They decided not to send you away." You told me how happy you were, that you had prayed, for if they had sent me away, who knows what would have happened to me, you said.

*I often read your words and I think about them. At the end you ask me what I am thinking about. In the night, I believe that I must give a long answer but it is not true, for your words need not an answer, they only need to be deeply thought of. Do you believe that it is precious to see something thickly, darkly covered time by time be revealed? And proving more and more bright and artificial. It is wonderful to go*

*somewhere in the darkness and slowly engross light and your foot*
*finds more and more a little place to go on. This is in the moment*
*nearly the only thing I wish to tell you. The German, I would apply in*
*German I would apply some other words, but I believe that you will*
*understand it in spite of that. But tell me, you tell me that you believe*
*to be one of these young persons who know certain things without ever*
*having lived them. You are realistic, how may someone be able, someone*
*who thinks realistic to know something which he only might have*
*learned by his feelings.*

*I never would name you with lieutenant, it is no use for me to do it.*
*I never would name the German soldiers with their military rank and*
*now I have no name for you.*

Dear Irmgard, today when I read these letters I have a sadness
because before there was no time to sit with them and read them
and let myself be washed over by the meanings in them. Sadder am
I still to think what a time we might have had to be able to talk at
length, with no constraints, in a time of peace. What if I had met
you in West Chester, Philadelphia, Paris? Or after the war? I could
have gotten to know your heart and your customs more directly. We
could have discussed how you saw me as realistic. You ask rightly if
I'm realistic—how could I say I know things without having lived
them, that is, how could I have intuited them? What a time we
could have had with that!

*Would you ever tell to your conqueror or to a man who feels like a*
*conqueror, "Here am I, here is my heart, deeply look into it." Now when*
*you wish to show anyone something of yourself, you always must stand*
*upon the same bottom. You always must meet with the same free will,*
*with the same readiness. It is different, it is difficult to translate and if*
*it is otherwise, I would be ashamed to tell only one word, which lies out*
*of necessity.*

*I like to make little presents, a little joy to someone and I never wish*
*to get anything for it. But in this question it would mean to throw myself*
*away when there not have the same conditions, the same foundations.*

*Why am I speaking to you? As first you know, as I wish to show you something of our real soul. For you told something about us which made me sure that we all don't know one from the other and it filled me with sadness.*

*I have learned to love this, the truth, therefore I will be sorry when truth lies hidden beyond a deep skin of misunderstanding, of bitterness, of badness, of bitterness of blank, blank, and though you will go back to America, I never will forget that once I showed a little of our true soul to a man who had such strange ideas of our soul. That must hurt a little an earnest person to a man whose people is an enemy. And I would have little joy in thinking that perhaps later, a man on the other side of the ocean, tells to his comrades, that I know that it is an idealizing thought, and I cannot change myself, "you don't know them right, I have seen it otherwise." Though I never wished that he should tell about me and second, it is natural that I am interested a little in a person with whom I began talking about problems. With whom I changed opinions and somewhat of who touched me after I tore away the sarcastic and bitter and proud outside.*

*But, this reason must not be spoke of, for if it were the only reason, I never were allowed to talk with you, who are our enemy and now I have a wish, please give back to me my letters, for it would not be good for you and for me if they would be found. And surely they will look at your things. I will do them all together and give you later, I promise. There no one will be lost, you do not see what I am doing. It is the worse thing when one loves his country to be looked at nearly like a treasure. You must not think I have fear, it is not truth and therefore, without sarcasm or making fun, fulfill my wish. If you cannot do it, I must finish my writing. My love of country is worth many sacrifices. The red sister does not know the content of the letters but she does not throw stones upon me.*

Dear Irmgard, you do not know how honored I was and how honored I am today to read your heart and soul in the thoughts you have written.

I no longer remember what I said to you, but I'm reasonably sure that it had to do with the Holocaust, the indecent and unforgivable murder of men, women and children. Their deaths sent a shudder through all of mankind. Nearly all of them were strangers to me, but they were my people. I'm proud to be a Jew, just as you were proud to be a German, and in your moral core, the core you showed me again and again, I was thrilled by your passion in telling me, "Do not look upon us all in that despicable way." You say over and again, "Look at me, at my heart and soul." You wanted to change my mind, person-to-person, heart-to-heart, standing on the same ground.

It is true, you tore away my sarcasm, and my bitterness and my arrogance. It is not easy to do without these as a prisoner of war. What was there to protect me? I agree with you that truth does lie hidden under a deep skin of misunderstanding, of badness, of bitterness, or whatever. It is exactly these qualities that I have spent over fifty years investigating.

You need never worry that I came back to America with any idea of mocking you. I hope you did take comfort in the fact that you lifted the curtain a little and showed a stranger, an enemy, a different picture.

I find again, as I have found before, that every letter you write contains many clear thoughts, but always, also, something that asks me to go deeper. But I should not be sad that there will never be a time for this. I have to be utterly grateful that I have already gotten so much from your letters.

I can only agree with you about showing your heart. I'm in sympathy with what you say, and there is only marvel in my being that you, so young, dared to do what you did under the circumstances that existed between us. It was an act of courage and love: know that I knew this then and that I know it even more now. Know also that you have made not a little present to me, but a great one which keeps renewing itself. I understand that you knew you were not throwing yourself away, that indeed we managed to create an equality of conditions, a ground of equal footing from which we could share our thoughts and feelings with open heart. The fact that danger lurked made our connection more precious, our fragile moments barely able to carry the weight of our feelings. I think this is what your music meant to me, for doesn't music always express the truth of the soul?

Now, from reading this letter, it is clear that I obey your wish; to this day I pay more attention to women in their mystery, in the greatness of their capacities. I gave you back each letter you wrote and had no doubt you would keep your word. I'm still inarticulate with pain and all the things we did not say. I still suffer the abruptness of our parting.

I have lived now many years, and my work takes me into people's lives. I can only repeat that what we shared was unique, liberating, frightening, exhilarating, and humbling. Our meeting could only have been God's plan. We, the young, ripen.

*I don't know if I've understood all you have written, but I hope so and will try to answer. I believe that I have understood you in some questions we spoke about and by the time I learned to know when you make fun or when you speak so bitter that it does not agree with your real opinion.*

*Naturally, I do not know you really but that means I will be able to unlock your heart and that would not be possible. That comment, I have thought about all people with whom I speak and longer I know that I cannot look into their heart but I think or I don't think lies in my feeling, if I should have any sympathy for them or not. If I should confide them a little so that I can talk with them about things which touch me, which lay out of daily life.*

*This does not mean that I agree with them, you are a prisoner of war, but when you have come later with your comrades, you know what I mean, I never would have talked with you in this manner. For they may come like conquerors like my doctors, and this would hurt me. Even if I never would feel like a conquered as the same manner as you never ought to be ashamed of your capture.*

*When they will come, they will have a manner and this is natural, which forbids for me to talk with them and so I never knew anything about them. Therefore, when I shall be too much hurt by their, in this moment, natural manner, I will think of their friendly enemy who I knew a little bit. Yes, you don't believe it but you never have had the heart and feeling of a woman. This would make all any easier, though he too is very arrogant. You must not always say my opinion is wrong, you must say, it is strange to you. For there is no straight answer in the world about our questions. Why should only your answer be a right one?*

*And you may find in the world then people would think, did you only like them because they think no matter what they think? I know that you try to find the truth in life, the deep sense of life but, it is no great fate when you say, I believe in myself. Look, it is true that one at first must know their own heart. That one must confide in oneself, but this is only the foundation on which one must build, on which the heart must grow.*

*I know believe that a strong character must not become bitter by disappointment. I know from experience that they hurt deeply, but I know that one grows wiser by them. Often you must be very strong not to become bitter, I know the word, "understand all is to forgive all," but must it always be applied? For if you understand all and you forgive it, there will never be any guilty in the world, there would never be any conflicts of conscious.*

*For example, all great dramas tell us from conflicts that the presence we can feel with them, we understand them but forgive it. But, I too believe that I cannot set to judge, I could yet tell many about this. We must try to understand for the reason to honor it.*

*You say I know all from theory, theory that is when I have learned it from books. All what I have seen and heard in the world. You name it wrong, I did not stand outside of life I was always in the middle of it, often in the middle of mud. I was frightened of it and I had only the wish not to be drowned there in.*

*According to your belief, people first must get a bad black soul, they must have been themselves till over their head in the mud to become wise. Though I know some of the bad side of love or just because of it, the fine side of love has become much brighter and once I wish it to fill my whole heart.*

*Once more I tell you that you don't know a woman's heart. I told you from the book by Isabelle Glommer in which I found a poem "The Night has a thousand eyes." In this book the young woman says, "you are right behind me, there does not lie anything heavy, difficult." No experiences which may give the belief that I am a woman who can help lean on someone in the manner as you mean, I never have shrugged. But, I believe that a woman, even a young girl, may have a knowing about things, which she has not the real lived, which is born with her. She needs not lived to be a woman-like. Sorrowing loving comrade, she does not take this role, a woman is predestined "to the state." You cannot think yourself in my world but I can think myself in yours and understand it. Women are different from men, we remain true to ourselves and in spite of that, we are able to give up ourselves.*

*I believe that when we find ourselves really, when we have given up ourselves. You must always forgive that many German girls are like me, must always figure. That you know little bit of the German people, you must forget my person. It becomes more and more difficult to talk with you, I don't wish to talk to you about the reasons, it does not matter and I don't give up talking with you. You know my conscious tells me the right way. The sister does not read my letter and she ignores yours too. Enough for the moment.*

Dear Irmgard,

When I speak with you I see you in all the simplicity of innocence, and for that alone I could fall in love with you again. See, I have become emboldened because it is safe; we are writing, talking, and now we are separated by time and space. I'm speaking to your spirit, which I know hears me.

You remind me at once in your letter of my old self. A self that spoke in that manner designed to protect me, my vulnerabilities. Here I think we share a loss—you for whatever reason, I because of my family's early poverty, which worried me endlessly.

You did not know your power, for you had already unlocked my heart. Otherwise, how could I have written letter after letter to you in these unnatural circumstances? When I wrote these responses I had always your face before me, I looked always into your eyes, your brown eyes, which softened as you talked to me. Did you know that? Your feelings were beyond your conscious control.

In a way, you are not fair about Americans coming as conquerors. My feeling is that they did not come and would not come with disdain or with arrogance. I believe we are a generous people. I love our America, and I hope that the Americans who came to your hospital showed you a quality that might have convinced you of what I say now.

You were right when you say that I must not say as I did, "you are wrong." Over the years I have come to listen to many, many people. Sometimes I still say "you are wrong," but, I hope, with compassion, and when I can I show them how and why they are wrong.

I would say this: there are many questions, many problems which do not have a straight answer. Today, however, I do think I have a straight answer to some of them, but your point is well taken. Your statements tell me you were a very headstrong girl who did not like at all the patriarchal establishment that took little or no heed of women. This would have been infuriating to thinking and feeling women, and you were certainly one of these. I understand your argument about bitterness, I must agree. I think that, with time enough, we might have found that we agreed on many things. Now that I respond once again to your letters, I feel that, all things considered, I've forgiven many people and ill deeds, and that I have gotten on with it. I do understand the saying, "To understand all is to forgive all," a little differently. We may forgive, but we do that for ourselves; the guilty still have to struggle with their guilt. I have not absolved them, I've absolved myself from them. I believe you have many times stood in the mud, but I believe you did not drown in it, but became wiser from it. I do believe that we must be in the mud to see our humanity.

Let me say that I understand what you say, I understand the depth of your heart. I understand now that you'd given yourself up to me—as you say, it was predestined. True, having known you, I know a little bit of the German people, and I know of a different kind of German who existed during the war years. Though I do know of Nazis, it is you I think of when I think of Germany, though your great human heart transcended distinctions like German and

American. I know why you say I have to forget you; I gather there's much animosity growing because you talk to me, from those who can see me only as an enemy, an abstraction to be hated and shunned. Your very goodness shines in your telling me you will continue to talk with me. Your conscience says it is right.

Other than this, I simply cannot imagine what kind of life you had.

# PHOTOS

*The author, aviation cadet Bernard W. Bail, Monroe, Louisiana (1942).*

*Passport picture carried by author on twenty-five WWII
combat flying missions (1943–1945).*

*The author receiving his wings, Monroe, Louisiana (1943).*

*Third mission officers (from left to right) Glickman, Segal, the author, and Carper (June, 1944).*

*Third mission officers (from left to right) Carper, Glickman,*
*Segal and the author (June, 1944).*

*WWII Air Force officers who flew with the author on his third combat mission to Germany. From left to right: Glickman, Segal, Carper, and the author (behind Segal) (June, 1944).*

*Crew of a flying mission, including Pete Henry and Al Winter.*
*Note plane riddled by flak (late 1944).*

*The author with friends (late 1944).*

*The author on his bike—Shipdham, England (1944).*

*The author and crew with Navy friend at an officer's club,
London, England (1944).*

*The author and stateside crew, including Slafka and Stroble,
Wendover Air Base, Utah (1943).*

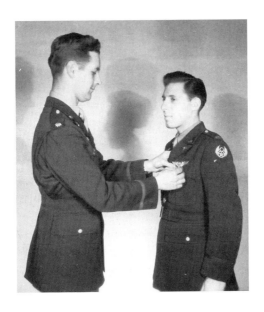

*The author being awarded his first air medal (1944).*

*Quonset hut and machine gun, Shipdham, England (1944).*

*Notification sent to author's family stating that he had been missing in action and was then liberated (1945).*

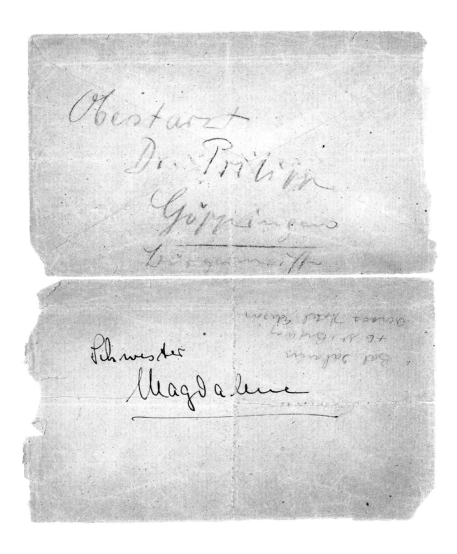

*Top: Signature of Col. Prilippi, head of the German station hospital in Goeppingen
where the author was held prisoner and met Irmgard, a civilian nurse (1945).
Bottom: Irmgard's signature showing her middle name, Magdalene (1945).*

*German station hospital in Goeppingen (1945).*

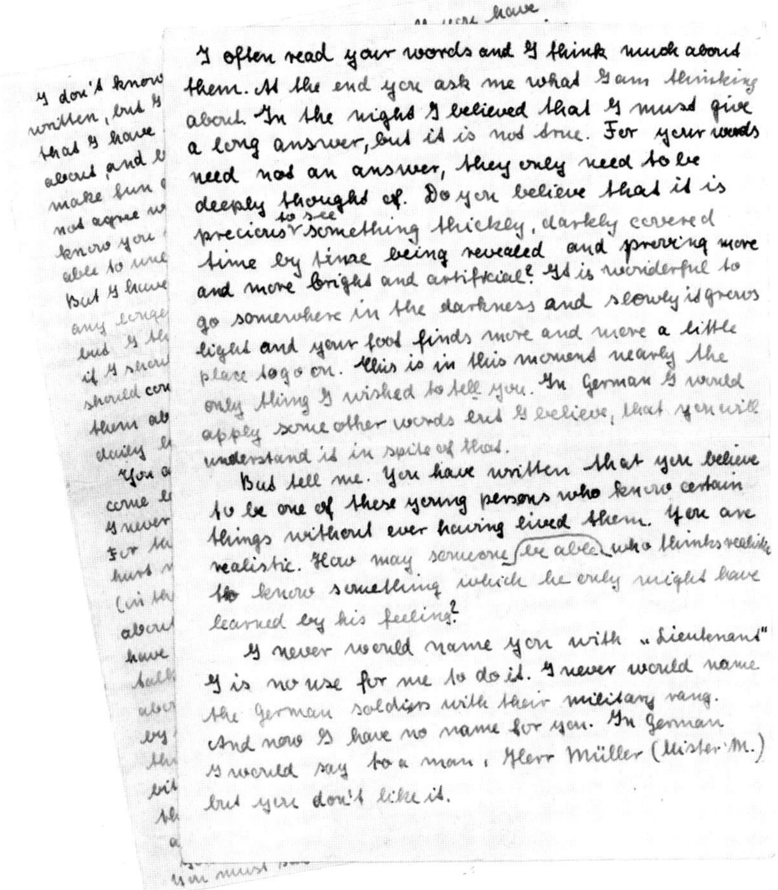

*Letter from Irmgard to the author (1945).*

*Letter from Irmgard to the author (1945).*

I have done something wrong. Surely you
were astonished when I spoke with Resi
in this manner. It wasn't fair to do
it in your presence. But I did not mean
it bad in doing it. When Resi spoke
the first time with you I talked with
U. Mosevich and suddenly he said "She
is the right woman for Benny." I was
surprised and asked "naturally the contrary." "We name such one foolish" said
he. And I did not forget these words.
And always when she was speaking to
you in this manner, which I don't like,
I thought of them. And I asked myself
what you think about her. I believed
that I must tell her that her behaviour
was a little strange but she did not
understand, I said each girl must have
a little proud, not national proud in this case
but proud of woman. She asked upon what
she should be proud. She had no proud. So it
will be in vain, trying to make her understand

*Letter from Irmgard to the author (1945).*

*Author's graduation from State Teachers College,*
*West Chester, Pennsylvania (1942).*

*The author graduates from medical school at Temple University,*
*Philadelphia, Pennsylvania (1952).*

*The author as an intern at Mt. Sinai Hospital, Philadelphia,*
*Pennsylvania (1952–1953).*

*The author as an intern at Mt. Sinai Hospital, Philadelphia,
Pennsylvania (1952–1953).*

*The author's graduating class at Mt. Sinai Hospital, Philadelphia, Pennsylvania (1953).*

_Guest List_

**Testimonial Dinner–Dance In Honor Of Alex Bail**

November 21, 1970
Grand Ballroom, Hotel Commodore

_Program from labor and civil rights celebratory dinner honoring Alex Bail_
_for his work (1970)._

## Irmgard, bitte melde Dich doch!

### Arzt aus den USA sucht Hamburgerin, die ihn vor 40 Jahren gesundpflegte

1945: Bernard Bail, der 23jährige Französischlehrer aus Philadelphia, als Angehöriger der amerikanischen Luftstreitkräfte

1984: Dr. Bernard Bail, renommierter Psychoanalytiker, der in seiner Praxis in Beverly Hills Hollywood-Prominenz betreut

Es klingt wie eine Hollywood-Story, aber die Geschichte ist wahr: Dr. Bernard Bail, Psychiater für zahlreiche Filmstars in Beverly Hills, sucht Krankenschwester Irmgard aus Hamburg, die ihn vor 40 Jahren in Göppingen gepflegt hat. Dr. Bail kommt am 24. Juli von Hollywood nach Hamburg und nimmt bis zum 2. August an einem internationalen Psychoanalytiker-Treffen teil. Bis dahin hofft der Prominentenarzt seine unvergessene Schwester Irmgard mit Hilfe des Hamburger Abendblatts zu finden.

Die Vorgeschichte beginnt im März 1945. Kurz vor Kriegsende war der damals 23jährige Luftwaffenangehörige aus Philadelphia mit seiner Maschine abgeschossen worden und schwer verwundet in deutsche Gefangenschaft geraten. Die deutschen Ärzte versorgten ihn so gut, daß er sich schwor, umzusatteln und Medizin zu studieren, wenn er heil nach Hause zurückkäme. Bernard Bail war Französischlehrer gewesen, als er zur US-Luftwaffe eingezogen worden war. Aber nicht nur das Können der deutschen Ärzte beeindruckten den Kriegsgefangenen und Verwundeten. Da war auch noch Schwester Irmgard, eine sensible, nachdenkliche junge Frau, die sehr gut Englisch sprach und sich mit ihm anfreundete.

Die Hamburgerin riskierte viel, denn sie wechselte Briefe mit dem Kriegsgefangenen. Atemberaubend kühn waren Sätze wie: „Du bist Kriegsgefangener, aber wenn Du mit Deinen Kameraden später gekommen wärest – Du weißt, was ich meine –, könnte ich nicht so wie jetzt mit Dir reden. Denn sie werden als Sieger kommen, als Machthaber, und das wird mich verletzen. Ich werde mich nie besiegt fühlen, ebenso wie Du Dich nicht schämen mußt, wegen Deiner Gefangennahme. Wenn sie kommen, treten sie natürlich in einer Art und Weise auf, die es mir verbieten wird, mit ihnen zu sprechen. Deshalb werde ich sie niemals kennenlernen. Aber wenn ich dann sehr verletzt bin, werde ich an den freundlichen Feind denken, den ich ein bißchen kenne."

Was sich da zwischen Irmgard und dem freundlichen Feind entwickelte, lassen die letzten Zeilen dieses Briefes ahnen. „Du mußt meine Person vergessen. Es wird immer schwieriger, sich mit Dir zu unterhalten. Ich möchte Dir nichts über die Gründe dafür sagen. Es ist unwichtig, und ich werde auch nicht aufhören, mit Dir zu reden, mein Gewissen wird mir den richtigen Weg weisen. Die Schwester (vermutlich die Vorgesetzte) liest meine Briefe nicht, und Deine übersieht sie auch."

Dr. Bail, der in den Wirren des Kriegsendes von seiner Krankenschwester Irmgard getrennt wurde, bevor er ihren Nachnamen und ihre Hamburger Adresse erfahren hatte, bewahrte die Briefe vierzig Jahre auf. Er hat inzwischen geheiratet, ist Vater von einem Sohn und zwei Töchtern geworden. Jetzt wird der 63jährige Arzt zum ersten Mal wieder nach Deutschland kommen, und sein größter Wunsch ist, Irmgard wiederzusehen. Er weiß, was für ein Institut Irmgards Vater in Hamburg gehabt hat, weiß, daß einer ihrer beiden Brüder im Krieg gefallen ist. Er erinnert sich auch noch, daß einer der jungen Ärzte in Göppingen Polster hieß, ein blonder kräftiger Doktor, der eine Brille trug und ungefähr 1,70 Meter groß war.

Dr. Bail ist offenbar optimistisch, daß sich Schwester Irmgard meldet, denn in der letzten Woche schrieb er an das Hamburger Abendblatt: „Bei dem Gedanken, diesen wunderbaren Menschen wiederzusehen, bin ich ein bißchen aufgeregt!"

Liebe Frau Irmgard, melden Sie sich bitte beim Hamburger Abendblatt unter 347 34 57 bei: HARRIET SCHWABE

*Clipping from Hamburg, Germany, newspaper: the author searching for Irmgard (1985).*

300

*The author working in his office (Beverly Hills, California, present day).*

Some of dais guests at testimonial dinner Nov. 21 in honor of Alex Bail, Executive Vice-President Emeritus of the RWDSU (center) include (from left) Local 1-S Pres. Sam Kovenetsky; Uzi Bloch, American representative of Histradrut, Israel's labor federation; Bayard Rustin, executive director of A. Philip Randolph Institute; RWDSU Pres. Max Greenberg and Sec.-Treas. Alvin E. Heaps.

## A Salute to Alex Bail

Alex Bail proudly displays Histadrut Medal of Honor presented to him at dinner. With him are New England Regional Director Thomas Leone and Eve Bail, who shared the limelight with her husband.

"Let My People Go," sings Bayard Rustin after speech in which he compared ancient and modern struggles for freedom.

A most personal gift—a portrait in oils he had painted himself—was presented by Local 147 Business Mgr. Caesar Massa to the guest of honor, Alex Bail, as well as a watch for Mrs. Bail.

Some of the 700 guests who turned out for Alex Bail testimonial listen attentively to speaker. The dinner, held at Commodore Hotel in New York, raised $35,000 for the Scholarship Fund of Histadrut, which helps needy Israeli students complete their high school or technical educations.

*The author's uncle and aunt, Alex and Eve Bail, being honored by the labor and civil rights movement (1970).*

302

*Dr. Alex Bail receiving award from President Lyndon B. Johnson (ca. 1967–68).*

*Vice President Richard Cheney awarding the author the Distinguished Service Cross, Washington, DC (February, 2006).*

*French Ambassador Jean David Levitte awarding the author the French Legion of Honor at the French Embassy, Washington, DC (June, 2006).*

*French Ambassador Jean David Levitte at the French Legion of Honor award ceremony at the French Embassy, Washington, DC (June, 2006).*

*The author with his wife, Ma Lan Bail, and (left to right) Major General Vinchon and Sergeant Major Bouvard at the French Legion of Honor award ceremony at the French Embassy, Washington, DC (June, 2006).*

*Author's maternal grandparents, Elizabeth and Joseph Miller (ca. 1910).*

*Author's fraternal grandparents, Jacob and Mary Bail (ca. 1910).*

*Elizabeth Miller, the author's maternal grandmother (ca. 1915).*

*Lillian and Abraham Bail, the author's parents (ca. 1917).*

*Lillian Bail, the author's mother (standing), with two friends (ca. 1915).*

*Lillian Bail, the author's mother, playing the guitar (ca. 1915).*

*Lillian Bail, the author's mother (ca. 1915).*

*Lillian Bail, the author's mother, with his older brother Paul (1917).*

*Paul Miller, the author's uncle on his mother's side, and Paul's wife;*
*Odessa, Russia (ca. 1938).*

*Alex Bail, the author's uncle (ca. 1945).*

# IRMGARD'S DRAWINGS

**Skizzenblock**

vom und ums Kgf.-Lazarett

Göppingen

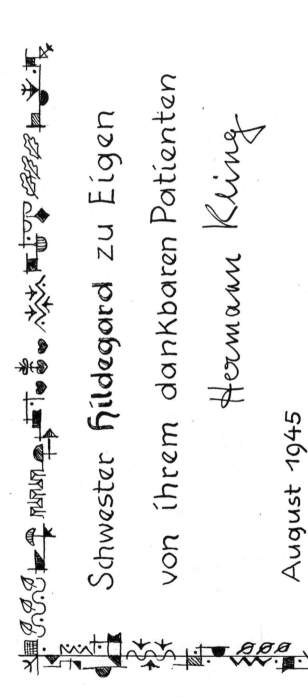

Schwester Hildegard zu Eigen

von ihrem dankbaren Patienten

Hermann Kring

August 1945

Das Tagewerk beginnt

Hohenstaufen

Ruine Staufeneck

Haupttor des Lagers

Lagerturm

Beim Sendehäuschen „Ursula"

„Ursula" bringt Nachrichten

Lagerstraße

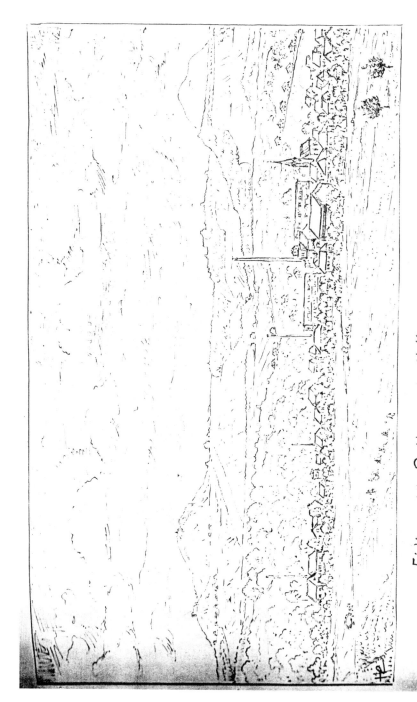

Eislingen, i.H. Rechberg und Stuifen

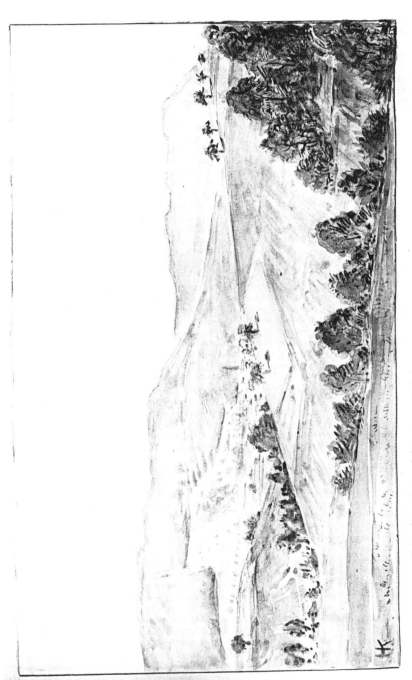

Schwäb. Albgebiet be Heningen

Freibad

Polospiel

Abendstimmung über Göppingen

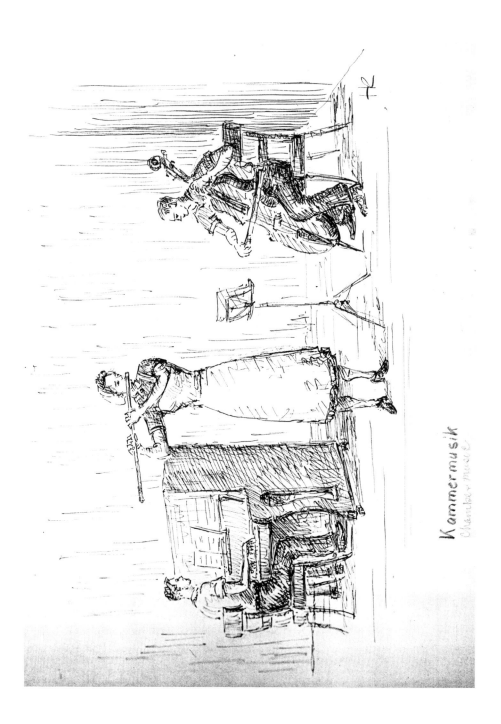

Kammermusik
(Chamber music)

„Ade, zur guten Nacht..."

Nun ruhen alle Wälder.....

www.bernardwbail.com

Mark pulled the woman to her feet and led her into the family room. At Gwen's request, and after his search yielded nothing more than a cell phone and a set of car keys, he reluctantly put away the handcuffs and led her to a chair. She sat and rubbed her bruised wrist. Gwen perched on the corner of the hearth, peering intently at the woman. She broke the silence. "Can I get you some tea or coffee?"

The woman lifted a puzzled look.

Cassie groaned. "Oh, for the love of—this isn't a social call, Gwen."

"I know, but look at her. I doubt she's a serious threat."

"Sweeter faces than hers have detonated suicide vests."

"I understand your point, but we're not in Afghanistan."

"Maybe." Cassie sat back, expression stony.

Gwen returned her attention to the stranger. "So, about that tea?"

The woman frowned. "You're serious."

"Of course."

She shrugged. "Sure."

"Where do you keep it?" asked Cassie as she rose from the sofa, shaking her head. "I'll only be a distraction here. May as well make myself useful."

Gwen told her where to find the tea, and Cassie left the room. Gwen returned her attention to the intruder, struggling to place where she'd seen her before.

"I should be taking you to the station in cuffs right now," Mark said. "You're lucky Gwen is as persuasive and compassionate as she is. Even so, I need to tell you that whatever you say here can and will be used against you in a court of law."

She rolled her eyes. "Thanks, but I'm familiar with Miranda."

"I'm not surprised. Still ... " Mark recited the remainder of the advisement.

"So, I'm under arrest?"

"I've got you breaking and entering, and resisting arrest. What do you think?"

Gwen knelt onto the floor in front of the woman. "Are you the same person we chased from the house a couple of days ago?"

The woman nodded briefly, then looked up.

Gwen sat back on her heels. "Wait. I've seen you someplace before."

Gwen halted on the landing, heart in her throat.

"Stay back!" Mark stiff-armed a restraining hand behind him, but kept his focus on the interloper. His voice lowered. "Put down the gun. You have nowhere to go."

The gunman said nothing, but began to back down the remaining two stairs, the pistol leveled. As the intruder came abreast of the archway into the family room, an aluminum rod flashed downward, crashing onto the extended arms. The stranger screamed, and the pistol clattered to the floor.

Cassie leaned through the archway and rammed the tip of her crutch into the prowler's rib cage. The hooded figure doubled over and crumpled to the floor.

Mark leapt forward, kicked the gun aside, and drove his knee down into the middle of the person's back. He looked up at Cassie. "You haven't lost your touch."

She shrugged, a satisfied smile curving her lips.

Gwen stepped forward. "Mark, be careful with your knee."

"Why should I?"

"That didn't sound like a man's scream."

He yanked back the parka hood, and dark hair spilled out, framing the face of a pale woman, cheek pressed against the floor.

Gwen laid a hand on his shoulder. "Maybe you can ease up a little. She's in pain."

"Don't be fooled." He pointed to the revolver lying against the wall. "A woman will pull a trigger as quickly as a man will." He pulled out his handcuffs and pulled her arms to her back.

"He's right," echoed Cassie. "No mercy for gender."

Gwen stepped to his side. "Can you wait a second?"

He glared up at her. "You're interfering, Gwen."

The woman spoke, her raspy voice quavering. "I wouldn't ... the gun's not real."

Cassie crossed the hall and picked up the revolver. "It's a starter's pistol. Takes blanks, and this one's empty."

Mark glared down at the woman. "I'm armed. One wrong move, and I would've shot you."

She lowered her face against the floor and closed her eyes. "I almost hoped you would," she murmured.

"And they matched?"

He nodded. "I'm thinking the housekeeper was Teresa. Since you found nothing in your father's financial records indicating he had secured a housekeeping service, I wanted to do a more thorough check for anything that might indicate a personal employment, maybe someone not associated with a legitimate house-cleaning outfit."

Gwen went silent at the flurry of possibilities Mark's comment evoked, some of them disquieting. Her father's slow withdrawal following her mother's death was one thing, but the thought of an unknown woman having independent access to his home was too much. Was she Simon's mother, and had her father remained in touch with his former lover over the years? Gwen's forehead heated. No, there was no way he could have kept such a liaison secret for so long. Perhaps they reconnected after her mother's death.

"Gwen?"

She opened her eyes to Mark and Cassie studying her. "Sorry, it's a lot to take in."

"Understandably," Mark said.

She turned toward the stairway. "Well, let's get to it."

"Mind if I stay down here and light a fire?" asked Cassie, glancing at the fireplace.

"Sure. Matches are on the mantle."

Gwen and Mark went upstairs to her father's study. She flipped up the light switch and propped her hands on her hips, surveying his desk. "So, where do we start?"

He moved across the room to a four-drawer file cabinet. "Let's look—"

Something bumped in the hallway, and they turned in time to see someone rushing toward the stairs. Mark bolted toward the door. "Oh, no you don't. Not this time." He careened through the doorway with Gwen close behind.

A figure in a hooded sweatshirt had passed the midway landing and was halfway down the lower staircase.

"Stop! Police!" Mark lunged forward, taking the steps three at a time. He hit the landing, vaulted the banister, and crashed onto the lower staircase four steps behind the intruder.

The stranger spun, pulling out a revolver and leveling it at Mark's chest. He grabbed the railing and pulled up short.

supervised. I think it would be more fun if you were to come along, though."

Cassie shrugged. "Why not?"

*** 

When the women arrived at the house, Mark's car was parked at the curb next to a panel truck with *Medford Locksmith* emblazoned on the side. Mark was conversing with the technician through the driver's window. They shook hands, and the locksmith backed out of the driveway just as Gwen's Corolla pulled in.

Mark squinted in through the windshield and flashed a surprised smile at Cassie. He opened her door. "Didn't expect to see you," he said, helping her out of the car. He kissed her on the forehead.

"I felt like getting out a little."

"Glad you did." He turned toward Gwen, who was closing her door. "Hope I didn't interrupt anything."

"You didn't." She looked at the panel truck. "I thought the locks would've been changed by now."

He handed her the new house keys. "They would've been, but there was a communications glitch, and the station didn't put in the request until this morning."

"The police station put in the request?"

"We get a good rate due to all the business we send their way, so I put the request in through channels and had them forward the bill to me. I thought you might appreciate the discount."

"Very much so. Thanks."

He leveled a grim expression at the front porch. "I don't like that the house sat all this time with the old locks. That's the other reason I asked you to come over, to make sure nothing else is out of order."

"Okay."

Mark steadied Cassie with her crutch as Gwen followed them up the icy porch steps. Once inside, they stowed their coats while Gwen tested each of the new keys in the locks. Task completed, she entered the family room and dropped the keys onto the end table. "What are you looking for in Daddy's paperwork?"

"The information Brent sent me on Teresa Hardy included an address here in Medford. It looked familiar, so I cross-referenced it to the false address the housekeeper gave the investigating officer after your father's death."

"The clerk tailed her to where she'd parked her car. Before she drove off, he snapped a picture of the car and license plate with his phone."

"Did you look up the plate numbers?"

"Yes, and you'll never guess where they trace to."

"Where?"

"Right there in Medford. I've already emailed the information to Mark. Oh, and one more thing. The clerk was smart enough to handle the license by its edges, so I have the Farmington PD pulling fingerprints from it. We'll see if she's anywhere in the system."

Gwen gripped the phone with both hands. "Oh, I so hope this turns out to be a solid lead. It's been driving me crazy to know I have a brother somewhere, but have no idea how to find him."

"Hang in there. We're getting closer."

At that moment, Cassie came into the room and signaled to Gwen, her phone in hand. Gwen nodded. "Can you hold a sec? Cassie needs something."

"I've got to go now anyway. I'll be in touch."

She smiled. "You'd better."

They signed off and Cassie handed Gwen her phone. "It's Mark."

"Oh. Thanks." She accepted the device. "Hi, Mark."

"Hi, Gwen. Have you heard from Brent?"

"Yes, just now."

"Good. Can you meet me at your house? I need to check out a final couple of things in your dad's paperwork, and I'd like you there. Besides, the locksmith should be finishing up, and he'll have your new keys."

"Um, sure. Right now?"

"Soon as you can."

She disconnected and handed the phone back to Cassie. "Mark wants to meet at the house." She paused. "Do you want to ride along?"

"Not necessary."

"Are you sure?"

Cassie tipped a smile. "It's pretty clear you're a one-guy girl. Either that, or you're an incredible actress."

Gwen laughed. "I stink on stage. My high school drama teacher wouldn't even let me stand near the prop table without being

I often read your words and I think much about them. At the end you ask me what I am thinking about. In the nights I believed that I must give a long answer, but it is not true. For your words need not an answer, they only need to be deeply thought of. Do you believe that it is precious to see something thickly, darkly covered time by time being revealed and proving more and more bright and artificial? It is wonderful to go somewhere in the darkness and slowly it grows light and your foot finds more and more a little place to go on. This is in this moment nearly the only thing I wished to tell you. In German I would apply some other words but I believe, that you will understand it in spite of that.

But tell me. You have written that you believe to be one of these young persons who know certain things without ever having lived them. You are realistic. How may someone be able who thinks realistic to know something which he only might have learned by his feeling?

I never would name you with „Lieutenant" I is no use for me to do it. I never would name the German soldiers with their military rang. And now I have no name for you. In German I would say to a man, Herr Müller (Mister M.) but you don't like it.

Letter from Irmgard to the author (1945).

The only reason, why I am writing you an essay and you do not do it, may be, that I must think to long to translate my opinions. But it is a very little reason. Sometimes it seems to me that I must be very little proud in doing so, but really it is not truth and I make vanish these thoughts. But if I knew, that you would smile at my efforts and my strange manner, I would be deeply hurt. I often tried to explain you the reason of which I am talking with you, and I don't know with which intent you wish to talk with me. — You have said, for personal reasons you don't wish to do away my letters and this I cannot explain. I truly will tell you what reasons order me to ask you for doing them away. At first, you know, that it is forbidden, and I am sure, you never would do it in my situation. Second, I do not speak about these questions to all peoples. I know I am different from them, with all my soul too

*Letter from Irmgard to the author (1945).*

*Letter from Irmgard to the author (1945).*

Alex Bail at White House Meeting

FIRST FAMILY GREETING Alex Bail, Exec. Vice-Pres. of the RWDSU. Occasion was a recent White House conference on pending labor and tax legislation.

*Dr. Alex Bail receiving award from President Lyndon B. Johnson (ca. 1967–68).*

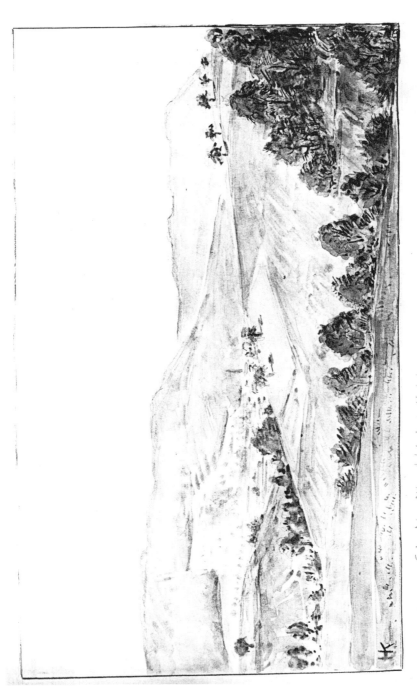

Schwäb. Albgebiet bei Heiningen

Kammermusik
(Chamber music)

Nun ruhen alle Wälder . . . .

www.bernardwbail.com